Philosophical ethics in reproductive medicine

Philosophical ethics in reproductive medicine

Proceedings of the First International Conference
on Philosophical Ethics in Reproductive Medicine,
University of Leeds, 18–22 April 1988

Edited by David R. Bromham
Maureen E. Dalton *and* Jennifer C. Jackson

Manchester University Press

Manchester and New York

Distributed exclusively in the USA and Canada by St. Martin's Press

Copyright © Manchester University Press 1990

Whilst copyright in this volume is invested in Manchester University Press, copyright in the individual chapters belongs to their respective authors, and no chapter may be reproduced in whole or in part without the express permission in writing of both author and publisher.

Published by Manchester University Press
Oxford Road, Manchester M13 9PL, UK
and Room 400, 175 Fifth Avenue,
New York, NY 10010, USA

Distributed exclusively in the USA and Canada
by St. Martin's Press, Inc.,
175 Fifth Avenue, New York, NY 10010, USA

British Library cataloguing in publication data
International Conference on Philosophical Ethics in
  Reproductive Medicine (*1st: 1988: Leeds, England*)
  Philosophical ethics in reproductive medicine:
  Proceedings of the First International Conference on
  Philosophical Ethics in Reproductive Medicine,
  University of Leeds 18th–22nd April, 1988.
  1. Man. Reproduction. Ethical aspects
  I. Title II. Bromham, David R. III. Dalton, Maureen
  E. IV. Jackson, Jennifer C.
  176

Library of Congress cataloging in publication data
International Conference on Philosophical Ethics in Reproductive
  Medicine (1st: 1988: University of Leeds)
    Philosophical ethics in reproductive medicine: proceedings of the
  First International Conference on Philosophical Ethics in
  Reproductive Medicine, University of Leeds, 18th-22nd April 1988 /
  edited by David R. Bromham, Maureen E. Dalton, and Jennifer C. Jackson.
      p. cm.
    ISBN 0-7190-3013-7
    1. Human reproductive technology – Moral and ethical aspects –
  Congresses. 2. Obstetrics – moral and ethical aspects – Congresses.
  I. Bromham, David R., 1945–   . II. Dalton, Maureen E., 1951–
  III. Jackson, Jennifer C., 1939–   . IV. Title.
    [DNLM: 1. Ethics, Medical – congresses. 2. Reproduction –
  congresses. WQ 205 I6035p 1988]
  RG133.5.I58   1988
  176 – dc20
  DNLM/DLC
  for Library of Congress   89-12914

ISBN 0 7190 3013 7 *hardback*

Typeset in Hong Kong by Best-set Typesetter Ltd

Printed in Great Britain by Biddles Ltd, Guildford and King's Lynn

Contents

List of contributors

David Bromham
Senior Lecturer in Obstetrics and
Gynaecology
St James's University Hospital
Leeds LS9 7TF
UK

Professor Alexander Campbell
Department of Child Health
Foresterhill
Aberdeen AB9 2ZD
UK

Dr Maureen Dalton
Lecturer in Obstetrics & Gynaecology
St James's University Hospital
Leeds LS9 7TF
UK

Professor the Revd G. R. Dunstan
(Hon. Research Fellow, University of
Exeter)
9 Maryfield Avenue
Pennsylvania
Exeter EX4 6JN
UK

Professor Anne Fagot-Largeault
(Dept. of Philosophy, Université de
Paris-X)
115–117, rue Saint Antoine
75004 Paris
France

Dr Raanan Gillon
Editor
Journal of Medical Ethics
London
UK

Professor Samuel Gorovitz
Dean of the College of Arts and
Sciences
Syracuse University
Syracuse
NY 13244–1170
USA

Professor Clifford Grobstein
Program in Science, Technology and
Public Affairs
University of California at
San Diego
La Jolla
CA 92093
USA

Dr John Harris
Reader in Applied Philosophy
School of Education
University of Manchester
Oxford Road
Manchester M13 9PL
UK

Professor Denis Hawkins
Professor of Obstetric Therapeutics
Institute of Obstetrics and
Gynaecology
Hammersmith Hospital
Du Cane Road
London W12 0HS
UK

Jennifer Jackson
Department of Philosophy
University of Leeds
Leeds LS2 9JT
UK

Simon Lee
Faculty of Law
King's College
The Strand
London WC2R 2LS
UK

Professor Richard Lilford
Professor of Obstetrics and
Gynaecology
St James's University Hospital
Leeds LS9 7TF
UK

Professor the Revd Jack Mahoney, SJ
Professor of Moral Theology
King's College
Strand
London WC2R 2LS
UK

Edgar Page
Department of Philosophy
The University
Hull HU6 7RX
UK

Jean Robinson
(Lay member, General Medical
Council)
56 Lonsdale Road
Oxford OX2 7EP
UK

Dr Pamela Sims
(Consultant Gynaecologist, Hexham
General Hospital)
6 St Cuthbert Terrace
Hexham
Northumberland NE46 2EL
UK

Professor Peter Singer
Director, Centre for Human
Bioethics
Monash University
Clayton
Victoria
Australia

Professor Richard Smithells
Deparment of Paediatrics and Child
Health
Leeds General Infirmary
Leeds
UK

Dr Robert Snowden
Director, Institute of Population
Studies
University of Exeter
Hoopern House
101 Pennsylvania Road
Exeter EX4 6DT
UK

James Thornton
Lecturer in Obstetrics and
Gynaecology
Welsh National Medical School
Heath Park
Cardiff CF4 4XN
UK

Dr Richard West
(Chairman, Ethics Committee,
Midlands Centre for Neuroswgery
and Neurology, Smethwick, West
Midlands)
23, Oxford Road
Birmingham B13 9EH
UK

Other delegates participating in discussions

Professor F. Beller
Universitaets-Frauenklinik, Munster,
Federal Republic of Germany

Dr. S. Botros
Lecturer in Medical Ethics, King's
College, London, UK

Dr. P. Braude
Clinical Lecturer in Obstetrics and
Gynaecology, The Rosie Maternity
Hospital, Cambridge, UK

Dr Iain Chalmers
Director, National Perinatal
Epidemiology Unit, Oxford, UK

M. Chesney
Tutor, Rochdale Midwifery School,
UK

Dr J. Cohen
Consultant Embryologist, Humana
Hospital Wellington, London, UK

M. L. Cox
Consultant Obstetrician and
Gynaecologist, George Eliot Hospital,
Nuneaton, UK

Rev. Dr R. Gardner
Consultant Obstetrician and
Gynaecologist, Sunderland, UK

S. Garnett
Chairman, Fertility Action Campaign
for Treatment, UK

Professor T. Glover
Hon. Senior Research Fellow,
Department of Obstetrics and
Gynaecology, St. James's University
Hospital, Leeds, UK (*formerly*
President, Fertility Society of
Australia)

Dr J. Goodall
Consultant Paediatrician, City
General Hospital, Stoke-on-Trent,
UK

Dr W. Greengross
Chairman, Ethics Committee,
Humana Hospital Wellington,
London, UK

S. Holm
Institute of Neurophysiology,
University of Copenhagen, Denmark

Dr P. Hoyte
Medical Defence Union, UK

G. Jarvis
Consultant Obstetrican and
Gynaecologist, St James's University
Hospital, Leeds, UK

Dr M. Johnson
Reader in Experimental Embryology,
University of Cambridge, UK

Dr I. J. Keown
Lecturer, Faculty of Law, University
of Leicester, UK

Professor Dr E-H. Kluge
Professor in Philosophy, University of
Victoria, British Columbia, Canada

Dr U. Levy
Community Physician, Ministry of
Health, Israel

W. Lindsay
MSL Division, Upjohn Ltd, Crawley,
UK

Dr A. M. McWhinnie
Buckinghamshire College of Higher
Education, UK

Dr M. G. Mott
Senior Lecturer, University of Bristol,
UK

Dr A Murray
Consultant Obstetrician and
Gynaecologist, Arrow Park Hospital,
The Wirral, UK

H. Murray
Lay member, North Manchester
Community Health Council, UK

G. Pickup
Lecturer in Law, Manchester
Polytechnic, UK

Dr J. Robson
Department of Psychology, University
of Sheffield, UK

Professor D. M. Serr
Director, Department of Obstetrics
and Gynaecology, Tel Aviv
University, Israel

B. Smith
The National Childbirth Trust, UK

Dr J. H. Solbakk
Norwegian Medical Research
Council, Norway

L. Somorjay
The National Childbirth Trust, UK

P. Spallone
c/o Women's Reproductive Rights
Information Centre, London, UK

Foreword

The conference

The purpose of the conference was to bring together doctors, scientists, philosophers, theologians, lawyers, paramedics and representatives of relevant patient support groups to discuss the many ethical problems that surround the theory and practice of reproductive medicine at the moment. In 1988, 10 years after the first 'test-tube baby' and 20 years after the Abortion Act began functioning in Great Britain, both topics were still being discussed in Parliament.

The organising committee for 'Philosophical ethics in reproductive medicine' (PERM) included ourselves, Professor David Holdcroft, Department of Philosophy, University of Leeds, Tim Bilham (later replaced by Mrs Cornelia Shirley ably assisted by Mrs Hilary Helms), Department of Continuing and Adult Education, University of Leeds, Dr Raanon Gillon and Professor Richard Lilford. We are very grateful to Allerton Medicare Plc, Hoechst UK Ltd, Roussel Laboratories Ltd, Serono Laboratories UK Ltd, Wyeth Laboratories and Upjohn Ltd for their sponsorship of PERM.

Approximately 200 delegates took part from many parts of the world: Israel and Canada, Australia and the United States, Finland and South Africa. Many shades of opinion were represented and considerable discussion followed not only the main lectures but also the 50 free communications that were heard. Inevitably, on no topic was consensus reached, but this has never been the intention of the conference. PERM took place to provide an open forum for public debate on these matters, and we are very grateful for the press coverage that we received in national and international newspapers and for the presence of two independent television companies.

Many people holding particular shades of opinion felt that their point of view had been under-represented. The frequency with which such comments were matched with those from the opposite 'camp' suggests that the balance was right.

The proceedings

Only the main lectures from the conference are reproduced in this volume. Space, unfortunately, does not permit us to reproduce the material given as free communications, although a selection of these have been published elsewhere. The chapters in this book have been grouped in Parts equivalent to the Conference sessions. Chapter 1.3, 'IVF and the Australian Law', by Professor Peter Singer, was given as a special guest lecture sponsored by Serono Laboratories UK Ltd and we have included it in Part 1. Iain Chalmers' lecture, 'Public support of well controlled experimentation', was based on a previous publication (Chalmers, 1986) and, for brevity, has been omitted from these Proceedings. Abbreviated transcripts of the discussion following the papers have been included. Much of this material is of relevance to other parts of the book: for example, the discussions following Chapter 1.1, 4.1 and 4.2 and the discussions on Parts 5 and 6. We will leave readers to enjoy tracing these overlaps for themselves. Chapters 4.3 and 4.4 are transcripts of lectures prepared at very short notice. They were included to cover a highly relevant topic that had arisen on the day before PERM commenced. Although some of the issues raised have had subsequent clarification, we have not deleted them as the principles behind those uncertainties remain valid. Chapters 5.1, 6.1 and 6.2 were also prepared from transcripts.

In addition to the authors who, by and large, submitted their chapters on time and adhered, by and large, to the publishers' formatting instructions, we owe a big debt of gratitude to a large number of typists, too many to mention by name, who converted the various contributions into a unified manuscript.

For those who receive this volume following their attendance at PERM, we hope it reflects your recall of the Conference. For others we hope it whets your appetite for PERM 2 in 1991.

D. R. Bromham
M. E. Dalton
J. C. Jackson
Leeds, 1988

References

Bromham, D., Forsythe, E. & Dalton, M. (eds.) (1989). *Ethical Problems in Reproductive Medicine*. London, National Association of Family Planning Doctors.
Chalmers, I. (1986). Minimizing harm and maximizing benefit during innovation in health care: controlled or uncontrolled experimentation? *Birth*, **13**, 155–64.

Part 1
The embryo

The moral status of the human embryo

The first speaker in a conference on serious and controversial issues has a heavy responsibility. There is no danger, given the strength of mind of those who will follow him, that he will skew the discussion in one direction or another. Yet he can establish a character, a tone. He could polarise the discussion, setting himself provocatively at one pole and so initiating an adversarial engagement with those ranged at the other. He could, on the other hand, affect a pose of neutrality, as though the engagement *could* be without tension; that is, as though the status of the human embryo were not a moral issue at all. Neither course would serve us well. Between the two lies a third, traditional in Anglican divinity. It is the way of comprehension, of holding the extremes together in tension. And when the criteria for moral action are looked for, they will be found within that tension, within a cluster of related moral claims.

It will have been noticed that I have already turned an abstract philosophical question, the moral status of the human embryo, into a practical question, moral action concerning the embryo. This is inevitable. Until recently the question of status was in fact subsumed under the question of permissible action: what may licitly be done to the embryo, and when? We have, however, in recent years, encumbered ourselves with the language of rights – and this at a time when the currency of 'rights' has been devalued by inflationary use, by investing with the status of a 'right' anything which an individual or a group wishes to enjoy. It was not so in the moral and legal traditions of the West. Traditionally we have spoken of duties. We have affirmed a duty to protect the embryo or fetus *pari passu* with its own morphological development. The extent of the duty was measured by the compensation, canonical penance or legal penalty due for causing an abortion.

This tradition has its relevance, as I shall try briefly to show. It also has its dangers. We must not be trapped, in our present enquiry, by a mentality formed by the discussion of abortion. Abortion means the premature ejection of the fetus from the womb. The embryo with which we deal is not yet in the womb, and may never be. At the stage critical for scientific investigation and consequent clinical application, we are discussing a pre-embryonic process of cellular division without commitment of cells to particular destinations. This is not a reductionist statement. I have not used the pejorative words 'mere' or 'merely'. The status of those cells is inherent in their genetic composition. The question wide-open is the extent of their claim to protection. Is it absolute or qualified? If qualified, qualified by what?

Let us survey the range of options. At one extreme stands the view that the pre-embryonic cells are simply biological material, morally indifferent: that is, without moral significance, usable and disposable without question, to say nothing of qualm. I have never met an embryologist or medical practitioner who holds this view, but propagandists for an opposite view sometimes say they hold it. The attribution may be false. If true, it would have no good foundation in science. Genetically those cells can be no other than human cells – even though few of them, if any, will develop into a human being. To deny them any moral significance is to deny moral significance to humanity itself.

At the other extreme lies an absolutism of another sort. This view ascribes an absolute 'right of life' from 'the moment of conception'. The assertion can be made only by a loose use of the language of rights and an over-simplistic view of the process of conception, which has no 'moment'. In strict usage, even the child in the womb is not a legal person, is not a bearer of rights, until born alive. That is not to say that we have no duty to protect it; it is simply to state the fact. So let us state the absolutist claim in better language. It asserts a strict duty to protect the conceptus from the time when fertilisation begins – presumably even before the fusion of the pro-nuclei. This is the assertion of the pro-life groups, and the sanction of religion is claimed for it. The Roman Catholic Church is the most rational and consistent expositor of this protectionist view. But if I have learned properly from Fr Mahoney (1984) and others, we may distinguish between a practical absolutism, represented by the formal prohibition of *in vitro* fertilisation and its attendant embryonic manipulation, found in papal pronouncements and magisterial instructions – even as recent as that of 1987 on *Respect for Human Life* – and the cautious approach of Catholic moralists who, recognising the impossibility of determining 'when life begins', expound as the safer course the duty to protect the embryo from its beginning, lest we commit the sin of homicide. A closely reasoned critique of even this position – resting on a rigorous analysis of the relevant biology and of the historic Catholic moral tradition is given by Ford (1988). And it may be observed in passing that the recent Vatican Instruction is not without its critics within the Catholic Church (*The Tablet*, 1988).

Somewhere between the poles stands an attempt by embryologists, followed by some philosophers, to determine the claim to protection by the observed growth of the central nervous system. Professor Clifford Grobstein (1979, 1981) has written on this. I have for long wished to ask him whether he was consciously echoing Dante (*Purgatorio* 25) when he cited the capacity for sensitivity and awareness as indicators of growth sufficient to warrant protection – for Dante used these words also to indicate the readiness of the fetus for ensoulment by a rational soul, the mark of its humanity. But if the argument is that interference with the embryo, as, for instance, in manipulative or destructive research, is morally licit up to the point when the embryo may be capable of feeling pain, it is fairly easily rejected (Marshall, 1988).

The superficial appeal of the theory, however, is strengthened by coincidence. The central nervous system is said to be capable of sensitivity and awareness at about 6 weeks of gestation, at about 42 days. For more than two millenia the West has lived with a tradition which held that the human embryo was sufficiently formed to be animated by a rational soul at upwards of 40 days. For myself, I can attribute no moral force to that coincidence, but I do attribute moral force to the principle inherent in the tradition, that protection due is related to morphological growth. I believe we now have scientific criteria for dating the claim to protection earlier than 40 or 42 days.

The tradition itself is sketched historically and evaluated philosophically elsewhere (Dunstan, 1988). It was given scientific and philosophical precision by Aristotle: that an organism or body – in this case the embryo – formed into a recognisable human shape must be deemed to be animated (we should say organised) by a rational (that is, human) soul. The concept was well enough established in Ptolemaic Alexandria to influence materially the translation of the Hebrew Old Testament into the Greek version known as the Septuagint. Whereas the Hebrew text of Exodus 21:22 preserved an old law which graded the damages for causing a woman accidentally to miscarry according to the social status of the husband, the Greek version graded compensation by the criterion of embryonic growth: if the fetus were formed, *exeikonismenon*, into the human likeness, the compensation due was that for taking a human life: if it were not so formed, a lesser payment would suffice.

From this vital point of transition, the moral tradition of the West derived. It is abundantly evidenced in the writings of the early Fathers, including St Jerome and St Augustine; in the moralists, penitencers and canon lawyers, including Pope Innocent III; in the Scholastic theologians and philosophers, including Albert the Great and St Thomas Aquinas; in the English common law, explicitly in Bracton, then (in a mutated form) in Coke and Blackstone and hence into the early Statute Law. It survived in Roman Catholic canon law and casuistry until formally abolished by Pope Pius IX in 1869; and it is alive and well today in reflective Roman Catholic moral theology. The tradition descended through the Arabic physician–philosophers also, and is embodied in Islamic law unto this day.

But what now is its present relevance? We cannot build much on Aristotle's pre-microscopic observation of embryonic growth. We cannot make much use of Aristotle's psychology, his theory of the soul, now that that whole area of thought has been clouded by Platonic dualism, and Christian sentiment has been clouded with it. But two key points remain, and on these I would build. The first is the fact of *process* in our physical coming-to-be. The second, that protected status is *attributed* – by the decision of rational human minds: it is not inherent in the biological process, nor given to us by self-authenticating incontrovertible authority from outside. It is a matter of moral decision. At what point, then, do these two considerations converge?

The science of embryology is now well enough established to give us some understanding of the pre-embryonic cellular process, which begins with the fusion of ovum and sperm in fertilisation, and ends with the beginning of embryogenesis out of the primitive streak and the first neural groove on the embryonic plate, at about 14 or 15 days. This is a time (I understand) of fluidity, in which cells, at first totipotential and later multipotential, are not committed to any particular destination in either the embryo itself or in the placenta or other membranes which will be discarded before or at birth. While these cells are undifferentiated and not committed, no individuality is possible: twinning can occur, or a non-human growth like the hydatidiform mole; or nothing can occur at all. Growth may simply cease. Once the primitive streak is established, so is individuality. From this point on embryogenesis, the differentiation into tissues and systems – neural, cardiovascular and so on – can begin; to be followed by organogenesis and the forming of the fetus. Now it has for long been established in Western philosophy that there can be no human personality without individuality. Boethius is quoted down the centuries: *persona est individua substantia rationalis naturae*: a person is an individual partaking in rational nature. And rational nature is, of course, the common property of humanity. An *individual* there must be, to become eventually the bearer of rights, the embodiment of human attributes and moral agency – friendship, kindness, justice and the like. Without individuality there can be no moral agency, no accountability, no identity.

To attribute protectable status, therefore, at the point when individuality is established, so far as present-day science can establish it, would seem to me to be a proper application of the perennial moral tradition of matching protection to growth, to progress towards maturity. This point of attribution does not leave the pre-embryonic cells without human significance; neither does it entail an *absolute* duty of protection for the emerging embryo or fetus. The pre-embryonic cells are humanly significant because they are compounded of human genes, and they are of supreme value for the genetic information which they contain. This information, if not expressed in further development, can be read scientifically and form the basis of knowledge, sacred in itself, and valuable for beneficial application. For the growing embryo or fetus, on the other hand, there is a strong presumption in favour of its life, as there is for any life in being. The presumption is rebuttable only if challenged by an overwhelming moral claim. Undoubtedly we have, in modern society, weakened that presumption by cheapening, trivialising, the counter-claim: by an over-ready resort to abortion. We may acknowledge that abuse without abandoning the moral position of which it is an abuse. And, as I suggested earlier, we are to avoid the trap of reading back the arguments about abortion into the pre-implantation stage in which not all the relevant criteria can apply.

The genetic potential of the pre-embryonic cells is sometimes used as an argument for their inviolability. Because (it is said) the pre-embryo is a potential human being, it must be protected as though it were a human being. The potential is morally equated with the actual. This equation philosophy has for long denied. Aristotle dealt with it tersely in the *Metaphysics*: 'as becoming is between being and not being, so that which is becoming is always between that which is and that which is not' (994a). And again, 'that which exists potentially and not actually is the indeterminate' (1607b) (Smith and Ross, 1908). His word, 'indeterminate', is precise and apt to the condition of these cells: they are literally indeterminate, in relation to what they may become – until individuality is established. Roger Bacon, in the same century as St Thomas Aquinas, makes the point in a rather complex argument:

> thus the embryo in the mother's womb is not called 'man', especially before it receives the rational soul. Nevertheless, after the animal essence is transmuted and pushed onward to the point where it becomes a human species, it is necessary for that which develops beyond the essence of the genus, before the infusion of the rational soul, to possess the nature of man, since it is suited to receive a rational soul and not the soul of an ass or anything else. Therefore we do not say that it is a man, and yet it does belong to the same species as man according to incomplete being. (Lindberg, 1983)

In short, it is logically possible to recognise the pre-embryonic cells as having the potential of the human species without attributing to them full protection proper to the actual embodiment of the human species; and, given the right indications, it is morally possible also. Karl Rahner has written: 'The reasons in favour of experimenting (sc. on the pre-embryo) might carry more weight, considered rationally, than the uncertain rights of a human being whose very existence is doubted' (McCormick, 1981).

It is inevitable that a Conference on philosophical ethics related to reproductive medicine should reflect the ambient restrictive mood. To put it crudely, the question now widely asked – and vigorously debated in Parliament – is: 'How far can we let these scientists and doctors go, and how far will they go if we do not stop them?' That mood may permeate even our discussions. But must not the philosophical mind ask another question? What do we *expect* and *require* scientists and doctors to do, and what should we enable them to do? In our much exploited fear of what they may do if unrestrained, might we forget that a disciplined curiosity is natural and proper to the human mind – a sheer desire to know, and pure satisfaction in knowledge? And that the harnessing of knowledge to beneficial use in technology and practical skill is a duty arising from the social and benevolent nature of man? Do we forget the great maxims which have come down to us in the philosophical tradition? Aristotle's *Metaphysics* opens with the words 'All men by nature desire to know' (980a). The Christian Scholastic philosophers used to assert that to search with the mind is a duty entailed by the command to love God with the mind, the *amor intellectus Dei*. Albertus Magnus could affirm that 'the aim of natural science is not simply to accept the statement of others, but to investigate the causes that are at work in nature' (Weisheipl, 1980). And Peter Medawar, in our own generation, when his creative life had not much longer to run, could write: 'If the generative act in science is imaginative in character, only a failure of the imagination – a total inability to conceive what the solution to a problem *might* be – could bring scientific enquiry to a standstill' (Medawar, 1985). There is nothing particularly noble or Christian in the mood which says, ' We know enough: why seek for more?', or, 'Knowledge is dangerous: we have done harm enough with our knowledge already'. I would hope that a gathering of philosophers with medical scientists and practitioners would wish to affirm, to validate, fundamental research and innovative medicine as proper duties and indeed a high vocation for the human mind. Christians would say that it is proper work for man made in the image of God.

The practice is not without moral restraint. Those who profess the disciplines of science and the arts of medicine are themselves moral agents in the human community, the first line in ethical guidance and restraint in what is done. The extra, external, controls (Research Ethics Committees, the Law and the Courts) are second lines of defence in case the professional conscience, corporate as well as personal, should falter. Human gametes and the human embryo exert their proper and respective claims to ethical regard, to discipline in treatment and in use. It is but a decade since the first IVF baby was born. It is but 4 years since the Warnock Report was published. These are short periods for the formulation of an ethics of practice. If you compare the debate in the House of Lords on 15 January 1988, on the Government White Paper setting out its proposals for legislation on Human Fertilisation and Embryology, with the debate in the same House on the Warnock Report, you will see what a remarkable advance there has been in understanding. Peers have begun to speak from knowledge, and from appreciation of the serious ends being pursued by appropriate means.

Much of this advance must be due, I believe, to the corporate sense of responsibility shown by the practitioners in the IVF centres in this country: their constant testing of hypotheses and experimental procedures and their proper caution in trying to improve what is, on any comparative count, still a very low rate of success. Instances of the bizarre, in outcome or in intent, shake public confidence from time to time, and they are easily inflated and exploited by some of the media. They may yet imperil regular practice.

The Government is now committed to legislation, and to a Statutory Licensing Authority to exercise control. The pattern of control now envisaged is well tested in experience, in a century of control of experiments on animals exercised through the Home Office and, latterly, that exercised over IVF by the professions of science and medicine consensually through the Voluntary Licensing Authority. The critical question remaining open is whether the Statute, when enacted, will allow our present liberty of beneficial research and experiment to continue, or whether it will prohibit it under penal sanction. That question may well turn partly on the confidence generated by the practitioners themselves, and partly by the quality of the discussion generated in gatherings like our own today. Ideas, once freed, have pinions. Philosophers and scientists must be alike in this, that both require liberty for the pursuit of truth; and both are bound to a discipline proper to its pursuit.

References

Dunstan, G. R. (1988). The human embryo in the western moral tradition. In: *The Status of the Human Embryo. Perspectives from Moral Tradition*, eds G. R. Dunstan & M. J. Seller, pp. 39–57. King Edward's Hospital Fund for London, London.

Ford, N. (1988). *When Did I Begin?* Cambridge University Press, Cambridge.

Grobstein, C. (1979). External Human Fertilization. *Scientific American*, **240**, 33–43.

Grobstein, C. (1981). *From Chance to Purpose: An Appraisal of External Human Fertilization.* Addison-Wesley, Reading, Mass.

Lindberg, D. C. (1983). *Roger Bacon's Philosophy of Nature.* Clarendon Press, Oxford.

McCormick, R. A. (1981). *How Brave a New World?*, SCM Press, London.

Mahoney, J. (1984). *Bioethics and Belief.* Sheed & Ward, London.

Marshall, J. (1988). Experimenting on human embryos: sentience as the cut-off point? In: *The Status of the Human Embryo. Perspectives from Moral Tradition*, eds G. R. Dunstan & M. J. Seller, pp. 58–61. King Edward's Hospital Fund for London, London.

Medawar, P. B. (1985). *The Limits of Science.* Oxford University Press, London.

Smith, J. A. & Ross, W. D. (1908). *The Works of Aristotle. Vol. III, Metaphysica.* Clarendon Press, Oxford.

The Tablet. 20 February 1986, pp. 218–19; 16 January 1988, p. 68; 13 February 1988, pp. 181–2.

Weisheipl, J. A. (1980). *Albertus Magnus and the Sciences: Commemorative Essays.* Pontifical Institute of Theological Sciences, Toronto.

Discussion   Chairman: Professor Richard Lilford

Gorovitz: You said that social mechanisms like committees and policy boards are a second line of defence in case the conscience falters. With respect to many of the issues we are discussing, the conscience is itself unfocussed. Where new problems are not addressed by the history of moral thought, the conscience motivates the desire to have this sort of deliberation.

Dunstan: We still regard the medical practitioner as the responsible moral agent in decision. This does not mean that he is a solitary omnipotent power. His judgements must be consistent with the ethics of his profession and what is accepted as ethical by the society which he serves. Neither do we assume that in an area of developmental medicine and a new science, he is going to form his conscience entirely unaided. Given human nature and the nature of science, and especially the capacity for exploitation of the science and the practice, there is need for further points of reference, sometimes further control. Hence ethical committees, which are voluntary in their constitution, and the cross-reference between scientists and practitioners on the ethical committees. Hence, standing behind them, levels of regulation, not always statutory, appointed by government. Standing behind them, statute and the courts of law. We have our protective lines spread out, but the first line of defence for the patient, and for the human being, must be the practitioner himself, and I think we do a grave disservice to humanity if we try and take that away from him and give it to a committee.

Serr: I refer to your interpretation of the Septuagint as translated in Alexandria from the original Hebrew text in which there is the fight between two men which may bring about a spontaneous abortion. Nothing is mentioned about form, it is only mentioned that this is an abortion, and it is proved by the fact that one can compensate for it monetarily. The next sentence goes on to say, however, if a life is taken, not referring to the fetus, then the famous sentence 'a life for a life, an eye for an eye, and a tooth for a tooth'. This was later taken up in the Talmud as 40 days, which was actually thought to be when the soul enters the fetus, which again is not morphological, and was later taken up by Islamic thought as 120 days. It is still one of the guiding features of both those religions.

Spallane: This concentration on the status of the embryo constantly sweeps the woman under the carpet. The subject of all of this is not in fact the embryo. The woman is the central subject, woman, whether we are talking about an embryo in the womb or in a Petri dish. Statements have been juggled around the idea of what is invasive: 'experimenting on an embryo is observation not experimentation because it is not invasive'. Again the woman is swept under the carpet. Women's groups I am involved with have made a formal note of this to the DHSS, to the Voluntary Licensing Authority and to the Progress lobby here, and I think that in other countries women are doing the same. I found Professor Dunstan doing a kind of juggling to buttress the moral arguments about experimentation and about protection of the embryo. You cannot talk in those terms scientifically because life is a continuum and you can go all the way back to the genes. Even you use them as an identity marker for humanity.

Grobstein: As an embryologist, it seemed to me fascinating that there was an embryology of morality as well as an embryology of humans. Is it necessarily the case that the embryology of morality conforms to the embryology of mammals? There may be some degree of non-correspondence between our developing morality and our developing scientific knowledge.

Dunstan: The major question and the danger always is, when constructing a case, to select those points which conform to the idea you want to present. That is what we all do in order to make a case for discussion. When forming a thing like an ethics of practice, we have to formulate the thing ourselves, we have to articulate our judgements and articulate what we think it right to do and what not to do. This cannot be done in monologue and it cannot be done claiming utter consistency. However, by repudiating, as I must, the control of absolutes over this area of scientic endeavour and medical practice, I am bound to face probable inconsistencies and to choose the best I can.

Millican: I would like raise two points. The first one is I am not persuaded that you can get where you want without appealing to the potential of the human embryo and running a danger of speciesism.

It is not clear to me that you can justify a special status for human life without appealing to the qualities which human life brings, but which are not present at such an early stage, unless you wish to appeal to some theological perspective that will give human life a special status above all others. The second point is whether determinism is such an important matter. Supposing a terrorist shoots into a crowd at random. I do not think that that is morally better than shooting at individuals. Likewise, it does not seem to be obvious that because the pre-embryo is indeterminate in terms of its identity, that it itself does not seem to be of obvious moral influence.

Dunstan: I should like, if I may, an embryologist to take that one up. What I thought was *not* that the cells have any moral value or lack of value because they are indeterminate, but because there is no guaranteed human destination for them.

Braude: The question of whether something is indeterminate or not is important because it may well be that a group of cells is never ever going to form an embryo, i.e. it would start out as a group of 2, 4 or 8 cells, and those cells have equal potential to become embryos and to become placentae. It would seem quite ridiculous to decide that what you have is something that is definitely going to be an embryo. We do not have that knowledge. The cells that would form, for example, the main cell mass, may fail, and all you would have is a placenta. These are exactly the same indeterminate cells and to regard that group of cells as a person or a potential person would be ignoring the biological facts. It is not a simple philosophical theoretical argument.

Millican: It would seem to me that the terrorist who fires into a crowd is no less culpable just because he might not hit people. The issue of determinism is a relative argument if we are talking about fetal rights, because if we are talking about rights there has to be an individual who has those rights. Professor Dunstan's concern was to get away from the concept of rights and to concentrate on our duties towards the pre-embryo, and that the fact that it might not have the potential to be a human being might weaken our obligation, but does not do away with it, if it is admitted that we do have a moral obligation once it becomes determined.

Dunstan: That is where we divide. I have not said we are without obligation to the pre-embryonic cell, they are so valuable we must not waste them, they are precious in themselves and in the knowledge that they give. But I deny that they have the same protectable status as an organism which has passed that area of uncertainty, indeterminancy and hazard and is on its way, its steady growth, towards being born. Undoubtedly we have matched protection to it according to its growth and I am resting on that. I do believe that there is a material discontinuity between the pre-embryonic fluidity and the stability of the embryo and fetus, and on that I think I can draw a valid moral distinction.

Lilford: I suppose that when the pregnancy is implanted you know that it is going to continue?

Dunstan: You assume it is going to continue.

Lilford: Nevertheless, I think it a point of interest that those who believe the embryo should have complete protection presumably have to be against the coil as a method of contraception, because that probably causes an abortion of the same embryonic stage.

Dunstan: There is an inconsistency there because some of the highest authorities who forbid contraception and forbid abortion have ruled it permissible for a girl who has been ravished to resort to the pill which prevents implantation. They explain, in doing so, that this is not an abortion because there is nothing yet to abort, but they agree it is a defensive measure even though, on their terms, the zygote itself has the claim of human life. Even those who profess to live by certain absolute rules recognise this necessary concession to a human accident, and this is a major inconsistency, and one which I defend.

Keown: In this reference to the morning-after pill are you referring to the Catholic Bishops condoning its administration in cases of rape?

Dunstan: It was not a matter of condoning it, it was a case of saying that this could be held to be licit.

Keown: It was not because they conceded that there was no worthwhile or viable life. It was because they took the view that there was an acceptable risk that there was nothing there at all. My other question is that you mentioned the distinction between formed and unformed fetuses. How do you think the Christian Church regarded the abortion of an unformed fetus?

Dunstan: The question posed by the canonists and moralists was: 'Is it homicide to terminate a pregnancy?', and the answer certainly was: 'If it is *formatus et animatus* it was homicide; if it is not it is not homicide'. Augustine expounded this very carefully. In the Celtic Penitentials you find that it was 7 years on bread and water to cause a women to miscarry if the fetus was not formed and 14 years if it was. The short answer is that to cause the growing human being to cease to grow was always a sin but was never homicide until *formatus et animatus*.

Keown: But it was always regarded as mortal sin?

Dunstan: Well, a grave sin. This is important. If you read the documents carefully they condemn, as one sin, spilling your seed on the ground, giving a women potions to cause her to be sterile or not to conceive, or causing a fetus to miscarry. These three were equated under one condemnation and it gives you an example of the sort of sin it was. I do not know whether you regard it as mortal or not.

Keown: Did the Church not regard it as a mortal sin?

Dunstan: The mortal and venial distinction was a bit later in the tradition. They did not think in those terms in the earlier days.

Keown: In the early days of the Church it was regarded as homicide. It is important to stress that this question of formation simply relates to canonical penalty and the tradition of the Christian Church was always that abortion at whatever stage of pregnancy was a very great wrong.

Dunstan: I do not deny it was held to be a sin but all the texts refuse to equate it with homicide until formed and animated. Now, if homicide means the taking, whether licitly or illicitly, of human life and if to take the life of an unformed fetus was not homicide, logically it requires you to believe that they did not equate unformed life with fully protectable human life. Gregory of Nyssa knew perfectly well what he was saying about this. Sin yes; homicide no.

Singer: To return to speciesism, my sympathies are with Peter Millican. If you eschew the argument of potential, then, simply to say that this is a human life, or even an individuated human life, is not enough to give a basis for saying that therefore it is worthy of moral protection. To say that simply because it is a member of the species *Homo sapiens* is no better than to say that it is worthy of protection because it is a member of a particular race. I also wanted you to say a bit more on sentience. My own view follows from the refusal to take the fact that a life is of a certain species as morally significant. You have to look at certain characteristics, which make a moral difference as they develop. The most obvious one would be when the developing embryo or fetus is capable of suffering. You refer to this as a view that can easily be refuted.

Dunstan: If the argument is that provided it feels no pain you may do as you wish, it leads you into quite dangerous waters. You can remove pain by anaesthetic but that does not give you licence to do as you wish.

Beller: It is said we do not know when life begins but we know when it ends. Do we know that? Why do we discuss brain-stem death so intensively? Nobody brought up the question of when brain life begins? We have proposed, when considering the anencephalic, that the fusion of the neural tube may be the beginning of brain life because the conceptus may have the potential to feel pain.

Genetic manipulation and experimentation

My assignment is to discuss genetic manipulation and experimentation from the perspective of philosophical ethics in reproductive medicine. I should begin by saying that professionally I am not a geneticist, a philosopher or a physician. My training and research experience were in embryology and developmental biology and my interest and activities for more than a decade have been in public policy in relation to advances in reproductive knowledge. This includes the ethical, legal and social status of early human developmental stages and the public policy options regarding newer reproductive technologies and their applications within the human sphere. I have paid particular attention to interventions in human heredity and this is my focus in what follows.

Clarity is more likely to be achieved if I state my conclusions first and then go back to indicate the facts and reasoning that lead to them. To begin, it is my belief that the manipulation of human heredity, for carefully defined purposes and under appropriate oversight, is both ethically acceptable and socially desirable. Accordingly, research in that direction should not only be pursued but should be more widely recognised as advantageous and necessary to probable future human objectives. To accomplish this, however, will require broader public understanding, as well as new foci and means of decision-making and careful ethical analysis at each step taken. This paper is intended to be a contribution in the direction indicated.

The argument for the position I have stated begins with the relevant scientific facts and, particularly, with what has turned out to be the surprising simplicity of the basic hereditary material. Informationally rich deoxyribonucleic acid (DNA) is a very long double-stranded chain of only four different elementary chemical units or nucleotides. The sequence of the nucleotides can determine, albeit in complex ways, either an identical sequence of nucleotides in a new DNA strand or the sequence of amino acids in a particular protein. In the first instance, the DNA is *replicated* as a genotype or genome, in the second case the genotype is *expressed* as a phenotype. The first process is the foundation of heredity, the second is correspondingly the foundation of development. Together the two constitute reproduction in all living organisms.

There is an important further fact to be mentioned. The replication of the genome through successive generations, while remarkably effective in biological terms, is not perfect. In various ways imperfections creep into the replicating genome. Major ones are quickly eliminated because they lead to lethal effects early in the new generation, moderate ones may persist for varying times in new generations depending upon circumstances, minor ones may be passed on through generations indefinitely, again depending upon circumstance. These imperfections are the source of genetic variation and the more advantageous of them become the raw material for building evolutionary progression. Similarly, they are the source of the individual variation we so much prize in ourselves.

One further fact completes the scenario. As understanding of heredity has emerged, first through accumulated experience and then through increasingly sophisticated science, it has been integrated into various technological practices, for example in agriculture and medicine. It has also taken root in our dominant attitudes and habits of thought. The latter effects are now producing some turbulence in intellectual and policy circles because they are recognised as a quantum jump in human capability to intervene in human heredity via the remarkably accessible and manipulable DNA. In this vision, the scenario suddenly seems to leap from the status of spectacularly successful science into the realm of philosophy and even theology. Is Creation itself, some ask, becoming the possession of possibly profane human hands? Are we at a watershed at which divinity and humanity confusingly overlap and both become ambiguous? Are mere humans seeking to 'play God'?

I shall concentrate on this aspect of the matter because it seems most appropriate to this occasion. But first allow me to scan briefly the nature of the policy problems raised by the possible application of genetic technology directly to human begins. The issue arises most acutely in medical science and practice in relation to gene therapy. This form of therapy refers to treatment of hereditary disease by replacing or over-riding a defective gene with a normal one. Of the several thousand diseases known to have a demonstrable genetic aetiology, a relatively small number are based on a defect in a single gene. Among these are certain of the thalassaemias, haemoglobinopathies and immune deficiencies, all involving the continually propagating cells of the bone marrow. These have become the target of a proposed therapeutic strategy.

[*Note*: the immune deficiency disease referred to here and later in the chapter is a rare *inherited* disorder and should not be confused with Acquired Immune Deficiency Syndrome or AIDS. (Eds.)].

The first step in the strategy is to isolate the DNA containing the normal human gene that has undergone the defective change. The second step is to insert the normal gene into a suitable carrier or vector that is capable of entering human cells, in the present instance a retrovirus. The third step is to show that stem cells of bone marrow, the precursors of the defective cells in the targeted diseased individuals, will incorporate into their genome the retrovirus containing the desired gene and both replicate and express it as the cells multiply and mature. The fourth step is to return successfully treated cells to the patient's bone marrow under circumstances that will allow them competitively to replace the defective precursor cells. Theoretically, if the four steps are successfully accomplished, the patient should show clinical improvement because cells derived from the treated stem cells will be normal.

The several earlier steps have been accomplished, though with less than impressive quantitative results in the third step, as carried out in animal studies. It is the fourth step, a clinical trial in actual patients, that poses the difficult policy issues. The first issue that is widely discussed asks whether deliberate intervention in the human genome is acceptable under *any* circumstance, given its central importance as a fundamental biological definition of humanity. The answer given by virtually all responsible groups charged to examine the matter (Walters, 1986) is that gene transfer to the human genome is acceptable under current therapeutic standards if it will provide benefit to the individual patient and usual practices for innovative therapies are observed. The argument is that gene transfer to *somatic cells*, which have no role in producing a new generation, is not ethically different from other established forms of therapy that alter the cellular genome – for example, the use of chemotherapy or radiotherapy for cancer. In emphasising somatic cells, the argument sharply distinguishes between cells whose descendants are limited to the individual under treatment (i.e. somatic) and cells whose descendants include gametes (i.e. *germ line cells*). Decision as to the acceptability of germ line treatment is reserved for further deliberation since it raises larger issues than simple therapy that is limited to non-germ-line or somatic cells.

In this view, it is germ line genetic modification and not gene transfer itself that raises the really difficult issues. The concern here is with intergenerational rather than with intragenerational consequences. Lurking not too far in the background is anxiety over possible eugenic use, i.e. deliberate management of human heredity in the alleged interest of 'human improvement', however and for whatever purpose improvement may be defined.

This is the issue we will focus on here. Should germ line modification be practised on the human genome and, if so, under what circumstances and for what purposes? I shall begin with a scenario that offers conceivable circumstances under which germ line modification could be regarded as an acceptable option. Assume that gene therapy is developed successfully to relieve the somatic symptoms of immune deficiency disease. The lives of young children suffering from the disease might therefore be preserved sufficiently to allow them to marry and raise offspring. But, in the absence of germ line treatment, the offspring will be at significant risk to develop immune deficiency disease similar to that of their parent. They would, therefore, also require somatic gene therapy or repetition of the cycle would occur in each subsequent generation.

Under these circumstances the rationale for the definitive solution provided by germ line therapy would seem compelling. On what grounds, in such cases, would one deny the claim to reproductive health while bestowing somatic health on those who are genetically afflicted?

The scenario once again makes clear that the policy problem lies not in the *procedure* for gene transfer but in the *values* implicit in its purpose and consequence. To restore *full* health to an afflicted child is, in itself, a benefaction that few can resist. So long as germ line therapy could be confined to such a context it is likely eventually to be accepted. But, if successful, will or should it necessarily be confined to that context? Or will it, once available, be applied to perhaps more questionable contexts? This, of course, is the usual slippery slope attack vigorously pursued by opponents of many innovative technologies. How much weight should be given to a possible slippery slope in the particular case of gene transfer for therapeutic and other possible purposes?

To assess the matter further, let us consider two other scenarios. Some serious consideration is currently being given to the possibility not only of extraterrestrial human exploration but of actual colonisation of the Moon and Mars and, further down the road, even of other solar systems. The travel distances to such sites of colonisation are measured roughly in units of days, months and years for the three possibilities respectively. Assuming such intervals, travel to the Moon need not seriously interrupt family production and rearing, but travel to and from Mars certainly would impose some limits. However, when we consider travel to the nearest star, at 4 light-years, we must assume essentially complete reproductive isolation. Moreover, given the logistics of space travel, the colonising party cannot be large, very likely it would entail not more than a hundred women, men and possibly children. These are to be the founders of eventual much larger populations, just as the founding coloniser-parties have been on Earth for oceanic islands.

It is well known that the survival of such small founder populations depends heavily on the characteristics of their gene pool. This is because the close inbreeding that is inevitable in small populations leads, as compared to larger populations, to more frequent phenotypic expression of disadvantageous recessive genes that occur in significant number in all natural populations. This threat to human colony survival might be addressed in several ways, among which the most definitive solution would be genetic screening of founder-candidates for disadvantageous recessive genes and replacement of them by more advantageous variants. After all, in the language of what many would regard as a suitable rationale, why infect a New World with the mistakes of an older one? However, such a solution, if practicable, clearly would be a form of eugenics, earlier defined as a strategy to improve the human species on Earth. But, whether on or off the Earth, who is to define advantageous versus disadvantageous? How can one disclaim the reality that such application of gene transfer *is* creation of new and, in a limited sense, improved humanity?

One final scenario may be permitted to round out the issues that arise in connection with gene transfer to the human germ line. The nuclear accident at Chernobyl in the USSR renewed the concerns and debates of three decades ago, when nuclear testing in the atmosphere led to wide anxiety about the health and genetic effects of radioactive fallout. Various estimates were provided of the probable increase of cancer incidence and mortality in the areas exposed to the Chernobyl fallout. What, in fact, is traced in such assessments is the geographics of a 'genetic scar' in the affected population, i.e. the number and distribution of individuals whose DNA had been altered in ways that increase the likelihood of serious delayed effects.

The destructive impact of an actual major nuclear war has also been estimated. Here the level of genetic scarring is a relatively minor concern in relation to the vastness of the less subtle physical devastation that can be anticipated. Nonetheless, assuming there to be sufficient survivors to reinstitute sophisticated medical care, the consequences of genetic scarring would be substantial, both for the immediately exposed population and for generations thereafter. Indeed, isolated small groups of survivors would each become a founder-population in its local area. Under these circumstances, means of genetic repair, including gene transfer, might become an essential technology for the continuance of humanity.

The scenarios described are not forecasts, although they are not entirely contrived, like plots in science fiction. They are introduced to convey a sense of the possible direction of future development but also, more particularly, to indicate the context within which policy issues are likely to be judged. Quite clearly, these issues, together with the issues raised by Professor Dunstan in the preceding chapter, indicate that advancing knowledge is challenging values that are very near the apex of existing ethical hierarchies. In fact, they disturb assumptions about the source and authority of a number of our most encompassing and salient human values.

This profound challenge, however, is not my subject here although it is certainly part of its background. My immediate objective is to clarify what kind of public policy process can deal with our rising capability to intervene in and to manage the human genome, in whatever degree this may prove feasible. This is a matter that has its origins in biomedical science and technology but that must find an accommodative and sound solution in a human society that is pluralistic in its background beliefs and values. In such a context, the preceding scenarios seem to me to justify an affirmative answer to the question of whether germ line gene transfer in humans should ever be attempted. But when and how particular decisions should be made remains an urgent item on the current policy agenda.

With respect to that persistent question, I shall again first offer my own summary conclusion and then attempt to provide a persuasive rationale. I regard the issue of deliberate intervention in the human genome as too profound to be left either to happenstance or even to considered individual decision, no matter how well-informed or wise the decision-maker may be assumed to be. I take this position because in my view the human genome is, in its very essence, a fundamental *collective* property of humanity – past, present and future. Therefore, deliberate intervention should never occur without collective deliberation. The question thus becomes a political one in the widest sense; it requires formal decision by a process stipulated and carried out within the body politic. The truly difficult question is how to define the relevant body politic and the mechanisms to assure to all relevant parties a suitable decision role. I shall offer some thoughts on each of these questions in now outlining the rationale for the conclusion I have just stated.

First, biologically, the human genome as a concept is fundamentally collective in nature. Though it is true that each individual human has a unique genome (setting aside identical twins as a special case), the human genome as we are here discussing it refers to that of the species as a population. In this conception, each individual genome is best thought of as a node in an overall hereditary web. Linking the nodes within the web there are kin relationships among members of a generation and also between succeeding generations. It is the substance of the web of linkages with which we are concerned when we consider the implications of gene transfer to germ-line cells. That substance is the collective human genome and its meaningful message is written in nucleotide sequence. Interestingly, we know now that the human genome and that of the pigmy chimpanzee, believed to be our closest neighbour-species genetically, are more than 99% identical. In these genetic terms, the large behavioural and cultural (phenotypic) differences between humans and chimpanzees involves less than 1% of our genomic heritage. The differences among ourselves as humans are based on an even smaller percentage of our total genetic heritage: a small fraction of 1%. Thus, looking at individual human genomes within our species, commonness rather than difference is overwhelming. It is this commonness that is our collective heritage and property as human beings. And it is about possible changes in this collective property, which is both a characteristic of the human species and something that is commonly 'owned', that all human beings have a right to be consulted. All of ancestry (past) and all of descendancy (future) are at stake in this lineage that is becoming ever more clearly of rising cosmic significance. It is appropriate then that the human genome be viewed as a focus of both universal human dedication and full human participation in decision.

A second major point to be made is that, despite the universal implications of intervention in the human genome, it is also clear that specific decisions necessarily will be made within more restricted jurisdictions – in accordance with the current realities of the organisation of the world body politic. Its fundamental units, of course, are the nation states that exist in varying combinations and systems of interaction up to the level of the United Nations.

With respect to policy governing human gene transfer, supranational bodies may offer significant but limited general guidance. But the operation of everyday public policy depends upon national or infranational decision. This is not to neglect the significant impact of non-governmental institutions, particularly those such as religious groups that deal actively with issues having high moral content.

In considering appropriate policy at the national level, I shall rely primarily on developments in the United States, simply because it is that situation that I know best. I shall, however, try to speak only of aspects that may be generalisable, not only to other nations but also conceivably to the world scene.

A third general point, then, is that possible gene transfer to the human germ line needs to be approached with great caution and within a regulatory oversight that emphasises open deliberation as to objectives, risks and possible unanticipated consequences. In the USA, public concern about human gene transfer in general seems to have been assuaged when worries were brought to the attention of President Carter in 1980 in a joint communication from three prominent religious organisations. In response, the President's Commission for the Study of Ethical Problems in Medicine and Biomedical and Behavioral Research, which was in existence at the time, initiated a major study (1982). This study within the Executive Branch was augmented by one in the Congressional Branch that reached generally similar conclusions (United States Congress, 1983). As summarised at a recent symposium sponsored by the Institute of Medicine and the National Academy of Sciences (Nichols, 1988),

> The ethical issues raised by human somatic cell gene therapy are the same as those raised by other new forms of therapy. . . . The issues surrounding germ line gene therapy are more complex, because genetic changes would be passed on to future generations. Government, religious, civic and scientific leaders should encourage widespread discusson of the pros and cons of germ line gene therapy, even though it is unclear whether the approach will ever be technically feasible for human beings.

While public education and discussion are certainly highly desirable, none of these reports makes clear what would constitute an acceptable motivation for human germ line therapy and what would not. In legislation passed in 1986, the Congress created a Congressional Biomedical Ethics Board charged, among other things, to examine the issue of gene therapy. The Board, comparable in its structure to the Congressional Office of Technology Assessment (OTA), was appointed but a Scientific Advisory Committee, called for by the legislation to conduct actual studies, has not come into existence. A stalemate reportedly developed because of concerns within the Board about attitudes of suggested nominees towards the knotty subject of abortion.

Meanwhile, research on germ line gene transfer moves forward on non-human species. In mice the technique has been successfully used, for example, to create special strains useful in studies of gene expression. In cattle and other domesticated species it is being used in an effort to achieve economic objectives, such as improved body structure for increased meat yield per carcass or secretion of desirable pharmacological products into cow's milk. Such studies will enhance technical background for possible human application but will need to be more specifically augmented if acceptable objectives and purposes for human application are defined. For the moment, the only governmental loci for such studies or their support appear to be the OTA, the Human Gene Therapy Subcommittee of the Recombinant DNA Advisory Committee or the program on Ethics and Values in Science and Technology in the National Science Foundation.

What questions would such studies address? Two general approaches to the problem of human germ line modification can be conceived, the formulation of *ad hoc* general principles or analysis case by case. An example of the former would be a prohibition against application of gene therapy to any offspring without consent of both parents. An example of the latter is approval of a specific protocol for use of gene therapy to cope with a particular life-threatening genetic disease. It has been generally assumed that in consideration of somatic cell gene therapy the process should go case by case, possibly leading to the emergence of principles as experience is gained. This is a reasonable approach. But is the same approach necessarily applicable to germ line modification? This is a question that could usefully be discussed at the present time, particularly since there appears to be general consensus that germ line modification raises new issues of principle that are much more consequential than those raised by somatic cell therapy. What are these issues of principle and how much consensus is there on each? Can preliminary agreement be reached on some of them so that they can be set aside? Which are the ones that most need fuller public discussion? In what format can this best occur?

With these considerations in mind, and recalling the somewhat turbulent history of the recombinant DNA debate in the 1970s, the following course of policy-making seems reasonable and feasible. A first necessary step is establishment, in each national jurisdiction involved in gene transfer research, of a deliberative body specifically and exclusively devoted to possible human genomic modification. The body, referred to as the Commission on the Human Genome or the equivalent, should prepare to receive and, subsequently, consider for approval any and all proposals within its national jurisdiction that are intended or likely to involve substantial modification of the human genome, whether in individuals or in populations.

In exercising its oversight role, the Commission should be constituted to include relevant expertise as well as respected public leadership; should be responsible for assuring adequate public education and information in its area of activity; and should maintain liaison with comparable bodies in other national jurisdictions with the objective of providing a concordant international policy.

Suitable powers of enforcement should be conferred on the Commission by statute or regulation and it should have adequate resources to exercise continuing oversight with respect to research on, and practice of, human genetic modification.

Second, in exercising its responsibilities the Commission should give particular attention to anticipating the road ahead, i.e. to scouting out and assessing potentials and pros and cons of human genetic interventions that are or may be technically feasible in the near term. This activity should be proactive rather than reactive, with the Commission seeking to anticipate and even to guide, in both a positive and negative sense, the course of research and development. In so doing, the Commission should view itself as an active participant in the ongoing process over which it has oversight, not as a deadweight to be overcome but as a supportive partner representing the national and overall human ethos.

Third, in carrying out its delicate leadership role, the Commission should continuously reformulate and publicly articulate objectives, criteria and judgemental mechanisms as experience with consideration of possible genetic intervention grows. The experience should initially be case by case, but the effort should be increasingly to generate principles for guidance as suitable and effective strategies are clarified. In this sense, over extended time, human purpose and judgement may become a conscious and deliberate factor in human genetic progression.

Fourth, based on the foregoing, it may become possible, in the very long term, to formulate a prospectus for the role and limits of genomic intervention in the human future. Such a prospectus could provide models for sound management of the human genome as it is tested in diverse colonisation sites beyond the Earth. Such policies may be essential to proceeding with due caution to reap the benefits while avoiding the hazards of our dawning use of genetic intervention in our own fundamental continuity and kinship – the ultimate expression of philosophical ethics in reproductive medicine.

References

Nichols, E. (ed.) (1988). *Human Gene Therapy: Annual Session of the Prestigious Institute of Medicine.* Harvard University Press, Cambridge, Mass. and London, p. 171.

President's Commission for the Study of Ethical Problems in Medicine and Biomedical and Behavioral Research. (1982). *Splicing Life: The Social and Ethical Issues of Genetic Engineering with Human Beings.* US Government Printing Office, Washington DC (Stock No. 83–600500).

United States Congress, Office of Technology Assessment (1984). *Human Gene Therapy – A Background Paper.* US Congress, Office of Technology Assessment, Washington DC (OTA-BP-BA-32).

Walters, L. (1986). The ethics of human gene therapy. *Nature,* **320,** 225–7.

Discussion   Chairman: Professor Richard Lilford

H. Murray: Would you envisage that this forum for debate, the deliberative body, would consider individual cases which, as we know, soon become precedents?

Grobstein: One of the things that would have to be decided is whether or when to spin off from this body something comparable to the local kinds of arrangements that exists to deal with biomedical issues.

Lilford: Do I understand correctly that, in the USA, such commissions were formed, one by administration and one by congress and they got dead locked?

Grobstein: No, what was formed was a bioethics board which was instructed to look into the matter of gene therapy. One would hope that out of it may come a scheme of this general sort but it is blocked at the moment in that what would be the guiding committee, a primarily but not entirely scientific advisory committee, has not come into existence because of the issue of abortion.

Mott: You thought gene therapy would be used for replacing an abnormal gene or where it might restore full health to somebody who did not have it. Going on currently, with existing technology, some Olympic athletes are having blood taken and reinfused to give them a competitive advantage when they come to race and normal children are having injections of recombinant human growth hormone in order to make them bigger and stronger. Do you not think that the advent of gene therapy is as likely to go along that route as towards replacing defective genes?

Grobstein: Neither of the examples that you give are ones that would involve gene therapy as I defined it. The hypothetical mechanism which I described would take up exactly the question you are raising and in my view would reject those sorts of purposes for the use of gene therapy.

Mott: The specific growth hormone example was one of the first transgenic experiments in another species, mice. You can inject growth hormone gene into mice and produce supermice. So it is perfectly possible to do this in the human situation. I am merely pointing out it is being done without gene therapy to get at the issue. We are talking about gene therapy as a technique rather than getting at whether its use may be ethical or otherwise in given defined circumstances.

Lilford: Those examples are similar to somatic gene therapy but different to embryo gene therapy which carries forward to a new generation.

Grobstein: Correct. What is described in the mice requires a procedure that I think would be totally unacceptable if feasible in the human. You are using 'the slippery slope' approach as I did too. In the case that we are discussing, the important question is whether we will invent the social mechanism that will insure that we will go as far along a slope as is beneficial, without necessarily blocking off an area that can be useful.

Gillon: Professor Grobstein, your position has been that removal of deleterious genes is acceptable in general, whereas improvement of the speices is something that we must be much more worried about. I have a science-fiction scenario in mind. What would your reaction be if it were possible to improve the genetic structure of human beings by incorporating a chlorophyll-generating gene into the skin? Suppose it were possible, would it be so unacceptable, given the starvation which exists in the world, to experiment, at least among consenting adults on behalf of their children?

Grobstein: If something is imagined that will be highly beneficial, and it involves genetic modification, should it be excluded or accepted out of hand? My answer to that is, if by some social mechanism such as I outlined, it were agreed that this were a distinct advantage, and there was a consensus in favour, then from a public policy point of view, not a moral one, this should go ahead. If it turns out subsequently that this has unforeseen negative consequences, it should be stopped. So long as the process of decision is appropriate it is we who ultimately are responsible for these judgements, and have to live with them and have to be willing to make them.

Beller: Do you request a unanimous decision of that commission?

Grobstein: I would assume this commission would work on the basis of consensus rather than unanimity. That means negotiation and accomodation within the commission. Its recommendation, to become policy, would then have to be endorsed by a congress or whatever you have. The commission is a deliberative body and would exist alone only at the beginning. One of its objectives would be to move decision making down to a more local level.

Holm: With the time scale in the experiment on human germ cells you would wait at least 20 years to find out if you are completely successful.

Grobstein: I do not think that I specified what the time scale was. The mechanism that is set up has to be flexible enough to deal with different rates. I am primarily concerned to get the process initiated and cannot adequately forecast how rapidly this committee would face practical questions. The important thing would be for it to get ready to fact them.

Kluge: I am a member of the ethics advisory panel of the British Columbia Ministry of Health and one of our functions is to suggest legislation in the area of health, particularly in this area and our divided opinion is somewhat more practical. Who should own any particular section of the genome, that might be incorporated so as to produce a beneficial effect? We are dealing with communal human property in general and the very practical question as to the ownership, not simply as a matter of its position but as a matter of right concerns us. Have you any ideas on that?

Grobstein: This is exactly the kind of issue that ought to be confronted by the sort of mechanism outlined. I would oppose individual ownership, in the sense of control and exclusion of others, of any portion of the human genome.

Gorovitz: Your main procedural thesis is fraught with optimism about the effectiveness in reaching some kind of closure on controversial issues by a broad-based diverse deliberative body. I have days like that myself. You have cited in your remarks some instances in which our own efforts to have such deliberations proceed effectively have been thwarted by unrelated political considerations. That is not the only example. *In vitro* fertilisation has, for close to a decade, been singled out and subjected to a moratorium on federal research support, because of political intrusions in precisely the kind of deliberative process you describe. My question is, how well founded is the optimism your suggestion reveals? When we try to do precisely what you suggested all too often it fails because of extrinsic interruptions.

Grobstein: We have moved substantially in this area in a favourable direction over the last decade or two with respect of recombinant DNA and with respect of *in vitro* fertilisation. So I think there are some empirical grounds for optimism.

Millican: Steptoe and Edwards did their work without any governmental commission, and got on with it. Now, is there anything to prevent a group somewhere, not so government conscious as the USA or Great Britain, getting into this field and then their people emigrating to our own countries? Can this be contained?

Grobstein: That is a difficulty. The only hope is that there is a general climate created that may isolate that phenomenon. We should understand that no one nation, by its policy, could change the course of human genetic progression. In the population of the world of, at the present time around five billion, there is very little that any small group can do to change the total gene pool.

Millican: There are at least two main objections to genetic manipulation. One of them is that it is undesirable for us to play God and these things should be left to nature, there will be natural changes in the genome but we must not do it because it is wrong for us to do it. The other objection is that it brings perhaps disastrous consequences. A global policy is not so obviously the right thing although superficially it is appealing. If you have a global policy, it implies that any changes that are made will be much more systematic. Given that there are random changes in the human genome anyway, the possible disastrous consequences of genetic manipulation arise from the fact that the human genome changes systematically as governed by man, with totally unforeseen conse-quences.

Grobstein: I did not intend to advocate a global policy. Rather what I advocated was national policies, which would not necessarily mean a uniformity of policy in the various countries involved. Again, I find it a difficult time to imagine that any concerted policy could significantly effect the total human genome. This is going to be significant where one deals with small subpopulations isolated from the main population. This is a far-out concept, but it is not unreasonable to assume that such small populations will eventually have to be considered as a practical problem

Millican: Do you think it is a good thing that systematic, population-wide genetic manipulation is not feasible.

Grobstein: Yes.

Lilford: A point people working in science make is that legislation is a protec-tion for the scientist to allow him to work without worrying or frightening the public.

Grobstein: The *in vitro* fertilisation experience is the strongest indicator of that. There is a real desire to be clear on what public policy is and not to carry the burden of making the decision.

Harris: Your argument seemed to be that because affect on the human gene pool affects us all there has to be public consent. Consent of the population of one nation does not secure that kind of consent because the human gene pool is worldwide and affects everybody. Since you are not in favour of global policy, I do not see how national consent secures the objective that your argument seemed to indicate.

Grobstein: I think that in some degree the policy should be global. There has to be participation but that is different from urging a uniform policy or a recommended model law for all countries. I do not advocate that or a concerted worldwide eugenic programme.

Harris: Changes in the gene pool affect humanity at large but national consent can only be from a particular population at a particular place.

Grobstein: I agree, but here we are talking about the genome as a human property. We are talking over a long period of time, between three million and three billion years. In that time frame it is a common human property but in the time frame of what we do this week or next month not so. On the other hand the patenting problem is an issue of ownership and therefore ought not to come under the exclusive control of any one individual or any small group.

Braude: When we are talking about genetic manipulation we are talking about very sophisticated techniques, about committees to regulate them and how to effect the total world gene pool. It is a small number of people who might be involved in this. A much stronger manipulation of the world gene pool is in our own hands. For example, let us say that we come up with a potent mixture that enables anyone to choose the sex of a child to be entirely male. This may not be a scientific development, it may have been picked up totally incidentally by a scientist. It is now within the grasp and you might find many cultures decide that they will have only male children. This is not now within the realm of any commission to stop.

Johnson: I am more concerned about how you envisage this whole thing taking its first decision: given what we know about transgenesis in animals, of site-specific expression differences, of mosaicism in the germ line as well as the cell line and the problem of actually transferring technology between species where you do not usually get the same result.

Grobstein: You are asking how do you get this sort of thing started and how are you going to implement it in a policy? That is going to vary at each national jurisdiction. In the USA legislation was actually passed that would set up just a mechanism for an initial evaluation and set of recommendations. I am assuming that this is the way. Hopefully it would involve more and more.

Johnson: What do you envisage as being an acceptable condition on which to undertake this?

Grobstein: I do not have in mind any particular situations apart from my first scenario. Having succeeded over a period of time with somatic therapy, the question would be of possibly generalising it to the germ line, in that specific case, with that particular gene. That might either be immune deficiency, or it might be haemoglobinopathy. Is that what you had in mind?

Johnson: Even doing that, which is the logical way to go, requires a fundamental change to go from colonising the haemopoetic tissue to colonising the embryo.

Grobstein: The technical means to make that transfer are not so difficult. If the focus were more strongly on developing gonadal tissue as proliferating and continuing strains it would become much simpler than at the present time. You are suggesting that because the transfer has to be made very early. Now, in standard clinical terms it is very hard to see how the set-up would allow you to make pro-nuclear transfers in humans in a total ethical and social sense. But on the other hand, if you have gametogenic tissue propagating and producing gametes than it does not become all that difficult in a logistical sense.

Johnson: How would you transfer primordial germ cells to embryos of the required age. It seems to me logistically far easier to go to the foundation embryos.

Grobstein: It would not be easier, in a clinical sense, to get earlier stage embryos for this purpose.

Lilford: Do I understand, Dr Johnson, that in animals it has worked, albeit at a low frequency?

Johnson: You can effectively make transgenic animals, but your success rate is low. The site of insertion may cause damage. Recent evidence suggests that insertional mutagenesis is higher than previously thought. So unless you can direct your insert, you will create as many problems as you solve. The technical aspects for this are enormously distant.

Grobstein: It is an uncertainty, whether such techniques will become feasible, at a level of a practical discussion.

Serr: You would find a consensus more easily obtained for gonadal cell manipulation than for preimplantation embryo. It is the philosophical or moral approach to manipulating preimplantation embryous and the more easily acceptable idea of manipulating a germ cell.

Grobstein: It seems to me very important to emphasise that. Whatever the process it has to go through a moral filter.

Johnson: I do not understand why one is more moral or legitimate than the other. Why one will be more easily accepted by this committee.

Grobstein: You do not set this up to block every proposal. You would then pass a law. You do not need a valve if you are going to have an uncontrolled flow.

Johnson: All you are doing is missing a generation of transgenesis. You are not going to make the person carrying this transgenic mutation transgenic, just the offspring.

Singer: The question was why the committee would not have consensus on embryo research. Your comment was simply referring to current attitudes which are rather restrictive on embryo research, whilst Dr Johnson is saying there is no sound ethical basis for that.

Beller: We are sitting here with people from the western third of this world. Two thirds of the world have, for the meaning of a given word, completely different ideas – democracy, peace, or even psychiatry. They have completely different ideas about moral ethical issues: more so with the oriental. So how are you so optimistic? If you look over the global strategy I am pessimistic.

Grobstein: I am not optimistic, in the sense that I believe that in every person in the world good is always done. I do not believe that. In the countries you are naming I might expect the bad factors rather than the good ones to operate.

Beller: I meant optimistic to bridge one third of the world with two other thirds which are not homogeneous and may be completely on different terms.

Grobstein: At this particular time. I think the issue that we are discussing will probably be discussed for a millenium as it is a fundamental issue.

IVF and Australian law

Introduction

In the field of reproductive technology, Australia has a number of distinctive achievements. An Australian team, based in Melbourne, Victoria, was the second in the world, after Edwards and Steptoe, to succeed in bringing a child into existence by the *in vitro* fertilisation technique (IVF). The same team pioneered the use of hormone stimulation to produce multiple ovulation in IVF; a technique now used almost universally by IVF teams. The first pregnancy from a donated egg occurred in Australia, and so too did the first birth from an embryo that had been frozen and thawed, and later the first birth from an egg that had been similarly treated.

These achievements were headline news throughout the country. Many Australians took pride in the fact that Australian scientists were world leaders in a new and momentous field. Moreover, unlike so many other areas of science, the benefits were both tangible and photogenic: newborn babies cuddled by delighted parents. Yet there were other Australians who were gravely concerned. Some of the concerns related to the fact that the multiple ovulation technique resulted in the fertilisation of several eggs, only some of which were transferred to the uterus, and very few of which survived to become infants. This aroused the opposition of anti-abortion groups, and of the Roman Catholic Church. Beyond this issue, however, there were questions about the length of the waiting lists for IVF programmes and who should be on these lists. Only married couples? Only couples in stable relationships? Single women? Lesbian couples? Other issues raised included the adequacy of counselling for infertile couples, the welfare of the offspring, and whether IVF was a proper use of public resources; while, in the near future, a tangle of legal problems could be discerned once egg and embryo donation, and embryo freezing, were employed.

Australia soon gained some less welcome distinctions. One which received wide publicity was to be host to the first frozen embryos to be 'orphaned' by the death of both their parents[1]. Even before this bizarre event had taken place, the public demand that something be done had led state governments to set up committees of inquiry. Since Australia has a federal system of government in which the powers to legislate about medical research and practice are largely retained by the states, Australia has almost certainly had more official committees of inquiry per head of population than any other country. More significantly, an Australian state (Victoria) passed, in the form of the Infertility (Medical Procedure) Act 1984, the first legislation anywhere in the world to deal specifically with IVF and associated issues. Victoria's legislative experience in this area provides a valuable model for any other country considering similar steps.

The background to legislation

Before we consider the legislation itself, some background is necessary. The first ethical guidelines on IVF in Australia from an official source – and again, probably the first official guidelines to go into effect anywhere – were issued by the Australian National Health and Medical Research Council (NH&MRC). This body funds a substantial proportion of Australian medical research, much as the Medical Research Council does in Britain, and the National Institutes of Health do in the United States. Since 1976 it has had a 'Statement on Human Experimentation' which established guidelines for research on human subjects. This statement was added to from time to time by way of 'Supplementary Notes', the most important of which, Supplementary Note 1, specified that all research involving humans must be approved by an institutional ethics committee with specified functions and composition. The NH&MRC (1982) issued a Supplementary Note 4 on *in vitro* fertilisation and embryo transfer. This Note states that IVF can be a justifiable procedure, under certain conditions. These include the keeping of detailed records, the exclusion of any element of commerce between gamete donors and recipients, and the limitation of treatment to 'an accepted family relationship'. Research on 'fertilised ova' is regarded as 'inseparable from the development of safe and effective IVF', but embryos are not to be kept *in vitro* beyond the stage at which implantation would normally occur. Freezing is accepted, but not for longer than 'the time of conventional reproductive need or competence of the female donor', while cloning to produce multiple genetically identical offspring is deemed ethically unacceptable.

The NH&MRC guidelines are not legislation. The only possible sanction for non-compliance is loss of NH&MRC funding. Nevertheless, the guidelines are significant because they suggest an alternative to legislation which has gained a high degree of acceptance by IVF research scientists. An audit carried out in 1985–86 (National Health and Medical Research Council Medical Ethics Research Committee, 1987) found that all 12 Australian institutions carrying out IVF were in broad compliance with the guidelines. The only discrepancies were in minor matters such as the constitution of the institutional ethics committee.

Though the NH&MRC guidelines may have satisfied the medical and scientific communities involved with IVF, they clearly did not allay public anxieties; for, within the next 2 or 3 years, committees on IVF and related matters had been set up by the State Governments of Victoria. Tasmania, South Australia, Queensland and Western Australia, while the New South Wales Government had referred the matter to its Law Reform Commission. At the Federal level, the Family Law Council, a body established under the Family Law Act to make recommendation to the Attorney-General on matters relating to family law, set up a sub-committee on reproductive technology. Subsequently the Australian Senate established its own select committee on the specific topic of embryo experimentation.

The Waller Committee

Of the various state committees, the most influential has been that established in Victoria, under the chairmanship of Professor Louis Waller, a professor of law. This was no doubt because of the prominence of the Melbourne IVF teams, the first of all the Australian IVF committees. Moreover, since New South Wales, the only state larger than Victoria in population, had taken a different approach by referring the matter to its Law Reform Commission (which at the time of writing is still to issue its final report), the reports of the Victorian committee set the framework for consideration of the issues and came to serve as a model for other state bodies.

The Victorian Government Committee produced an Interim Report (1982). This dealt with IVF in what the committee called 'the most common situation' in which IVF is employed in Victoria – that is the situation in which a husband and wife supply their own genetic material for the production of an embryo, or embryos, which will be inserted into the uterus of the wife in order to produce a child. The committee found that IVF in this situation was acceptable.

In its two subsequent reports (1984a and b) the committee was no longer unanimous, but a majority approved of the use of donor sperm, eggs and embryos, and of embryo freezing, all under specific conditions. The committee had even more difficulty in deciding whether to permit experimentation on embryos. Three options were canvassed: a complete ban; permission for experimentation only on excess embryos; or permission for experimentation on excess embryos and in addition permission for embryos to be created specifically for research. Two members insisted on a complete ban, arguing that a fertilised embryo is a human being and should be respected as such. A majority of five members recommended permitting research on excess embryos only, up to 14 days after conception. The report defended the restriction to excess embryos in the following terms:

> From a moral perspective, it may be said that, regardless of the particular level of respect which different sections of the community would accord an embryo, this individual and genetically unique human entity may not be formed solely and from the outset to be used as a means for any other human purpose, however laudable. Where the formation occurs in the course of an IVF procedure for the treatment of infertility, the reasons which lead to the embryo's existence are not 'means to an end' ones. (1984b, para. 3.27)

The reason offered for the fourteen day limit on development of the embryo after fertilisation was that: 'It is after this stage that the primitive streak is formed, and differentiation of the embryo is clearly evident.' (1984b, para. 3.39)

In handling the issue of the status of the human embryo, the Waller committee seems to have been unsure how to handle the moral arguments with which it was confronted. The only position which is clearly stated and firmly held (although only by two members of the committee) is that the embryo has the same status as any human being. In accepting the idea of destructive experimentation on excess embryos, the majority must have rejected this idea. But why? Although strong philosophical objections to the claim that the embryo has the same moral status as a human being are readily found in philosophical and bioethical writings on this topic, and indeed were presented in submissions and oral testimony before the committee, one searches the committee's reports in vain for its reasons why the embryo might not be entitled to human status. There are only repeated references to the pluralistic nature of the Victorian community. In the dissent of the medical scientists, this appears to be wielded as an argument against restricting the scope of scientific research; but again there is no developed discussion of the role of law in a pluralist community. If there is an argument from pluralism against restrictions based on the views of only some sections of the community, why do those members of the committee who favour some forms of experimentation still suggest restrictions, such as the 14-day limit and the requirement that minimum numbers of embryos be used? They present no evidence that there is a community consensus in favour of these restrictions.

Legislation in Victoria

The Waller Committee's reports were followed by the Victorian Infertility (Medical Procedures) Act 1984, which enacted several of the Committee's more important recommendations, but changed some of them significantly. In part this was the result of the political situation in Victoria, where the Labour Government does not control the Upper House. As a result the opposition parties can, if in agreement, force amendments on the Government, which then has the alternative of accepting the amendment or not proceeding with the legislation at all.

The Victorian legislation permits IVF, the use of donor gametes, and embryo freezing, when carried out in specially licensed insitutions, under specified conditions. Three of these conditions are worth mentioning. One is that only a 'married woman' can receive IVF. In the original Bill as introduced by the Government, this term was defined to include women in *de facto* marriages; this definition was deleted in the Upper House. The second is that no couple may be admitted to the programme unless they have been under treatment for infertility for a least 12 months. This condition stems from a recommendation of the Waller committee, to the effect that a couple should not be admitted to the programme unless their infertility had proved unresponsive to treatment *or* they had sought treatment for at least 12 months. The deletion of the first of these options means that even if a woman has had both fallopian tubes surgically removed, she must still seek treatment for her infertility for 12 months before she can be admitted to an IVF programme! Parliament did not indicate what form of treatment it recommended in such cases. Thirdly, the legislation requires IVF teams to provide qualified counselling to all patients. The Act also gives effect to the Waller Committee's recommendations on embryo experimentation, by prohibiting the creation of embryos except for the purposes of transfer to a woman's uterus in order to create a child. Thus an embryo cannot be created in order to carry out research on it; but the Act leaves open the possibility of research on embryos which were created with the intention of transfer to a woman, but which subsequently became 'spare'. The Act sets up a Standing Review and Advisory Committee on Infertility, one of the functions of which is to consider proposals for experiments on such embryos.

The Victorian legislation gave rise to several question of interpretation. Most prominent among them was the question of precisely when an embryo comes into existence. The debate possesses, on this issue, significance beyond the Victoria experience because it can now be foreseen that it will occur whenever a jurisdiction seeks to prohibit, by statute or regulation, experimentation on embryos. Moreover it has turned out to have important consequences for researchers and infertile couples. It therefore merits examination in some detail.

The syngamy debate

Section 6(5) of the Infertility (Medical Procedures) Act 1984 states that it is an offence, carrying a maximum penalty of 4 years imprisonment, to fertilise eggs removed from the body of a woman for purposes other than implantation of the resultant embryo in a woman's uterus. Thus, as we have already noted, the creation of embryos specifically for research purposes is prohibited. After the proclamation of most sections of the Infertility (Medical Procedures) Act, the research community in Victoria felt that – despite the non-proclamantion of some crucial sections of the Act, including section 6(5) – all planned embryo research should be submitted for prior approval to the Standing Review and Advisory Committee on Infertility (SRACI). As it happened, this committee was also chaired by Professor Waller and most, but not all, of its members had served on his previous committee.

Accordingly, in October 1986, a group of Monash University researchers submitted a research proposal to SRACI. The proposal concerned the microinjection of a single sperm into the egg, a procedure which would allow sub-fertile males to become (biological) fathers. The usual requirement for testing an innovation of this kind would be to examine the embryos so pro-duced for genetic and chromosomal abnormalities. This examination requires destroying the embryos concerned. Since the researchers did not consider it ethically defensible to implant the resulting embryos in a woman's uterus until a number of them (40 was the figure suggested in the research proposal) had been examined in this way, the eggs initially removed in order to be fertilised by microinjection would have been removed from the donor's body 'for purposes other than implantation of the resultant embryo ... '. SRACI therefore could not approve such research, regardless of its merits, since it clearly would contravene section 6(5) of the Act. Strictly speaking, the problem was not section 6(5) since this had not been proclaimed, and so had no legal force at this time. Section 29, however, required SRACI to have regard to the spirit and intent of the Act in its work. The committee held that this required it to have regard to section 6(5) even though it had not been proclaimed.

Since destructive examination of the embryos would be unacceptable, the researchers proposed to carry out a more limited research plan. Monitoring the feasibility of sperm microinjection does not necessarily require that the fertilised egg be allowed to develop to an advanced stage. Whether or not the procedure is reliable can be assessed by the success of the sperm in entering the egg, before the genetic material of the egg and sperm has combined – the stage known as syngamy. Another parameter that can be assessed prior to syngamy is the fertilisability of the egg. This provides a check on whether injecting the sperm under the zona pellucida has damaged the egg. Fertilisability would, in these cases, be determined by establishing whether or not the egg is able to complete its maturation and participate in fertilisation.

At this point problems of definition arise. In the meaning of the Act, is an egg fertilised as soon as the sperm has entered it? If it is, then testing the egg at this state is contravening the Act, because it amounts to fertilising eggs for purposes other than implantation. If, on the other hand, passage of the sperm does not amount to fertilisation, then testing at this stage is within the legal boundaries of the Act. The central problem, however, is that the Act fails to specify just what counts as fertilisation, and so does not provide for a clear ruling on the legality of the research procedures in question.

In order properly to understand the nature of the issue here, we need to understand the scientist's use of the term 'fertilisation', and the reasons for this usage. Briefly, the matter can be put in the following way. As knowledge of the earliest stages of human life has spread, it has become more common to view human fertilisation as a complex process, lasting for about 24 hours (Harrison, 1978). The reason for this is that the union of the sperm and egg (the ordinary meaning of 'fertilisation' in sexual reproduction) seems to be best identified not with the bare fact of the sperm passing into the egg but with the processes, initiated by the entry of the sperm, which culminate in syngamy. In outline these processes are as follows: the sperm enters the egg, the egg completes maturation, the genetic material of each condenses into chromosomes, and finally the male and female contributions come together to form the new genotype. This first formation of the new genotype is syngamy; and, because the union of the two gametes does not seem to be complete before syngamy has occurred, the proper scientific use of the term 'fertilisation' includes the entire process which begins with the sperm passing through the zona pellucida and comes to completion at syngamy.

Given this scientific meaning of fertilisation, the proposed research does not contravene the Act. But was the term properly understood in this way when used in the Act? There were no precedents to go by. In other debates on when a human life begins – for instance, in the context of abortion – the fact that the sperm has passed into the egg is not known until long after syngamy has taken place. One might say that the legislators ought to have foreseen the problem; but this is unfair. For all of human history prior to the development of *in vitro* fertilisation, it had made sense to regard fertilisation as an event, rather than a process, because no-one had been able to observe it, or to interfere with it, between the time the sperm entered the egg and the time when syngamy was complete.

In March 1987, SRACI discussed whether the research proposal came under the Act, and was therefore prohibited by it. Opinion was sharply divided amongst the members of the committee; and when a vote was taken, there were four members in favour, and four against. The Act did not give the Chairman a casting vote.

The Victorian Government was now in an unenviable situation. To resolve the dilemma, SRACI proposed that the Act be amended to allow the committee to approve research proposals involving the initiation but not the completion of the process of fertilisation outside the body of a woman. The amendment would therefore permit the approval of research proposals which allowed development to proceed beyond the passage of the sperm through the egg membrane, but which would be stopped before syngamy. Although SRACI was evenly divided on the question of whether the Act as it stood already allowed such research to be approved, a majority of 7 to 1 supported the idea of amending the Act so as to make it clear that fertilisation is a process which is completed at syngamy, and that a new human life begins once fertilisation is complete. This view was the heart of the controversy which the proposal created. Does syngamy really mark the beginning of a new human life?

In favour of taking the moment the sperm enters the egg as the beginning of a new human life, it was urged that this is the first time that there is a single unified entity with the potential to generate a new human life; moreover the genetic identity of that individual was said to be determined at this stage. Even though the genetic material from the male and female do not combine until syngamy, the entry of one sperm normally prevents the entry of any other sperm, and thus of any additional genetic material (cf. St Vincent's Bioethics Centre, 1987; Dawson, 1987). Against this view, and in favour of syngamy, it was suggested that the entry of the sperm does not amount to the creation of a single unified entity, since the male and female pronuclei remain separate and distinct until syngamy; they could still be considered separate entities within a single outer layer, much as Siamese twins with separate brains could be separate individuals within a single body. Or to put it in another way[2], if the formation of a new genotype is the formation of a new biological individual (a criterion which is at least plausible for creatures which reproduce sexually), then syngamy is the appropriate landmark for creatures like us.

It is not clear whether it was these arguments, or public agitation from infertile couples, or merely the recommendation of the Standing Review and Advisory Committee, that moved the Victorian Government, and subsequently the Parliament of Victoria; but in November 1987 Parliament passed a Government Bill which became the Infertility (Medical Procedures) (Amendment) Act. The amendment [sections 4(2) and 4(4) (d)] specified that, subject to the approval of the Standing Review and Advisory Committee on Infertility, eggs could be fertilised outside the body for experimental procedures 'from the point of sperm penetration prior to but not including the point of syngamy'. Syngamy itself is defined as 'the alignment on the mitotic spindle of the chromosomes derived from the pronuclei'. After the passage of this amendment, SRACI approved the research proposals submitted by the Monash group of researchers.

I shall add a few words to this debate. Although there are defensible grounds for taking syngamy, rather than the point at which the sperm enters the egg, as the beginning of a new human life, we should remember that even if it is concluded that syngamy *is* the beginning of a new human life, the *moral significance* of syngamy is not thereby established. To settle factual or definitional questions about the beginning of a new biological life is not to settle the moral question of how we should treat such biologically defined entities. Since I have elsewhere (Singer, 1979; Kuhse & Singer, 1986; Dawson & Singer, 1988) developed my own views on this topic, I shall here restrict myself to three points, stated dogmatically:

(1) The term 'human being' can mean two things: a member of the species *Homo sapiens*, or a being with certain characteristics, such as some

minimal level of self-awareness, or rationality, or ability to communicate with others. In the former sense, there can be no doubt that the newly fertilised egg is human; in the latter sense, there is equally little doubt that it is not. The question therefore arises: which sense is morally significant? I think it requires only brief reflection to see that it can only be the second. Mere membership of a particular species cannot itself be morally significant. If I were suddenly to reveal to you that I am a Martian, I hope you would not therefore promptly conclude that my suffering or death is a matter of complete indifference. Similarly, an anencephalic infant is a member of the species *Homo sapiens*; but while we may grieve over its birth, since it is quite unable to experience anything itself, I do not think we need to attribute to it a right to life. The same applies to an early embryo, which, like the anencephalic, is unable to experience anything.

(2) It will be said that a human embryo has a special moral status – one which makes it wrong to destroy it – because of its potential. Since those who put forward this argument do not attribute the same moral status to human eggs or sperm, they need to distinguish the potential of the embryo from that of the eggs and sperm. I do not believe that this can be done. The argument from potential runs into difficulties whether it is applied to embryos *in vitro* or *in vivo*, but they are considerably more acute in the *in vitro* situation. An *in vitro* embryo has, given the present state of the art, only a small chance of becoming a human being. Since fertilisation is one of the easier steps in IVF, an egg surrounded by sperm in a glass dish in the laboratory has virtually the same prospects of becoming a human being as does the *in vitro* embryo. If it is said that the difference is that the genetic identity of the future human being is determined only after fertilisation, the anticipated success of the micro-injection technique, to which I referred earlier, will back-date this to the point at which the sperm is selected for microinjection. Will advocates of the argument from potential then regard the egg, sperm and syringe as constituting a system which it is wrong to interrupt? If not, they will need to offer a convincing explanation. I doubt that they will succeed.

(3) I will no doubt be asked at what point I believe the embryo should be protected. In brief, my answer is that just as a warm, breathing human body needs no further protection – for its own sake – once its brain has been destroyed, so a developing embryo needs no protection for its own sake until it has a functioning brain, and can experience something. (There is one qualification; if an experiment will *not* destroy the embryo, then of course the future child does need to be protected from harmful consequences that experimentation may have.) I should add that to say that a being needs some protection, once it is able to have experiences, is not to say that it has a right to life, let alone a right as stringent as that

possessed by beings who are rational and able to have desires about their future existence.

Australian legislation outside Victoria

Until March 1988, this would have been a very short section: for no other Australian legislature had then passed legislation dealing with IVF. But in that month the South Australian legislature passed the Reproductive Technology Act 1988, based on the report of the Select Committee of the South Australian Legislative Council. The Act takes a different approach from that of the Victorian legislation. It sets up a 'Council on Reproductive Technology', with a specified membership consisting of scientists and lay members. The legislation specifies that, as far as practicable, the council is charged with laying down a code to govern IVF and embryo experimentation. IVF and embryo research are permitted only in accordance with the code, and at an institution licensed by the Council. The code will have the status of regulations under the Act, and thus can be changed without a further Act of Parliament. The Act does, however, lay down that the Code, or licenses subsequently issued by the Council, must prohibit embryo flushing, embryo freezing for longer than 10 years, any experimentation that is detrimental to the embryo, and maintaining an embryo in culture beyond the stage of development at which implantation would normally occur. IVF itself is restricted to married couples, but this includes couples who without being legally married have cohabited for at least 5 years.

No other state has got to the point of introducing legislation on IVF. At the Federal level, most political discussion has been about embryo experimentation. In 1985, a conservative senator introduced into the Australian Senate a bill which sought to prohibit all non-therapeutic experimentation on human embryos. The Senate set up a select committee of inquiry, consisting of seven senators, to report on the desirability of legislation to control human embryo experimentation. In the Senate Select Committee Report (1986) a majority of five senators recommended that destructive embryo experimentation be prohibited. Two senators, however, wrote a dissenting report which argued that destructive embryo experimentation should be allowed when it is in accordance with the wishes of the couple from whom the gametes have come.

The Federal Government did not accept the majority recommendations of the Senate Select Committee. Instead it accepted the major recommendation of an earlier report from another Federal body, the Family Law Council, to establish a national bioethics advisory committee[3]. The committee's chairperson has indicated that the committee is unlikely, initially, to take up contentious issues such as *in vitro* fertilisation and genetic enginerring (*The Age*, 19 March 1988).

The reasons for the reluctance of the Federal Government – and of the governments of New South Wales, Queensland, Western Australia and Tasmania – to move towards legislation are probably political rather than ethical: legislating on matters relating to the status of the human embryo is more likely to disaffect those voters who object strongly to the legislation than to win over any who approve of it.

Conclusion

It has often been said that the new reproductive technology has created a legislative minefield. If we may employ such a hackneyed metaphor, we could say that Victoria has acted on the principle that the best way to get through a minefield is to run – not blindly, but at considerable speed – across it. Other Australian legislatures have hung back and watched. On the whole, what they have seen has discouraged them from trying to cross the field. I cannot altogether blame them, but in the end, somehow, we will all have to get to the other side.

If a complete ban on embryo research is adopted as an easy and final option it could only create a further but different ethical problem. IVF has at present only a limited success rate. Improvements are occurring, often as a result of experimenting with the culture conditions for the gametes and embryos. Is this embryo research? If it is and if it were banned in some all-embracing restrictive legislation we could see an end to the progress being made with no further improvements in the outcome from IVF. Under those circumstances scientists, doctors and health care resource allocators must ask themselves whether it is ethical for society to continue with this form of treatment on the basis of its present chances of succeeding.

Acknowledgements

The paper which is embodied in this chapter was supported by an Australian National Health and Medical Research Council Grant to myself, Helga Kuhse and Beth Gaze. Parts of it are drawn from work carried out jointly with Stephen Buckle, Karen Dawson and Pascal Kasimba, Research Officers at the Centre for Human Bioethics. I am grateful to all of those I have just mentioned for their assistance.

Notes

1. For details of the orphaned frozen embryos, see *Newsweek*, 2 July 1984; *The Age* (Melbourne), 20 and 21 June 1984 and 4 December 1987; *The Australian*, 4 December 1987.
2. 'Individuals and Syngamy', a submission to the Standing Review and Advisory Committee on Infertility by Stephen Buckle and Karen Dawson, Centre for Human Bioethics, Monash University; for further discussion of this issue, see Stephen

Buckle, Karen Dawson and Peter Singer, 'The Syngamy Debate: When Precisely Does a Human Life Begin?', *Law, Ethics and Health Care*, **17**:2 (1989) 174–81.
3. Family Law Council, *Creating Children: A Uniform Approach to the Law and Practice of Reproductive Technology in Australia*; for the Federal Government's response, see *Hansard*, Australian Senate, 18 December 1987, p. 3483.

References

Dawson, K. (1987). Fertilisation and moral status: A scientific perspective. *Journal of Medical Ethics*, **13**, 173–8.

Harrison, R. G. (1978). *Clinical Embryology*. Academic Press, London.

Kuhse, H. & Singer, P. (1986). The ethics of embryo research. *Law, Medicine and Health Care*, **14**, 133–8.

National Health and Medical Research Council. (1982). *First Report by NH&MRC Working Party on Ethics in Medical Research: Research on Humans*. Australian Government Publishing Service, Canberra.

National Health and Medical Research Council Medical Ethics Research Committee. (1987). *In Vitro Fertilisation Centres in Australia: Their Observance of the National Health and Medical Research Council Guidelines*. Australian Government Publishing Service, Canberra.

St. Vincent's Bioethics Centre. (1987). Identifying the origin of a human life. *St. Vincent's Bioethics Newsletter*, **5**, 4–6.

Senate Select Committee on the Human Embryo Experimentation Bill 1985. (1986). *Human Embryo Experimentation in Australia*. Australian Government Publishing Service, Canberra.

Singer, P. (1979). *Practical Ethics*. Cambridge University Press, Cambridge.

Singer, P. & Dawson, K. (1988). IVF technology and the argument from potential. *Philosophy and Public Affairs*, **17**, 87–104.

Victorian Government Committee to Consider the Social, Ethical and Legal Issues Arising from in Vitro Fertilisation (1982). *Interim Report*. Victorian Government Printing Office, Melbourne, 1982.

Victorian Government Committee to Consider the Social, Ethical, and Legal Issues Arising from In Vitro Fertilisation. (1984a). *Report on Donor Gametes in IVF*. Victorian Government Printing Office, Melbourne.

Victorian Government Committee to Consider the Social, Ethical, and Legal Issues Arising from In Vitro Fertilisation. (1984b). *Report on the Disposition of Embryos Produced by In Vitro Fertilisation*. Victorian Government Printing Office, Melbourne.

Discussion   Chairman: Dr Maureen Dalton

Jackson: The low success rate of *in vitro* fertilisation and the cost – emotional and financial – is common with all sorts of medical technology for example transplant surgery. If they are allowed to continue they may have tremendous improvements. Are there any special reasons why this should not be so with *in vitro* fertilisation?

Singer: The way improvements come is through research, not just through practice or we would have seen greater improvements. There is a learning curve. The success rates of new *in vitro* fertilisation units are far lower generally than in units working for 2, 3 or 4 years. But we have been doing this now for about 10 years and there are many teams with more than 5 years experience. Their success rates have topped off and it would only be through further research that we would expect to find out why the implantation rates are relatively low.

Serr: As regards the process of introducing one single sperm into the egg, Professor Waller had said that this was playing God by you deciding which sperm would go into which egg and this was his objection more than actual legal objections.

Singer: Professor Waller is a close colleague of mine but I have not heard that that was his view. He voted with the majority of the committee in favour of amending the act to allow research to proceed until syngamy, so I think it is probably not a correct account of his current view. I could not guarantee that it was not an initial view.

Cox: Would Wood and Trounson be happy with a 14-day limit on their experimentation?

Singer: They are currently restricted to research up to syngamy. If they were able to work to 14 days they would be able to achieve all of their objectives in their immediate research programme. There may be further research which would go beyond that point: it is a possibility. Dr Trounson does not really believe that 14 days marks a morally significant point. He is not quite clear when I put to him my view that the development of sentience is more important. Maybe he would share some view like that if he were able to create exactly the legislation that he desires.

Bromham: Coming back on the point about the financial continuation of learning curve. This applies equally to all developments in medical science. However, infertility and its treatment represents one particular area, where at a congress or meeting, you will almost inevitably run into a paper on fund raising and resource allocation. I do not think the British Paediatric Association, when they met in York last week, contained many papers from people telling others how to raise funds. The infertility meetings and clinical symposia abound with papers on this topic. It seems almost that the diseased non-functioning reproductive system has been singled out as a system which does not need help. The infertile couples tend to be told, 'You have got your health, why worry about your fertility?'. You would not go to someone who was in a wheelchair with osteoarthritis and say, 'You have got your health, why are you worried about your immobility?'. But as far as infertility is concerned, it comes way down on everybody's priority.

Singer: That is clearly true. One reason is that, when compared with paediatrics, it does not have these appealing little babies there for whom you can say, 'You have got to save this baby's life'.

Botros: Strongly in favour of more research in *in vitro* fertilisation is the argument that because of the low levels of success in *in vitro* fertilisation, the cost is in the loss of embryos, and these would actually balance out or be greater than the loss of embryos in research.

Singer: You are saying that there are more embryos lost because of this? It is a kind of utilitarianism of embryo loss. I am not sure that opponents of embryo research would accept such an argument, because they tend to be absolutist rather than consequentialist. Rather than say: 'I am prepared to sacrifice this embryo in order to save those embryos', they would probably say that embryo research is wrong because you would be using the embryos in research as a means to save other embryos. People who hold an absolutist ethic would not allow that.

Botros: On the point you made about embryos that are deliberately created and simply used as a means, whereas those produced in *in vitro* fertilisation are not used as a means. Could you say a little bit more about that?

Singer: It was a view put forward by the majority of the Waller committee. There is a kind of a Kantian philosophy behind it in that every individual has to be considered as an end in him or herself rather than as a means; a thing to be used for other individuals. There are many problems with applying Kantianism to embryos because they are certainly not rational beings but if you regard that as simply an error that this general Kantian view is being applied to a clearly non-rational entity, then the idea is that when you deliberately create an embryo, this embryo has no other reason for existing except that it will serve someone else's purpose or goals. Whereas if you take one that was created differently and then say, 'Ah well, here we have this embryo which is not required, we could allow it simply to expire, but why not, rather than allow it to expire, since it will not suffer anything, use it for research', you are reaping an incidental benefit as a by-product of the unfortunate fact that this embryo has no future.

Levy: How is GIFT covered by this legislation because the fertilisation is in the tubes?

Singer: Originally, it was thought that the legislation did not effect GIFT. But because it referred to the removal of an egg for purposes other than the transfer of the resultant embryo to the woman's body, it actually caught GIFT and prohibited it or at least there was legal advice received to that effect. When the amendment, to which I referred, about syngamy went through there was a clause tacked on that GIFT was not prohibited by the legislation.

Glover: Professor Singer has produced a very convincing argument that under no circumstances must we have legislation associated with *in vitro* fertilisation, that this is one of the great disadvantages, as far as Victoria is concerned. The Victoria legislation encourages research workers from Victoria to do their research in Queensland. This is the silly situation which has arisen in Australia. You can do what you like provided you are in the right part of the country. There are in Australia an awful lot of alternative checks and balances other than the legal ones. The Bioethics Committee, for example, which has been set up consists of not only scientists and medical people but also lay people. All the *in vitro* fertilisation units have to be registered by the Fertility Society of Australia which consists of non-medical people as well as medicals and scientists. The difficulty with legislation is that it is very difficult to repeal or amend. The discussion so far has shown that legal definitions are so difficult. If Professor Waller had heard Professor Dunstan's talk at this conference it would have given food for thought.

Singer: We have to face some kind of legislation and the only way to have the flexibility required is to have the legislation merely providing a framework for some statutory licensing authority to oversee and supervise. It is a bit like the South Australian legislation which was a good idea. Setting up a Council on Reproductive Technology specifying various lay and scientific membership and then handing over the field to that council would have provided the needed flexibility. Unfortunately amendments got tacked on saying that you cannot do any experimentation detrimental to the embryo.

Braude: You equated 14 days and implantation which is untrue. Implantation probably occurs somewhere between 6 or 8 days and not 14 days. One would have to look at that as separate from a 14-day rule.

Singer: It was actually NII&MRC that talked about implantation and then this somehow got regarded as being 14 days, but I accept that that is inaccurate.

Gorovitz: Legislation sometimes is not restrictive but enabling. Some enterprises do not proceed because of the liabilities in an area that is uncertain: for example, legislation that allows physicians to refrain from providing treatment at the end of life, holding them safe from prosecution for a civil liability when they simply acted in accordance with the patient's wishes. It may be the case that some legislation would actually be helpful in some jurisdictions in making it easier or safer to gain certain pursuits.

Glover: The difficulty with any form of legislation is definition because you run into this problem, such as the time of implantation, not always appreciating what goes on scientifically.

Gorovitz: I do not wish say anything in defence of badly phrased legislation. Done well it can be enabling rather than simply restrictive. We have had researchers in the USA move to different States, in order to be able to pursue research they could not do where they are. They might go to another country. How serious a problem is that?

Singer: There has been one case where a major team from South Australia went over to California. That was before the South Australian legislation and I think the reasons were financial more than legislative but the prospect of legislation may have been a factor. It has been said that Professor Wood is establishing a base in Queensland in case things in Victoria are too bad. Australians are not quite as mobile as Americans, but there could easily come a point where the impossibility of doing the research that they want to do makes them move.

Craft: You say that you felt that one might question whether you could carry on doing *in vitro* fertilisation without research, is that correct?

Singer: The question has to be raised. In terms of the cost both financial and psychological to those involved, the justifiability of doing *in vitro* fertilisation, in may view, would be questionable unless we can expect success rates to improve.

Craft: Would not that be the patient's choice who was fully informed of the success rates. I am not aware that Dr Trounson's success rates are lower than those of other people in the world who might be doing research.

Singer: On a worldwide basis the success rates have not climbed. His are certainly not worse than other people's but the research is not being done. As to whether it is up to the patients, perhaps yes if the patient is paying the full cost, in Australia the patients do not pay the full cost, they are reimbursed from Government health funds for roughly 75% of the cost. So perhaps, without a high success rate, the Government could withdraw from funding procedures and that would greatly reduce the number that were done.

Beller: In Germany we had to work on conditions set by our own council. For 2 years it had a recommendation on *in vitro* fertilisation which included experimentation on embryos under the condition that all the objectives were clarified with the State. Then the mood of the population changed dramatically and it was just changing one word from 'using' embryos to 'producing' embryos that caused a wave of hysterical reaction of the public. We are facing now a law which makes any experimentation on embryos a criminal offence but, interestingly enough, does not state, clarify or define what research means.

Solbakk: Are there any distinctions between destructive and non-destructive research on embryos and do you believe destructive research on embryos to be non-therapeutic research on embryos and non-destructive to be therapeutic?

Singer: Both the terms have been used, as well as this expression 'detrimental' which appears in the South Australian legislation. They are all undefined; if challenged they would all need to go to Court. Obviously, if you biopsy an embryo, you have destroyed it. It is clearly also non-therapeutic, it is not helping that embryo. What would count as therapeutic or as non-destructive has been discussed a little, amending the culture fluid, for example. You could argue that that was both therapeutic and non-destructive.

Millican: A clarification of the Victoria Act. Embryos can only be created for the purpose of transfer back to the woman. That does not actually rule out research on embryos which are later to be transferred back. It is more difficult to defend that sort of research.

Singer: The Victoria Act also sets up a committee and the proposal to carry out research on embryos to be transferred to the uterus would have to be approved by it. I think the committee would be very hesitant about approving any research which had any prospect of leading to a damaged child. If the committee were convinced, say on the basis of animal experimentation, that the technique existed and could be safely employed, it would be in its power to allow it.

Part 2

Society and assisted conception

Taking surrogacy seriously

Introduction

Modern surrogacy has gone too far to go away. In this chapter I start from the assumption that it cannot be ignored and that we should therefore consider what is required if it is to become a legitimate way of having a family. I shall argue that it needs a supportive framework of structures of its own, not adaptations of structures designed for adoption and custody.

In the present situation if a surrogate mother gives up the child, as planned, the commissioning parents can only hope to become its legal parents by adoption. A well-known case in which this happened is that of Kim Cotton, an English surrogate mother who had a baby for an American couple. If, however, the surrogate mother refuses to give up the child the case is treated as one of custody, bedevilled by the surrogacy contract. The legal tangle that this can produce, with appalling consequences for the surrogate mother, the commissioning parents and the child, is well illustrated in probably the best-known surrogacy case, that of Mary Beth Whitehead, known as the Baby M case, in New Jersey, USA.

Whitehead was a surrogate mother for the Sterns in 1986. She refused to give up the child for them to adopt. The courts first upheld the surrogacy contract, deprived Whitehead of her parental rights and allowed the commissioning parents to adopt the baby. Later, in 1988, this was reversed on appeal. The surrogacy contract was then ruled not valid, the decision to allow the child to be adopted was revoked, Mary Beth Whitehead was reinstated as the legal mother, but custody was given to the commissioning parents. After the appeal Whitehead was granted extensive visitation rights.

Some people think that this notorious case constitutes the ultimate proof that surrogacy should be prohibited. In my view many of its distressing features might have been avoided had there been appropriate legal and institutional structures.

Weak surrogacy

The New Jersey Supreme Court judgement in the Baby M case made it plain that there is no 'legal prohibition against surrogacy when the surrogate mother volunteers, without any payment . . . and is given the right to change her mind and to assert her parental rights.'

On the other hand, it strongly suggests that when the child is born the surrogacy contract will have no bearing on the eventual outcome. I shall call this weak surrogacy.

There are two main problems with weak surrogacy. First, a successful outcome is dependent on adoption and therefore on the test of whether it is in the child's best interests. Secondly, the surrogate mother might change her mind about giving up the baby. Together these mean that the outcome is by no means certain.

Strong surrogacy

With the stronger form of surrogacy that I shall advocate, surrogacy is taken seriously as a distinct way of establishing a family and is set clearly apart from adoption. By seeing adoption and surrogacy in relation to social norms connected with the family, it is possible to argue that adoption occurs in aberrant circumstances, that is when the child has no parents able and willing to look after it. Surrogacy, on the other hand – which at present is also regarded as an aberrant activity – would not be aberrant given suitable legal and social structures that take seriously the distinctive aim of surrogacy, which is the production of children for intending parents.

The difference between surrogacy and adoption is that surrogacy is aimed at the production of children for intending parents – commonly childless couples – whereas adoption is aimed at meeting the needs of existing children. Therefore, if surrogacy is to be taken seriously as a way of establishing a family, the first requirement is that the commissioning parents should be able to have reasonable certainty of becoming the legal parents of the child with the minimum difficulty and delay. Ideally they should automatically be the legal parents of the child when it is born.

This may seem to involve dangers for the child. There can be no presumption, it might be argued, that the commissioning parents will care for the child. If these fears are well founded it may mean that the commissioning parents should be screened and investigated in the way that prospective adopters are. But this could be done before the surrogacy arrangement is entered into. Indeed if the commissioning parents are to be ruled out it is better that it should be done before the surrogacy arrangement is made so that there will not then be a question of what is to be done about the child when they are found wanting after it is born.

It is, of course, possible that other restrictions on access to surrogacy may make screening less necessary than with adoption. For example, if surrogacy was restricted, as some have suggested it should be, to cases where one or both of the commissioning parents are the genetic parents of the child this might be some safeguard.

Surrogacy contracts

There is a question of how the commissioning parents could come to be the legal parents of the child automatically when it is born. It might be thought that the obvious way would be for surrogacy contracts to be legalised. But surrogacy contracts between individuals cannot and should not determine who has responsibilities, rights and duties with respect to infants. Such questions are seldom left to the free choice of individuals. In England privately agreed adoptions have no legal validity and it is a fundamental principle of the socio-legal framework within which the validity of contracts would be decided that babies are not freely transferable. It is probably only in the USA, and even there possibly only in the public eye, that surrogacy has been perceived in terms of surrogacy contracts that might actually have legal validity.

The alternative to the surrogacy contract as the mechanism by which the commissioning parents automatically become the legal parents of the child is a framework of legal and social structures that lays down clearly that it should be so. This would put surrogacy arrangements where they belong – in the sphere of family law.

I shall not here attempt a detailed discussion of the structures that would be required. Under any regulated system of surrogacy, however, individual surrogacies would need to be registered in advance. A condition of eligibility for the commissioning parents to be registered automatically as the legal parents of the child might be that the surrogacy arrangement had been registered at least 12 months, say, before the birth of the child. Other conditions such as prior screening and counselling of surrogate mothers and commissioning parents might then be made necessary for registration of the surrogacy. This would have many advantages.

What it the surrogate mother refuses to give up the child?

The most difficult question raised by surrogacy is whether the surrogate mother should be compelled to give up the child if she refuses to do so. This problem has been discussed mainly in connection with the surrogacy contract.

A very harsh contract view was displayed by a Californian surrogacy agent when he said, on British television, that if a surrogate mother refused to give up the child he would take her to court and 'sue her for everything she is worth'. If she had no money he would 'pursue' her, 'follow her all over the country' and 'make her life miserable'. No doubt he held the view that a contract is a contract is a contract.

Some people with less harsh attitudes support the general point that the surrogate mother has entered into a contract and should be expected to keep it. Indeed, I have heard it argued that it demeans women to suggest that surrogate mothers should not be required to stand by their agreement to hand over the child. Such people might think that it suggests that women generally cannot be expected to honour contracts and perhaps that it reinforces the cliched stereotypical view that it is a woman's prerogative to change her mind.

Nevertheless, many people, especially women, find the harsh contract attitude repugnant and believe that it would be wrong to compel a surrogate mother to give up the child even though she entered into an agreement to do so. There is a persistent disquiet and concern that the peculiar vulnerability of surrogate mothers is being disregarded.

There are at least four different strands or levels to the argument. First, there is concern about the immediate effects of pregnancy and childbirth on the mother's state of mind, her emotional ties with the baby, and the fact that forcing her to give up the baby at that time would be damaging and cause her unacceptable suffering and distress. Unfortunately, although these effects of pregnancy are widely acknowledged, they are often viewed as short-term effects that surrogate mothers could be expected to get over.

Secondly, loosely from a feminist standpoint, the contract approach to surrogacy is seen as representing a typical male view which systematically discounts or does not understand female experiences and concerns and is blind to the special character of the mother–child relationship. A female perspective could not contemplate forcing a mother to give up her child even if she agreed to do so, but not simply because of the immediate effects of pregnancy and childbirth. Women throughout their lives, not only in pregnancy, conceptualise their reproductive role differently from men and this importantly conditions the special relationship that exists between a mother and her child. Consequently, the effects on the surrogate mother of forcing her to give up the child cannot be thought of as short-term effects which will soon disappear.

Thirdly, people point to the fact that a mother cannot be bound by a prior agreement to surrender her baby for adoption when it is born. This seems to be for the protection of mothers. Therefore, it is argued, the same protection should be given to surrogate mothers. This is a strong argument but it does not take into account the fact that a woman who agrees when she is already pregnant to put her baby forward for adoption is probably subject to more psychological and social pressures than a prospective surrogate mother would be. However, it is not clear that protection for the natural mother in adoption is based on the fact that women who are pregnant might be led by their special circumstances to make decisions they will later regret.

Fourthly, there seems to be a widely accepted rule that a natural mother should not be deprived of her baby. While this obviously protects women there might be other reasons for it. For example, it is arguable that it is a constitutive rule of the family and thus is important for maintaining the family as a social norm. If this is so it should be seen as a rule of the wider socio-legal framework and set alongside that other important rule, mentioned above, that babies are not transferable.

I shall not develop these arguments further here. Suffice it to say that I am persuaded that an acceptable system of surrogacy must include some provision for a surrogate mother, exceptionally, to keep the baby. This should not be regarded as her right but rather as a provision for the rights she surrenders in becoming a surrogate mother to be restored to her in special circumstances. This of course leaves an element of uncertainty about the outcome which could cause anxiety for the commissioning parents. This, it seems to me, must be accepted – but it should not be exaggerated. The likelihood of the surrogate mother keeping the child is not high.

In recent years there have been hundreds and possibly thousands of surrogacy arrangements. It appears that the great majority of surrogate mothers voluntarily release the baby to the commissioning parents. It is possible that a properly regulated system of surrogacy would result in even fewer cases where the surrogate mother refuses to give up the child. Furthermore, it should be remembered that it would be extremely odd, if not weird, for a woman to become a surrogate mother as a way of getting a baby for herself.

In the majority of cases, then, it is reasonable to assume that the child will be handed over to the commissioning parents as planned. In these cases, I have argued, the commissioning parents should be able to register themselves automatically as the legal parents of the child. In the small number of other cases, if there are any, where the surrogate mother refuses to give up the child and it would be damaging to compel her to do so, some machinery would be needed to restore her parental rights and duties to her.

Earlier we saw that it may be necessary to screen commissioning parents in advance of surrogacy arrangements to make sure that they will be acceptable parents for the child. Now, recognising the need for a provision to allow the surrogate mother to keep the child in exceptional cases, it is clear that there will be an equal need to establish in advance of the surrogacy arrangement that the surrogate mother will be an acceptable parent for the child if she ends up with it. This is a point worth emphasising. It is widely recognised that surrogate mothers should be screened and counselled about having the baby and surrendering it to the commissioning parents. Seldom is it mentioned that she must also be seen to be a fit person to keep the child of it comes to that.

It might be thought that this should go without saying, as it does normally for natural parents. But the case of Mary Beth Whitehead shows how the fitness of the surrogate mother to rear the child can be brought into question after the event.

Special regulations for surrogacy

The foregoing argument shows that if surrogacy is to be taken seriously it needs to be a strong form of surrogacy.

In summary, the minimal provisions for such a system of surrogacy are:

(1) the commissioning parents should automatically be the legal parents of the child;

(2) surrogacies should have been registered not less than one year before the birth of the child for automatic registration of the commissioning parents as the legal parents;

(3) the surrogate mother, exceptionally, should be able to keep the baby and have her parental rights and duties restored;

(4) it should be established in advance of registration of the surrogacy that both the commissioning parents and the surrogate mother would be acceptable parents for the child.

Beyond these minimal provisions a system of surrogacy would need additional provisions and supportive institutions to deal with very important aspects of surrogacy, the details of which cannot be discussed in this chapter. It should be plain, however, that if minimal provisions of the kind indicated here had been in force when Mary Beth Whitehead became a surrogate mother her story could not have been the distressing chronicle that it was and continues to be. Either she would have been debarred from being a surrogate mother from the beginning, on the ground that she would not be an acceptable person to rear the child if she refused to give it up, or an exception would have been made in her case and she would have been allowed to keep the child without having to show then that she would be an acceptable parent for the child.

Taxonomy

I now move to a more theoretical, possibly more philosophical, discussion to examine some of the suggestions in the first part of the paper from a different angle. I shall connect the present discussion with my earlier work on surrogacy (Page, 1985b, 1986), some of which needs revision. The following terms will be used to refer to two main types of surrogacy.

Genetic surrogacy is when the surrogate mother has her own genetic baby, usually fertilised with sperm from the commissioning father by artificial insemination. Kim Cotton and Mary Beth Whitehead, mentioned above, were both genetic surrogate mothers inseminated artificially with sperm from the respective commissioning fathers.

Gestatory surrogacy is when the surrogate mother gestates and gives birth to a baby from someone else's embryo by *in vitro* fertilisation and embryo transfer. For the purposes of this discussion I shall assume that the embryo is the genetic embryo of both commissioning parents. Clearly, then, a gestatory surrogate mother is not the genetic mother of the baby.

Gestatory surrogacy is far less common than genetic surrogacy, no doubt because it requires more advanced medical technology and resources. The first gestatory surrogate was Shannon Boff, Michigan, USA, in 1986. Another case is that of the South African 'granny' surrogate mother, 48-year-old Pat Anthony, who gave birth to triplets in 1987 from genetic embryos of her own daughter and son-in-law.

Gestatory surrogacy and genetic surrogacy

The two main suggestions in the first part of this chapter were, firstly, that the commissioning parents should automatically be the legal parents of the child and, secondly, that exceptionally the surrogate mother should be allowed to keep the child and have parental rights restored to her. Intuitively we are likely to react differently to these suggestions depending on the type of surrogacy involved.

With genetic surrogacy we may find it difficult to accept that the commissioning parents should automatically be the legal parents. This is because the genetic surrogate mother is the natural mother and, intuitively, the true mother. By the same token we may think it not unreasonable that she should be allowed to keep the child if she cannot bring herself to part with it.

Our intuitions tend to go the other way with gestatory surrogacy. Here the baby is from the genetic embryo of the commissioning parents which is transferred to the surrogate mother for gestation only – on the understanding that the baby will be given back to the commissioning parents at birth. Intuitively, many people think it would be unjust to allow a gestatory surrogate mother to keep the baby, even exceptionally, and that the commissioning parents should automatically be the legal parents of the child when it is born.

This view is reflected in the court ruling in the case of Shannon Boff, the world's first gestatory surrogate mother, who gave birth in April 1986 to a baby from the genetic embryo of the commissioning parents in Ann Arbor, Michigan, USA. Before the baby was born, the court ruled that, subject to medical tests to show that the commissioning parents were the 'biological' parents, they would be the legal parents and their names, not the name of the surrogate mother, should appear on the birth certificate. This made legal history, it being the first time that a woman other than the birth-mother was registered as the legal mother of the child. It should be noted, however, that Warnock (1984, 1985) recommended that even in this kind of case the woman who gives birth to the child should be its legal mother.

Some people may think that the differences between genetic surrogacy and gestatory surrogacy are so great that legally and socially they should be treated differently. They might even argue that one but not the other should be legally permissible. I shall argue that they should both be included in a single system.

Birth-mothers or genetic mothers

To deal with these problems we need to ask how we are to decide who is the true mother of the child. We can take 'true mother' to mean the woman who ought to be the legal mother of the child. This was a central question in the Warnock Report, which says the woman who gives birth to the child is its true mother (Warnock, 1984). I call this the 'Warnock rule' or birth-mother rule.

The birth-mother rule is obviously correct for normal natural reproduction. Intuitively it is also correct for births from donated eggs or donated embryos although in these cases the birth-mother is not the same person as the genetic mother. It is not difficult to see what lies behind our intuitions here. Logically, donation of an embryo (or donation of an egg) implies the surrender and transfer by the donor of all her rights and duties with respect to the embryo and the resulting child. The donee's acceptance of the donated embryo also seems to imply the acceptance or assumption of all parental rights and duties. She thus becomes the child's true mother. It is as if the parental rights and duties were voluntary surrendered and transferred.

The fact that the birth-mother is the true mother when embryos are donated might make it seem that a birth-mother's right always overrides a genetic mother's right. However, in gestatory surrogacy this is extremely doubtful as we have seen. Here, although the embryo is transferred physically it is not donated and that fact seems to make all the difference. It needs to be asked: how could the birth-mother become the true mother of the child when the embryo is not donated? If the genetic parents do not voluntarily surrender their parental rights and duties by what process would they lose them?

This way of looking at the donation of gametes and embryos seems to presuppose or imply two underlying principles. These are:

(1) Genetic parents are the initial holders of parental rights and duties as the producers of gametes. This we might call the genetic (parent) rule.

(2) Parental rights and duties can be surrendered and transferred by donation of gametes or embryos.

I propose to accept these principles although some people may want to reject them. It is currently fashionable to deny that the genetic or biological relation between parents and children has any moral significance. But anyone who dismisses these principles on that account must address seriously the question of whether people have any rights and duties at all with respect to gametes and embryos from their own bodies. The assumption that people do have such rights and duties seems to be deeply embedded in much of our moral and legal thinking.

These principles imply that, although the birth-mother rule is correct for normal natural reproduction and for births from donated eggs or embryos, it is not correct for all cases. They seem to imply that a genetic surrogate mother is the true mother of the child, but not that a gestatory surrogate mother is.

The apparent implication that a genetic surrogate mother is the true mother creates a problem for the earlier proposals. It would be unsatisfactory to adopt a system of surrogacy in which the commissioning parents are automatically the legal parents of the child if both intuition and theory point to the surrogate mother as its true mother.

In utero donation and surrogacy

A possible solution to this problem is suggested by the above theory of donation. If parental rights and duties can, in effect, be surrendered and transferred by donation of the embryo, there is no reason why we should not take genetic surrogacy to involve donation of the embryo *in utero*. Normally, of course, we think of donated embryos as being outside the body; but there is no logical reason why embryos should not be donated *in utero* without being removed from the body.

Legal acceptance of this would mean that the parental rights and duties of the surrogate mother, with respect to the embryo and subsequent baby, could be surrendered and transferred to the commissioning parents from the outset of the pregnancy. The effect of this would be to put the commissioning parents in genetic surrogacy into the same legal relationship with the baby as are the commissioning parents in gestatory surrogacy. They would then be the legal parents already, when the baby is born, and there would be no question of the arrangement involving or anticipating the transfer of the baby.

The idea of *in utero* donation of the embryo can seem to support the view that the surrogate mother should be made to hand over the child if she refuses to do so, which would be a distressing feature of the theory to many people. This may be because it suggests a property contract model of surrogacy of the kind that I have already argued should be rejected. Donation, of course, does not imply such contracts. There is no reason why the surrender and transfer of parental rights and duties by donation should not be regulated and mediated by the institutions and legal structures of society.

The Warnock Report, we might recall, recommended that all donation of gametes and embryos should be regulated and controlled through a statutory licensing body within a framework of legislation. The recommended legislation would make donation of eggs or embryos 'absolute', in the sense that donors lose all their parental rights and duties in respect of the child, and would, in effect, result in donees being deemed to assume those rights and duties.

The tendency to think that *in utero* donation of the embryo would bind the surrogate mother to surrender the child can be dispelled by looking at forms of adoption that could be modelled on *in utero* donation. In England the natural mother's agreement to adoption is 'ineffective' if given before the child is six weeks old. This rule protects the mother. Important as it is, however, there could be forms of adoption without it. A system of advance adoption or, indeed, of pre-conception adoption is imaginable and could be understood in terms of *in utero* donation.

For example, if it was legally possible, a woman finding herself pregnant might be glad to arrange an advance adoption involving donation of the embryo *in utero*. Or a married couple with six or seven children already, say, might welcome a pre-conception adoption agreement, in effect, to donate *in utero* the embryo of their inevitable next pregnancy to a childless couple. Advance or pre-conception adoption should not be confused with 'pre-natal adoption', a term sometimes used for ordinary embryo donation. Pre-conception adoption would call for a modification of the characterisation of adoption as concerned with existing children. We would need to say existing children or children who will exist in any case whether the pre-conception adoption arrangement is made or not. This would distinguish pre-conception adoption from what I call *total surrogacy* where a couple have their own genetic child naturally for commissioning parents.

A system of advance adoption would be possible though of course I am not advocating one. Such advance adoption agreements would not be binding on the natural mother to hand over the baby, if there was also an overriding principle that a mother who agrees, in advance, to give up her baby, when it is born, must be free to change her mind. This of course does not make the agreement worthless. For one thing, the agreement would have legal consequences if the child was handed over as intended. Furthermore, many important agreements on which people do in fact rely are not enforceable; for example, an agreement to marry.

In utero donation does not change anything as far as compelling the surrogate mother to surrender the child is concerned. Nonetheless, it is a useful model. It can help us to see how and in what sense the baby might be considered to belong to the commissioning parents before it is born. Of course their rights with respect to the baby during the pregnancy will be considerably restricted by the surrogate mother's autonomy, privacy and rights over her own body. For example, she may have a right to terminate the pregnancy without their consent. In this respect the position of the commissioning parents might be compared to that of fathers normally. However, if the question of abortion arises because it is a Down's fetus, say, there would be a stronger case morally for giving priority to the preferences of the commissioning parents.

Male and female perspectives

A criticism of the theory of *in utero* donation and its application to surrogacy is that it presents a male-centred perspective that disregards the concerns of women. This kind of criticism is not always articulated in the form of an argument to which a man might hope to respond; and perhaps it cannot be. For example, an eminent, usually articulate and normally friendly woman philosopher said on one occasion: 'You obviously know nothing about women'. Others say: 'Only a man could think that', and so on.

This criticism and the implicit suggestion that there are different female and male perspectives needs to be taken seriously but if it is valid it is likely that men will be incapable of seeing how or why it is. How then is one to proceed?

Take the present theory, for example. I have argued against the contract view of surrogacy that leads people to say that a surrogate mother who refuses to give up the child must be compelled to do so. I have suggested that a system of surrogacy must have a provision for the surrogate mother to keep the child in such a situation. The importance of women's experience of pregnancy and childbirth seems to be implicit in the acceptance of the birth-mother rule in normal reproduction and when embryos or eggs are donated. The one situation in which the birth-mother rule does not hold is in gestatory surrogacy, but that surely is a special case. Admittedly, the theory involves a central proposal that surrogate mothers should not be regarded as the legal mothers of the children they give birth to. But that does not mean that a baby can be whisked away no matter how much the surrogate mother protests.

The roots of the theory lie in the earlier account of ordinary donation of gametes and embryos as implying the surrender and transfer of parental rights and duties. It will be recalled that this seemed to imply the existence of two fundamental principles: one, that genetic parents are the initial holders of parental rights and duties as the producers of gametes; the other, that parental rights and duties can be surrendered and transferred by donation. It was argued that these principles underlie our intuitive acceptance of the birth-mother rule.

What was not clear in the earlier argument was that it implies that when a woman has a baby from a donated egg or embryo she becomes the true mother solely because of the surrender and transfer of the donor's parental rights and duties and *not* because she is the birth-mother, that is, *not* because she gestates and gives birth to the child. So although the argument appears to recognise the importance of childbearing and childbirth, it does no such thing.

This means that according to the theory the birth-mother rule applies in cases that involve donated eggs or embryos, as a secondary rule, the primary rule being the genetic rule. But if this is true it means also that even in natural reproduction, where the birth-mother rule is obviously correct, the birth-mother is the true mother only because she is the genetic mother and not because she is the birth-mother. The birth-mother rule thus becomes theoretically dispensable.

The upshot of this is that no weight at all is given to gestation and childbirth in themselves, in this theory. They become mere accompaniments of genetic motherhood. They might be important for the woman subjectively but, on this view, they are not important for the question of who the child really belongs to. A consequence of this is that mothers and fathers are deemed to have symmetrical and equal relations to their progeny. This would fit with the modern view that mothers and fathers have an equal status as parents. But it flies in the face of the fact that a natural mother's relation to her child is very different from that of the father.

It seems obvious that men would find this theory more acceptable than women. This is probably because for a man the question of whether he is the true father of a child has always been simply the question of whether the seed came from his body. It is reasonable to suppose that this also determines the perspective from which men respond to the question: who is the true mother? Obviously, pregnancy and childbirth do not have a central place in a perspective dominated by concern for the seed. Nonetheless, one might wonder whether even men could seriously uphold such a view once its implications are explicit.

Plainly, women could not be expected to accept the view that pregnancy and childbirth are of merely incidental importance for the question of whose child it is. For a woman the most, or one of the most, important aspects of motherhood is likely to be the special relationship between herself and the child – a relationship conditioned by the fact that the baby is created, grows, is carried and is nourished in her own body and the fact that she gives birth to it. It would be extraordinary if this did not give a different perspective for women on reproduction and parenthood, a perspective that informs their reactions to theories, policies and actions in which they may detect the covert assertion of a different, hostile perspective.

It now seems clear that the above donation theory projected a male-centred perspective that failed to engage with female concerns and relegated the most important aspects of the woman's role in reproduction – childbearing and childbirth – to the sidelines, tacitly imposing a male priority that is indifferent to women's experience. We are left with the question of what can be done about it.

One possibility is simply to make the birth-mother rule a primary rule – to put pregnancy and childbirth at the centre of the picture, making them and the birth-mother important in their own right. This would be a move towards a more woman-orientated perspective, or perhaps we should say, towards a perspective in which the experiences and concerns of women and men have an equal place. However, it is one thing to say this but quite another to know how to develop it.

Would a woman-centred perspective include the genetic rule?

There is a question of whether the genetic rule would have a place in a woman-centred perspective. Some feminists consider the genetic relation between parent and child to be an exclusively masculinist concern – an aspect of the patriarchal interest in property.

It is probably true that the genetic relation has been of greater concern for men in the past than it has for women. This is understandable, perhaps, given the facts of human reproduction, but now that modern reproductive technology can produce circumstances in which the birth-mother is not the same person as the genetic mother it is not so clear that the genetic relation will remain an exclusively male concern. In any case, if the genetic relation is an intelligible and legitimate concern for men one might expect it to be so for women too, even though its importance for them may have been overshadowed by pregnancy, childbirth and lactation. But is the genetic parent-child relation a legitimate moral concern for either?

This is too big a question to be answered fully here. We cannot, for example, be concerned with the moral status of the genetic parents of a five-year-old child, say, where some people might want to say that being the genetic parents is no longer important.

We should, however, ask whether the genetic parents of a neonate have any special parental rights. Most people would probably accept that natural parents have the right to possess and rear the child if they are together and that a natural mother does if she is not with the father. They would probably agree also that if the mother dies, in childbirth, say, then the natural father has a right to possess and rear the child. This gives some support to the view that genetic parents have some rights.

We must also consider the rights people have in relation to their gametes or embryos *in vitro*. Warnock (1984) acknowledges the existence of such rights and often refers to them as parental rights. She says, for example, that donors of gametes or embryos should lose all their parental rights with respect to the resulting child, clearly implying that they have them, and it is difficult to see how anyone could deny that they have some such rights.

I argued above that people have these rights initially as the producers of gametes. However, this could be misleading. The mere fact that the gametes from which a baby develops come physically from the bodies of its parents is not the important factor. Parental rights cannot be based simply on the fact that people have property rights in gametes as physical products of their bodies. Parental rights are not on a par simply with property rights that people have in other parts or products of their bodies (such as blood, hair, teeth or urine) which may or may not have a value.

It is here that the genetic relation is important. Obviously, it underlies the common knowledge and belief that a child inherits characteristics from its natural parents; and this is important for our understanding of parenthood as it is valued in human life (Page, 1985a). The parents' knowledge or belief that the child is their progeny – their own 'flesh and blood' – conditions the parent–child relationship because of, or partly because of, the common belief in genetic inheritance.

If this is true, one would expect it to apply to women or mothers as well as to men. In particular we might expect the mother–child relationship to be conditioned not only by the fact that the child is produced physically from the mother's own body but also by the mother's knowledge that the child inherits characteristics from her. Of course, in natural reproduction women have never had reason to distinguish these two aspects of a mother's relationship with her child. But now that the birth-mother and the genetic mother can be different persons it may be necessary for them to do so. Consequently, we cannot assume that there would be no place at all for the genetic rule in a woman-centred perspective.

At this point let us return briefly to the comparison of gestatory surrogacy and genetic surrogacy. In theory the genetic surrogate mother's donation of her embryo *in utero* results in there being no difference from a quasi-legal point of view between genetic surrogacy and gestatory surrogacy. In both cases the child is deemed to belong to the commissioning parents at birth, not to the surrogate mother. However, from the surrogate mother's point of view we might expect that there would be a considerable difference between them.

Whatever is brought about by donation *in utero*, in the way of a transfer of parental rights and duties, the genetic surrogate mother knows that the baby is her own progeny. On the other hand, the gestatory surrogate mother knows that the baby she bears is not her own progeny but is the progeny of the commissioning parents who still think of the child as theirs. We need to ask whether this would be likely to make a difference to the surrogate mother's relationship with the child when it is born and her affective reaction to the prospect of surrendering it.

The above argument about the genetic relation suggests that a woman's knowledge that the child she carries is her own progeny, or her knowledge that it is not, is likely to affect the special relationship or bond that she has with it. If so, it is possible that a gestatory surrogate mother would not have the same affective relationship with the surrogacy child as a genetic surrogate mother or a normal natural mother. Thus it is arguable that there would not be the same reason for allowing a gestatory surrogate mother to keep the child, even in exceptional circumstances, as there is with genetic surrogacy.

This amounts to saying that a gestatory surrogate mother would be less vulnerable, in this respect, than a genetic surrogate mother; but some people argue against this. For example, without mentioning the genetic relation, Trusted (1986) argues that:

... the surrogate mother provides material from her body for the developing fetus ... She feels it grow and move. Fetus and mother react on each other ... Therefore whether the surrogate mother donated her ovum or accepted *a tenant embryo*, she has actually given part of herself over and above any germ tissue'. (*my emphasis*)

Perhaps the most we can say, if anything, is that it is possible that a gestatory surrogate mother would be less likely than a genetic surrogate mother to refuse to surrender the baby. However, this is no reason for saying that she must be compelled to give it up, if she does refuse, if it would cause her damaging distress. Consequently, the provision allowing the surrogate mother exceptionally to keep the child should apply to gestatory surrogate mothers as it does to genetic surrogate mothers.

Does the birth-mother rule over-ride the genetic mother rule?

In our earlier male perspective the birth-mother rule was derivable from the genetic rule and therefore could not conflict with it in a fundamental way. In our new perspective, however, the two rules can conflict. Of course, the birth-mother rule is now a primary rule but that means only that it is not derivable from other rules. It does not mean that it necessarily over-rides any other rule that might conflict with it.

At first sight we might think that in a woman-centred perspective priority would automatically be given to the birth-mother rule and that the genetic rule would always be over-ridden by it. On reflection, however, this is doubtful.

We saw above that when a woman gives birth to a child from a donated egg or from a donated embryo she must be regarded as the true mother. But this is not simply because she is the birth-mother. It is at least partly because the parental rights and duties of the donor (the genetic mother) with respect to the resulting child must be deemed to be surrendered and transferred in the act of donation. Therefore, we cannot conclude from cases involving donation of eggs or donation of embryos that the birth-mother always takes priority over the genetic mother.

There could be cases that do not involve egg or embryo donation where the birth-mother and the genetic mother are not the same person. Consider the following imaginary case.

Mrs A and Mrs B are both to have babies by *in vitro* fertilisation and embryo transfer at the same hospital. For Mrs A and her husband it is the only chance for them to have their own progeny, which they desperately want. Mrs B at first considered adopting a baby but then decided against it. Like Mrs A she wants her own genetic child.

In the event things do not go according to plan. Someone puts Mrs B's fertilised eggs into the freezer thinking they are for storage and all Mrs A's eggs, fertilised by her husband's sperm, are inadvertently transferred to Mrs B's uterus for implantation. By the time the mistake is discovered Mrs B is definitely pregnant with Mrs A's progeny.

The situation now is that Mrs B thinks that if she was going to have someone else's baby she might as well have adopted one. Yet being pregnant she is now set on keeping the child. At the same time, Mrs A is determined to claim her progeny from Mrs B when the baby is born.

It is impossible to say how such a case should be resolved. One thing seems quite certain: we cannot say simply that the birth-mother rule provides the right answer. It would be very surprising if a consensus among women emerged favouring the birth-mother rule in such cases. Both women have a strong claim to the child. An important part of Mrs A's claim is based on the fact that the child is her progeny. This suggests that the genetic rule has some importance although clearly many other factors are involved as well.

A factor we have left out is any claim that Mrs A's husband has, as the genetic father, and the fact that Mrs A herself might be influenced in her view of the matter by the fact that the baby that Mrs B now carries is from his sperm. Viewed from this standpoint the claim of the genetic mother and father together might seem stronger. It might even be thought to be so strong that Mrs B should be forced to give up the child when it is born. However, given our attempt to develop a more woman-centred perspective, we must not allow the claim of the father to dictate this. We need to know which factor – being the birth-mother or being the genetic mother – is the more important from a woman's point of view.

It should be noticed that this case does not involve any of the moral difficulties that make surrogacy controversial. For example, there is no suggestion that Mrs B is being exploited or that there are special dangers for the child. We might have thought, therefore, that it would be easier to resolve. But although it is different in many respects from gestatory surrogacy it is not easier. If anything it is perhaps more difficult.

To try to clarify this example we might reflect on other possible cases. First, suppose a woman finds out that spare eggs, or embryos, from her own treatment have been used to give someone a child without her consent. Does she have any rights with respect to the child? Secondly, suppose doctors discover that they have transferred embryos to the wrong patients by mistake with the result that two women learn that they are pregnant with each other's embryos. Which child could they each claim as theirs? Thirdly, it would be interesting to know how women would react faced with the perhaps medically unlikely choice between: (a) having their own pregnancy with a donated egg, or embryo; and (b) having their own genetic embryo gestated by a surrogate mother.

In order to be sure that we are not unduly influenced by a male view, in pondering such cases as these, we need to know how women generally would respond to such situations and the weight they would give to the genetic relation. On this question there is very little empirical evidence.

I shall take these questions no further. Given that the birth-mother rule and the genetic mother rule are both recognised in a woman-centred perspective there are clearly three possibilities. First, the birth-mother rule might outweigh the genetic mother rule; secondly, the genetic mother rule might outweigh the birth-mother rule; or, thirdly, they might have equal weight.

Let us suppose that the birth-mother rule outweighs the genetic mother rule – the hypothesis most likely to undermine my theory. It would mean that in the case of Mrs A and Mrs B, above, Mrs B would be the true mother of the child as its birth-mother and Mrs A, the child's genetic mother, would have no claim to it. In the case of the two women who are pregnant with each other's genetic embryos, as a result of the doctors transferring the wrong embryos to them, each would be regarded as the true mother of her birth-child, not her genetic child. The woman who discovers that her genetic embryos *in vitro* have been used to give someone else a child would have no claim to it. These cases seem clear.

At first sight it might also seem clear that the birth-mother rule would exclude the possibility of a system of surrogacy in which the commissioning parents are automatically the legal parents of the child. It might be presumed that the rule would mean that the surrogate mother is the true mother of the child and therefore its legal mother when it is born. But let us compare this with the existing situation. There is no question presently that in normal circumstances the natural mother of a child is its true mother and automatically its legal mother. But that does not seem to preclude the possibility of a system of surrogacy along the lines proposed above.

The important question is not whether the surrogate mother is the true mother. It is whether the rights and duties of the true mother are alienable and, indeed, alienable in advance. This question cannot be settled by the rule stating who, other things being equal, the true mother is.

Would a woman-centred perspective exclude surrogacy entirely?

Some people argue on general grounds that a woman-centred perspective would preclude surrogacy entirely. For example, some feminists argue that all developments associated with the new reproductive technology are contrary to women's interests because they involve the control of women's reproductive functions by a male-dominated medical profession, with a consequent denial of their reproductive autonomy (Corea, 1986). I shall not address this argument.

A more specific argument is that the special relationship between a mother and the child she bears is such that she should not be allowed, at least before the baby is born, to put herself into a situation where she can even be expected to part with it. This in effect is an argument that the mother's rights and duties are inalienable, i.e. cannot be surrendered and transferred, in advance of the baby's birth let alone conception. It is a variant on the argument that it is contrary to a woman's nature to have a child for the explicit purpose of handing it over to others and therefore that surrogacy should not be allowed.

This argument founders on the fact that it is patently clear that some women are willing or positively want to be surrogate mothers. It is not convincing to say they would not do so unless they were under some kind of duress, economic or otherwise. Therefore, to prohibit surrogacy for this reason alone would be an unwarranted restriction of individual liberty. It is one thing to say that women must not be compelled to part with the children they bear, as we have said throughout – it is quite another to say they must not be allowed to enter into surrogacy arrangements to have babies for other people if they so wish and to surrender them voluntarily. Consequently, it cannot be assumed that a perspective that puts the birth-mother at the centre would necessarily exclude surrogacy altogether.

Conclusion

The upshot of this is that our attempt to develop a more woman-centred perspective by making the birth-mother rule a primary rule does not seem to undermine the earlier proposals for a system of surrogacy and the supporting theory.

This might seem to be a surprising result. Indeed, the claim to have made the birth-mother rule a primary rule might even seem to be a sham because it appears to have made no difference to the outcome. This is not entirely just, however.

First, much of the animus of people who criticised the original theory as being male-centred and hostile to women's interests was directed at the fact that it countenanced compelling the surrogate mother to surrender the baby. This, I have argued, should be corrected by the provision allowing the surrogate mother to keep the baby if she is unable to give it up voluntarily. This itself involves a shift to a more woman-centred view but it does not turn on what I have called the birth-mother rule.

Secondly, although giving greater priority to the birth-mother does not undermine the theory of surrogacy it could and, in my belief, does have important consequences beyond the theory of surrogacy. By forcing us to weigh the genetic mother rule against the birth-mother rule it might lead us to question the importance of the genetic relation of the father to the child. If, when the genetic mother and birth-mother are different people, the genetic mother has no claim to the child against the birth-mother, how can the genetic father have a claim to the child against the natural mother who is both the birth-mother and the genetic mother? The importance of the genetic relation does not vary, surely, according to whether it is the mother–child or the father–child relation. Consequently, if real priority is given to the birth-mother as against the genetic mother, it is difficult to see how the idea that mothers and fathers have equal parental status can be maintained. But such consequences, important though they are, lie outside the scope of this chapter.

References

Corea, G. (1986). *The Mother Machine*, Harper & Row, London.
Page, E. (1985a). Parental rights. *Journal of Applied Philosophy*, 1, 187–204.
Page, E. (1985b). Donation, surrogacy and adoption. *Journal of Applied Philosophy*, 2, 161–72.
Page, E. (1986). Warnock and surrogacy. *Journal of Medical Ethics*, 12, 45–7.
Trusted, J. (1986). Gifts of gametes. *Journal of Applied Philosophy*, 3, 123–6.
Warnock, M. (*chairperson*) (1984). *Report of the Committee of Inquiry into Human Fertilisation and Embryology*. HMSO, London, Cmnd. 9314.
Warnock, M. (1985). *A Question of Life*. Blackwell, Oxford.

The family and artificial reproduction

Introduction

Artificial reproduction is the term used to describe those techniques which enable conception to take place in the absence of sexual intercourse. One of the most important aspects of these new techniques is that they can employ the use of donated gametes to achieve a conception. The emphasis in this chapter is on the social and psychological implications for marital and family relationships when gametes are donated by a third party.

The donation of gametes

Procedures which use donated gametes, such as artificial insemination by donor (AID) or embryo donation after *in vitro* fertilisation (IVF), are often loosely referred to as infertility treatments. However, procedures which use donated gametes to enable infertile couples to have children are qualitatively different from other infertility treatments, and not just different in degree. The use of donated gametes does not cure infertility; it does not enable the affected partner to become fertile and to reproduce. Donor procedures may solve a couple's childlessness but that is not the same thing as curing an individual's fertility. This is not just an academic point but is of profound practical importance to individuals who are infertile. For example, an infertile man whose wife has had a child following AID remains just as infertile as he was before the procedure. AID merely allows the wife of an infertile husband to bear another man's baby, and allows the infertile husband to nurture this child (Snowden, 1987). This procedure has profound implications for both parent and child, and also for relationships within the wider family network.

The family

In many respects the family is an illusive concept which describes relationships with which we are all familiar but which, on closer examination, we find difficult to define. It possesses deep and significant subjective influences of a very pervasive kind, while at the same time representing an institution which socialises individuals to become members of a particular society and permits the necessary values which maintain that society to be passed from one generation to the next. It is not surprising that sociologists point to the family as being a unique social institution (Beutler, 1988).

While definitions of the family are hard to agree, most observers accept that the family comprises a number of individuals linked by a set of enduring relationships and that the most important of these relationships are those which, in one way or another, affect and are affected by the birth process. As Davis (1984) has noted, 'all marital and familial phenomena ultimately come back to connection through birth'. We are born into families and the relationships with family members are permanent rather than transitory, and are ascribed rather than chosen. Relationships also extend across generations and the birth of a child has implications not just for the parents but also for a much wider and larger group of surrounding individuals. Our relationships with family members differ from interaction with friends or colleagues, both in their permanence and in their quality.

Family relationships are associated with perceived rights, duties, obligations and expectations; occasionally these are formally supported in law, but more often they are informally acknowledged. Nevertheless, the feelings of obligation and duty, and of expectation, between family members are extremely strong. The appropriate behaviour of relatives is defined by certain roles, for example, those of mother, father, son, daughter, uncle, aunt, etc., and these roles are largely based on perceived biological or genetic links or, as Davis (1984) put it, to connections through birth.

Until recently in our society the assumption was that the role of 'father' encompassed two main functions: (i) the provision of half the genetic material which at conception would contribute to the genetic make-up of the child; and (ii) the responsibility for the care and nurture of the child until that child reached adulthood. The role of 'mother' has three functions; in addition to the provision of the other half of the genetic input at conception and responsibility for the nurture of the child after birth, the mother also carries the child during the nine-month gestation period of pregnancy.

Gamete donation and the family

These assumptions about motherhood and fatherhood do not hold when gamete donation takes place. Because artificial reproduction procedures make it possible to separate out the various phases of the reproductive process, it is now possible for a child to be subject to multiple parenting with two different men fulfilling the differing functions of the 'father' role, and up to three different women the role of 'mother' (Snowden et al., 1983).

It can of course be argued with some justification that other situations also give rise to the circumstance of multiple parenting. In the case of adoption the child has two sets of parents. However, it is recognised that adoption may pose certain problems, and in our society adoption is formally regulated and supported by a framework of agreed social practices which are enforced in law. A child may also be born as a result of an extramarital liaison. However, it has to be acknowledged that such a situation, if known, is not socially approved and often leads to the breakdown of a marriage.

Artificial reproduction introduces procedures for which there are no established social roles and, for this reason, considerable uncertainty surrounds the practice. Using sperm donation in AID as an example, it is possible to examine the implications of procedures which involve the donation of gametes for the participants, the (potential) child, and their family relationships. Information collected by a resarch team at the University of Exeter (Snowden *et al.*, 1983), in interviews with 70 married couples who have one or more children who were conceived by AID, and from discussions with AID practitioners, donors and children serve as a basis, in this chapter, for exploring the psychological and social implications of AID for parents, children, and for wider family relationships.

The infertile husband and AID

Not many men are willing to talk about their infertility and as a result few people realise the relatively common incidence of male infertility. Among the general population infertility is erroneously believed to be almost totally confined to women. Many people (both men and women) confuse infertility with impotence and a lack of virility or masculinity, and they imagine that infertile men must be incapable of normal sexual feelings and performance. A diagnosis of infertility, therefore, often comes as a shock to a man who has experienced normal feelings of sexual arousal and enjoyed a mutually satisfying sex life with his partner. In addition, most men are apprehensive about the possible reactions of friends and colleagues were they to know of this infertility. One man said: 'If you tell most people you are sterile they think you are not virile, and you can be jibed about it and people just don't understand' (Snowden & Snowden, 1984). Male infertility is, therefore, a subject surrounded by stigma and taboo.

As noted earlier, AID does not cure male infertility. So what does AID do? Essentially AID is a procedure which upholds and maintains the belief that sexual relationships within marriage should be exclusive, and that a woman should have sexual intercourse only with her husband. AID merely allows a woman to have another man's baby without having a sexual relationship with him. When viewed in this way AID can be seen as a marriage-affirming procedure. Indeed, considering the stress, embarrassment, inconvenience and financial cost of AID, the willingness of couples to submit themselves to this procedure demonstrates a quite striking commitment to their marriage vows. There are simpler, cheaper and less public ways of conceiving another man's baby.

Although AID does not cure a man's infertility, it does offer him some solutions for his childlessness and allows him to fulfil the function of nurturing his wife's baby. Whilst AID does not enable a husband and wife to start a baby in a biological sense, it does allow them to create their own baby in a social sense. This creation of a child identifies a major difference between AID and adoption, for in adoption a baby is already in existence and is in need of parents. A child conceived by AID results directly from a decision made by a couple from within their own marriage; in this sense the resulting child is a carefully planned *social* creation of their marriage. One AID mother in the Exeter survey explained her preference for AID when compared to adoption by saying: 'I think it was because we both desperately wanted a child that was *ours* from the very start. [Her husband interjected, 'Part of *our* unit.'] We didn't want somebody just to come and knock at the door and say "Right, we've got a baby for you"' (Snowden & Snowden, 1984).

AID also allows a man to behave as though the baby his wife has conceived is the result of a natural conception and so to present a 'normal' front to the world. Traditionally, some of those who have provided an AID service have encouraged men in the denial of their infertility. They have supported the assumption that a man will naturally want to keep his infertility secret (Sandler, 1972). Men have been consoled that 'no-one need ever know' and they have been encouraged to pretend – to themselves as well as to others – that the baby conceived by AID has been conceived in the usual way and that they are the natural parent. The information booklet published by the Royal College of Obstetricians and Gynaecologists (RCOG, 1979) for couples deciding whether or not to undergo AID perpetuates this pretence. Wives are reassured that: 'provided you do not abstain from intercourse during the period in which AID was carried out, there can be no certainty that any child conceived is not your husband's'. Couples have also been assured that children need never discover the truth about their conception. Again, the RCOG booklet advises: 'Unless you decide to tell your child, there is no reason for him (or her) ever to know that he (or she) was conceived by AID'.

However, to try to solve a problem by denying the true state of affairs, and by evading or distorting the facts, is rarely successful. Denial simply buries rather than solves problems which often re-emerge to trouble the sufferer at some later date. Happily, public attitudes about AID are beginning to change. The recent White Paper on human fertilisation (DHSS, 1987) proposes that skilled counselling should be provided for infertile couples to enable them to explore and face up to the implications of accepting artificial reproduction procedures.

In the case of the infertile husband this is particularly necessary because AID does not address his basic problem of infertility.

AID does not enable a man to procreate children of his own who will continue his line of ancestors and descendents. Having children is a way in which parents can live on in future generations, almost a means of achieving immortality. One infertile husband told us: 'My major hang-up really was based on this rather metaphysical notion of genetic immortality. What depressed me most of all, and overwhelmed me mentally, was the idea that at this point my genetic channel stops. That's the end. And that was the most chilling thing I had to take on board'. The problem of 'genetic death' for the infertile male is, of course, not solved by his wife having a baby through the use of a donor's sperm. This same husband, who was the devoted father of two AID children, said: 'I must be frank and say that I still wish I could father a child. It doesn't intrude into my relationship with these two children ... but I think if somebody suddenly discovered that my fertility had come back I would want to try most vigorously to have a child'.

From the viewpoint of the husband, perhaps the central complexity of AID is that the child has two fathers. Our conversations with AID fathers left us in no doubt that conceiving a child by AID produced confusion about paternity. One husband struggled to describe his confused feelings about being the father of two AID sons: 'The fact that they were not mine – they are, I know they are mine – but it was in the back of my mind that it was never mine, never my child – I wasn't the one, the father – but I mean I know they are mine now, they always will be mine'. This confusion is to some extent inevitable. Although the husband is in all practical terms the father of the child, the person who provides for and loves and cares for the child, he is not the genetic father of the child. We may agree that the husband is much more important in terms of practical fathering, yet it is a fact that the donor, a more shadowy and perhaps less important figure, is still the genetic father of the child. Many of the men we interviewed referred to the donor as 'the real father' whilst at the same time they were in no doubt that they were also the child's father. Men tended to resolve this conflict in one of two ways. Some denied the donor's involvement altogether: 'I can't even picture it as a donor to be honest with you. It's just a medical treatment the same as an operation is a medical treatment. It's the medical treatment for the medical problem, just the same as you take aspirins for a headache. I've got infertility, so you take AID to solve the problem that way'. Others attempted to resolve this confusion about paternity by playing down the role of the genetic father and emphasising their own role of nurturing father. The semen donor's part was completed once the ovum was fertilised whereas the infertile husband had supported his wife during pregnancy and labour, had been present at the birth, and had taken on all the long-term responsibilities of fatherhood. To all intents and purposes, he was the true father. Nevertheless, a child is not the cure for infertility, and it seems to us that to consider AID as a satisfactory solution for male infertility is less than infertile men deserve and less than they can rightly expect. Research into the causes and treatment of male infertility is urgently needed.

The wife and AID

Although a wife who is married to an infertile husband does not share his infertility, she does share his childlessness. One wife said: 'When I was holding someone's baby, or even looking after little children, I'd play with them and do all sorts and it was lovely. But when I went home, I could have climbed up the wall because there was so much love inside of me that I couldn't give'. Wives often share the burden of their husband's infertility in another way; discussion with couples where AID has been attempted showed that it was very common for wives to pretend that it was they and not their husband who was the infertile partner. This was done to protect the husband from perceived stigma attached to male infertility; it was felt that female infertility was more sympathetically viewed by close relatives and by the general public. Nevertheless, this self-sacrificial act often increases the pain of childlessness for some women who find themselves being 'blamed' by in-laws and seen as inadequate marriage partners.

Wives take on their husband's infertility in yet another way. When a decision is made to seek AID, it is the fertile wife, who is suffering no malfunction or disorder, who becomes the patient and who suffers the indignities of intimate examinations and 'treatment'. In some practices she may also be subjected to investigations to prove her own fertility (even though there may be no reason to question it) before the practitioner is willing to start AID. It is interesting to speculate on the reasons for this. Does the doctor have a need to define the woman as a legitimate patient and then to 'medicalise' a procedure which, as we have discussed, has in essence a social rather than a medical rationale? AID is a simple procedure from a technical point of view, and some wives (and single women too) have circumvented any involvement with the medical profession and successfully undertaken the procedure themselves on a do-it-yourself basis.

Although the AID procedure is a detached and clinical one, wives are conceiving a child outside the usual marriage bond. Some perceive that their behaviour may meet with disapproval, particularly from the older generation. Some wives fear that if their AID became known their character might be compromised and people might question their moral standards. One wife explained that she would prefer to be able to talk about AID more freely but '. . . well, I always feel for instance that they're thinking, "Well, look at her, she's no good, it's not her husband's child"'. Wives who undergo AID are also very aware that their husbands might have reason to feel excluded from the process and be jealous; one commented 'To me I was getting everything. The baby was going to come with me; it would be more me than [husband], and I felt it was an awful lot to ask somebody. It seemed so unfair'. Many couples took care to make sure that the husband felt included and involved in the experience of pregnancy. One wife said to her husband: 'We involved you in everything didn't we? As soon as I felt the baby moving I let him feel it – everything. Just do it together. Whenever I had been to hospital I'd tell him everything that had happened so that he never felt left out'.

Women appeared less likely to be aware that they too might find it difficult to accept the fact that it was a donor's child they had borne rather than their husband's child. Sadly, it is possible for an AID child to be used to punish an infertile husband. One man wrote: 'My wife has always held it against me for not being able to produce children, which is very unfortunate, so in order to make her happy we both agreed to her having artificial insemination. I was so happy when X was born as she was such a beautiful child and still is. Since this separation I cannot see my daughter ... The last three years [my wife] has repeatedly told me I am only her guardian. I love my daughter very much and have always shown her a great deal of affection but the hurtful part of all this is that my wife has told her I am only her uncle which is very hurtful after five years ... '. It is not common for wives to be worried about their own reaction to their husband or to their expected child. They would give birth to their own baby and so they had few worries about how they would react to it. Their anxieties, if they had any, were for their husbands. When asked if she had any initial worries, one wife said: 'I think the only thing was how he would accept the baby when it was born; you know, whether he'd reject it or whether he wouldn't. I was almost certain he wouldn't, but you had that problem there as to whether or not he would'. It was apparent that many wives were hesitant to admit to having any thoughts at all about the donor for fear of hurting their husband's feelings. Wives who did admit to thinking about the donor described an attitude of fairly superficial curiosity rather than a desire to know who it was: '. . . what he did for a living, what he looked like, was he clever, how tall was he – all these things. But I really wouldn't want to know. It's just my curiosity. It would bring it too close to reality. I would be thinking "I've had your baby"'.

Wider kin

The birth of a child holds implications for other relatives as well as for the immediate parents. Not only does the birth of a child link a couple in the creation of a child which shares a mixture of their own genetic endowment, but the birth forges other links. A grandparent is linked with their new grandchild; a daughter-in-law becomes more closely linked with her in-law's because of the combined genetic inheritance which has now been passed on to the child. In the case of AID these genetic links are not present on the husband's side and there is inevitably a situation of imbalance, with only the maternal relatives having genetic links with the child. Parents of AID children are fearful that this imbalance may cause conflict within the family, with maternal grandparents feeling superior, and paternal grandparents finding it difficult to accept a newly born grandchild. However, the Exeter research project demonstrated that almost without exception where grandparents and other relatives were aware about AID, grandchildren (and nieces and nephews) were loved and accepted in the usual way by all family members. It appears that there is greater anxiety associated with the possibility of conflict than dealing with its actual occurrence. Because AID produces an imbalance in consanguineal relationships favouring the maternal grandparents, it could be supposed that couples would be more likely to inform the wife's than the husband's parents about AID, but this was not always the case. In some instances the wife's parents were not told, even though the husband's parents were aware; this seemed to be because the husband was already perceived to be disadvantaged in some other respect. The wife's parents may already be unhappy at what they consider to be an unfortunate match for their daughter, and to tell them about AID might exacerbate an already difficult situation. One wife said: 'A woman's family can feel that the husband has let her down, even if the wife doesn't feel that herself'. This illustrates an important point; infertility and AID must not be seen as isolated or discrete problems. AID is but one item in a complex of inter-relating issues and family pressures which may affect any relationship between close family members.

The donor

If a couple decide to have a child by AID, the one condition absolutely necessary for them is that there is another man who is willing to donate his fertile semen for their use. Unfortunately, the needs of this essential man, the semen donor, are often largely ignored (Handelsman et al., 1985). However, the donor, in complementary ways to the recipient couple, is also subject to complex social and psychological implications of his semen donation. He too is a member of a family for which his action has important implications. Perhaps the main reason for ignoring the part played by the donor is the perceived need for his anonymity; programmes are purposefully organised to render the donor 'invisible' and so his needs are often unrecognised. The use of frozen semen and sperm banks helps to depersonalise the procedure and the donor is discouraged from thinking of the couples who are to receive his donation and of any children who might be born. Medical students have been described as: 'a good source of donors because they can be recruited en masse (and) processed through standard selection procedures and tests with comparatively little sense of involvement and superficial motivation' (A. Klopper, 1985, unpublished). In short, donors are discouraged from thinking about the consequences of their actions. Nevertheless, profound consequences are likely to ensue and it is unrealistic to assume that a donor will always be able to shut them out of his mind (Daniels, 1986). The ethics of encouraging a man to donate semen without adequate consideration of the consequences must also be questioned, and has important implications for the notion of informed consent. The counselling of donors is as necessary as counselling for infertile couples, and there should be a formal requirement that before the donation of gametes, donors should be counselled by an independent trained counsellor.

Donors are asked to provide gametes and to be willing to reproduce biologically, but then to forego any knowledge of their offspring or any re- sponsibility for his/her nurture. An infertile, recipient couple will, of course, nurture the offspring as their own much wanted baby, and are likely to lavish all their love and care upon it, so superficially any disquiet a donor may feel about a potential child may be thought to be irrational. But men are not simply detached, rational beings; men also have strong emotions and deeply ingrained beliefs about their responsibility to their offspring. It is no simple matter for a donor to donate sperm which may result in the creation of a child who carries his genes, a child who inherits his appearance and traits. There is a very real sense in which we see ourselves as living on in the lives of our children, and these deep and complex feelings and emotions are not easily denied. It is not surprising that some men who donate semen in their youth do, later on in life, have regrets. Some doctors, now in middle life, do say that they regret their student involvement as semen donors. As their own children grow up and develop their own unique personalities, the fact that there may well be other, unknown offspring begins to bother and disturb them; they find themselves wondering how these other children have developed, and how they are faring.

Semen donation also has implications for the donor's kin. His wife (or indeed a future wife) shares with him the procreation of children and the responsibility for their nurture. She too may be bothered and disturbed by the possibility of unknown other children. This is sometimes dismissed as feelings of jealousy, but it is more than this. It is the denial of deeply ingrained beliefs and attitudes which are developed as a result of the socialisation process. A donor's parents are affected by his donation as they may have grandchildren who are unknown to them. A donor's own children may also have unknown half-brothers or half-sisters as a result of their father's action. This fact can be profoundly disturbing to an adolescent child as they themselves struggle to achieve a sense of their own independent identity.

Donation is characterised as an altruistic act, but this may exacerbate rather than reduce the stress for donors. It could be argued that a man who is motivated to act in a selfless way, and for the benefit of others, might be more than ordinarily susceptible to feelings of disquiet about any offspring for whom he has relinquished all responsibility.

Egg or embryo donation

With the advent of the procedures surrounding *in vitro* fertilisation (IVF), egg and embryo donation are now also practised. Although similar to sperm donation in many ways, egg donation is more complex because the recipient mother carries the baby for the 9-month gestation period of pregnancy and gives birth to the baby. Nevertheless the egg donor is the genetic mother, and she (and her family) is subject to all the psychological and social implications associated with the donation of semen described above. Indeed it could be argued that any anxieties and regrets among women donors could be even more severe, as females are more heavily socialised to care for their offspring than are males.

Following embryo donation, any resulting child will be nurtured by a couple neither of whom are the genetic parents of that child, and so in some ways embryo donation can be likened to adoption. Indeed some practitioners have used the term 'pre-natal adoption' to describe embryo donation. There is considerable evidence from adoption research that relinquishing mothers often suffer long-term grief over the loss of their baby. Will embryo donor couples also be subject to similar feelings of grief and loss? Will they in subsequent years find themselves wondering what has happened to their genetic offspring? It is also possible that an infertile couple who donate a 'spare' embryo to another couple may be faced with a situation where their own embryo replacement is unsuccessful. These are deep and complex issues of human emotions and it is vital that all donors of genetic material, in whatever form and for whatever purpose, are interviewed by a skilled counsellor about the social and psychological implications of their proposed action and given adequate time to consider what their course of action will be.

Donation between close relatives

It is relatively rare for a donor from within the recipient's own family to be used. Schoysman (1975) has detailed two cases of sperm donation between brothers; in both cases neither the wife nor sister-in-law was told that the infertile man's brother was the donor. According to Schoysman the outcome was happy but, in general, practitioners are reluctant to use a brother as a donor. In recent months it has been reported that sisters have donated eggs to their infertile sisters, and there appears to be an opinion among some practitioners that egg donation between sisters is less likely to be problematical than sperm donation between brothers. Perhaps the greater willingness to consider sister donors is because a recipient mother is felt to have a closer identification with the mother role (because she bears the child) than does a recipient husband in the case of AID. Or perhaps it is a matter of gender stereotyping where the female is seen as likely to be more caring and co-operative rather than success-oriented and competitive. Nevertheless, gamete donation between either sisters or brothers is bound to result in considerable confusion of relationships within the family. A child's aunt will also be his/her genetic mother, or a child's uncle his/her genetic father. Before the donation is made (and in the absence of any child), problems which this role confusion may cause may seem insignificant and unlikely to an infertile couple who desperately desire a child. However, once a child is born and begins to grow up within the family, it is possible to predict areas where conflict may well arise. These problems are likely to affect the social-parent/child relationship,; the 'aunt' or 'uncle'/child relationship: the relationship between the siblings and also between the in-laws. As previously noted, there are clear expectations within families about the behaviour appropriate for the roles of mother, aunt, sister-in-law and wife, and where these roles become confused it would be unlikely for conflicts (both intrapersonal and interpersonal) not to emerge. A donor 'uncle', seeing his genetic offspring grow up, may feel he has rights and duties over and above those of the usual uncle; a child may experience divided loyalties; a recipient social father may experience a sense of reduced worth and inferiority compared with his donor brother; a sister-in-law and brother-in-law may find it hard to know how to behave towards one another in the knowledge that they have together produced a child. And to keep the whole matter a secret, as Schoysman did, seems likely to introduce even more potential conflict within the family where some members are part of the secret and others are excluded from it. Even if secrecy is avoided, there remains one very important character in the drama to be played out who will have no say in any decision being made. This is the child who will be born if the donation results in a pregnancy.

The child and AID

When the decision about whether or not to try for a baby by AID is made, the interests of the potential child need very careful consideration. The principle that the child is of primary concern is often stated, but difficult to substantiate as the child does not yet exist. Some practitioners are honest enough to admit that it is the needs of the infertile couple, and their desperate desire for a baby of their own, which is being met by AID. But in meeting the needs of the potential parents, society's responsibility towards the potential child must not be forgotten: a child who will have to live with the repercussions of a decision in which he/she had no say. As Matthews (1980) has remarked, 'Yet to be designed is a consent form which the unborn child can sign'.

What are the best interests of the child? Lusk (1988) has suggested that rather than referring to 'the child' it is more helpful to think in terms of an individual. All children grow up eventually and if we think about adults we may be less prone to speculating about how children feel and think, and be more inclined to consider an adult's point of view and also to see the question from the angle of human rights. This point is illustrated by the results of a survey, carried out in 1985 by the popular British magazine *Woman* (12 January 1985), of its readers' views about artificial reproduction techniques. When asked to put themselves in the place of parents who had used AID, only about one-half said they would tell the child. By contrast, when considering how they themselves would feel as a product of AID, 80% felt they had a *right* to know how they were conceived and to know basic information about any third party involved in their conception.

Traditionally, the majority of parents of AID children have been reluctant to tell these children about their origins. This has been as much to protect the husband from the exposure of his infertility as to a desire to protect the child. However, the recommendations of The Warnock Report, and the suggestions for legislation put forward in the recent White Paper on human fertilisation and embryology, accept that it is preferable and wise for parents to be open and honest with their children about their means of conception rather than to try to keep the matter secret. The frequent and open discussion of the new artificial reproduction techniques in the press and on radio and television means that children who are growing up today will be much more aware that some children are born following the use of artificial reproduction techniques. They are very likely to be curious to know if this applies to themselves. In the same way that many growing children ask their parents, 'Am I adopted?', it is not difficult to imagine growing children a few years hence asking their parents, 'Am I a test-tube baby?' The Warnock Report recommended that a child conceived by AID should have access at the age of 18 years to information about the donor's racial origin and genetic health (Warnock, 1984). This is good in that it would inform the young adult of the manner of their conception but it would give them no more information than can be presumed already (i.e. that the practitioner chose a healthy donor and a Caucasian donor for a Caucasian recipient). McWhinnie (1988) argues that 'this will satisfy neither their needs nor their curiosity and goes little way to giving them the rights which we in Britain accord to others. It is an adult-oriented concept in which the adult world decides how much it is good for a child to know. And yet the child will be aware that records have been kept somewhere for the ascertainment of racial origin and genetic health'. The White Paper goes further than Warnock and proposes that a young adult conceived by AID should have a right of access to certain (unspecified) 'non-identifying information' about the donor. This is preferable to the Warnock recommendation; research among adopted children has shown that they find it helpful to know some details about the characteristics and life-style of their biological parents. However, the anonymity of the donor is to be preserved – at least for the time being. This is an example of the needs of the child not being given primacy in the proposed legislation. The proposal that the donor's identity should not be known takes account of the donor's (presumed) desire for anonymity and the practitioner's fear that his task of finding willing donors will be made more arduous were this anonymity to be removed, but does little to take account of the child's need for information. Not all young adults conceived by AID will wish to know the identity of their genetic father. Experience among adopted children who have this right would suggest that only a small minority will wish to do so. Nevertheless, research has shown that some people, particularly as they grow older, are motivated to investigate their genealogy. It is likely that as more young people become aware of their AID origins there will be pressure from some of them to achieve the right to knowledge of the identity of their genetic father.

The reactions of AID children

Until recently very little has been known about how AID children have fared as they have grown up within their families, and even now the information is based on the experiences of only a small number of individuals. Occasionally, usually in the popular press, one hears of the experience of adults who have become aware of their AID origins and who are disturbed by this knowledge. Often these individuals have found out about their origins accidentally or in a hurtful way during a family quarrel. It may be significant that the young people contacted in the Exeter project had all been told in a purposeful and planned way. These young adults had accepted their AID status equably and none of them had found it a particularly traumatic experience. They had certainly been surprised when they were told, but some of that surprise was because their parents had kept the matter such a close secret for so many years. None of them regretted the fact that they had been conceived by AID. They were enjoying life and happy to be alive and realised that they owed their existence to AID. They were also pleased to feel that their parents had wanted a child so badly, and that they were that child who had fulfilled their parents' wishes. One said, ' ... the realisation that I had been brought into the world, you know, they actually went to tremendous lengths because they wanted to have a baby. And I suddenly felt that they must love me a tremendous amount, that I was very important to them'.

In the cases where the father was still alive and in contact with the child, the fear that the father/child relationship would be damaged proved to be unfounded. Indeed, the relationship in some cases had been strengthened as the son or daughter came to realise the anguish which the father must at times have experienced. The young people were not overly curious about the identity of the anonymous donor who had begotten them and they did not spend time worrying about who he was. Nor did they have a feeling of lack of identity themselves, or a sense of not being sure who they were. They had identified with the father who had brought them up and considered him their father. From the experience of this small number of young adults, it would seem that many of the fears expressed by parents about their children are likely to be unfounded. Parents had found it possible to explain AID origins to their older children. This knowledge had not apparently damaged the personality of the

AID child nor had it disrupted family relationships. However, it would be foolish to pretend that the outcome of AID will always be successful and that resulting family relationships will always be smooth and harmonious and supportive. All family relationships have their ups and downs; divorce and unsatisfactory relationships between parent and child occur in many families. It would be too much to expect that AID families will escape these problems. Nevertheless, with adequate counselling help to enable the couple and the child to explore their own situation, and with an appropriate supporting framework of legislation and regulation, the best possible circumstances for a successful outcome can be constructed.

References

Beutler, I. F. et al. The family realm: Theoretical contributions for understanding its uniqueness. *Journal of Marriage and the Family*. (In press.)

Daniels, K. R. (1986). Psychosocial issues associated with being a semen donor. *Clinical Reproduction and Fertility*, 4, 341–51.

Davis, K. (1984). The study of marriage and the family as a scientific discipline. Paper presented to the American Sociological Association.

Department of Health and Social Security (1987). *Human Fertilisation and Embryology: A Framework for Legislation*. HMSO, London.

Handelsman, D. J., Dunn, S. M., Conway, A. J., Boyland, L. M. & Jansen, R. P. (1985). Psychological and attitudinal profiles in donors for artificial insemination. *Fertility and Sterility*, 43, 95–101.

Lusk, T. (1988). The importance to children of having knowledge about their parents. In: Bruce, N. (ed.). *Truth and the Child*. Family Care, 21 Castle Street, Edinburgh.

McWhinnie, A. M. (1988). The child, the family and society. In: Bruce, N. (ed.). *Truth and the Child*. Family Care, 21 Castle Street, Edinburgh.

Matthews, C. D. (1980). Artificial insemination – donor and husband. In: Pepperell, R. J. (ed.). *The Infertile Couple*. Churchill Livingstone, London.

Royal College of Obstetricians and Gynaecologists (1979). *Artificial Insemination*. RCOG, London.

Sandler, B. (1972). Donor insemination in England. *World Medicine*, 19, 87–9.

Schoysman, R. (1975). Problems of selecting donors for artificial insemination. *Journal of Medical Ethics*, 1, 34–5.

Snowden, R. (1987). AID: Facts and fantasies. *British Journal of Sexual Medicine*, 14, 118–20.

Snowden, R., Mitchell, G. D. & Snowden, E. M. (1983). *Artificial Reproduction: A Social Investigation*. George Allen & Unwin, London.

Snowden, R. & Snowden, E. (1984). *The Gift of a Child*. George Allen & Unwin, London.

Warnock, M. (*chairperson*) (1984). *Report of the committee of inquiry into human fertilisation and embryology*. HMSO, London.

Religion and assisted conception

Introduction

From time to time during the past ten years of public debate on developing techniques for assisted conception and artificial reproduction, I have indulged myself the following speculation: supposing a tribe of human beings existed who possessed no means of reproducing themselves, and supposing further that one day the scientists in that community informed their fellows that they had made a startling development, and had come up with a means of creating new human persons; what would be the various possible reactions within the community to this astonishing new power within its grasp? From the ethical point of view could not its only major response be one of delight at the new-found possibility of conferring the gift of life on new human beings and of welcoming new members into the human family to enjoy a share in its existence and its destiny? A moralist would surely be hard put to it to find any ground for objection or misgiving in reaction to such a procedure when it is phrased in such positive and beneficent terms. He might no doubt wish to enter various caveats and cautions along the way, but I think he would find it difficult to object profoundly or radically to such a new-found human capacity to impart and share the goods and values of human existence with new fellow human beings.

I have begun with this elementary scenario for two reasons. The first is because I think it serves to highlight the primary reality which should dominate all ethical consideration of assisted conception and artificial reproduction, that their end result and purpose is the bringing into existence of new human persons. And the second is because this primary reality of bringing new human beings into existence also provides a unifying focal point for the various religious considerations which can be, and have been, brought to bear on the whole subject of assisted conception and artificial reproduction. Those various religious considerations I would identify as: firstly, how the human capacity to initiate life relates to the divine prerogative of God as creative life–giver; secondly, how the commissioning by God of our first human forebears to 'increase and multiply', or in non-biblical terms to reproduce, is considered to provide natural structures and ethical conditions for humans in the discharging of that God-given commission; and thirdly, how the interests of the offspring of such reproduction affect the motivation and the methods invoked in the process of assisted conception or artificial reproduction. More briefly, I shall address in turn the three considerations of God, parents and child, which are raised by religion as it considers the developing techniques of assisted conception or artificial reproduction.

God

It is a fixed constant of the judaeo-christian tradition of thought that God is the originator of all that we know as life, that human life began with him and is destined to return to him. Sometimes this relationship between God and his human creatures is depicted in human terms and categories of justice, so that he is regarded as Lord of life whereas we humans possess at best not the complete disposal of the gift of life but only a stewardship of creation in general and of human life in particular. It is this perspective of justice in our relationships with God which is the ultimate basis for Christians of the sanctity and inviolability under God of every human life which he has created, and which then generates moral conclusions in terms of the right to life in such areas as abortion and mercy killing. It is this context of justice to the only author of life which also forms the basis of respect for our own lives, as resulting in a moral responsibility towards God which proscribes suicide and voluntary euthanasia, and which positively enjoins on us a responsibility to protect ourselves and to take care of our lives and health in the variety of possible human situations.

Alongside this strong Christian tradition of viewing God as the author of life who has claims of moral justice with respect to how we dispose of human life, there is another strand of religious thinking which expresses the human relationship to God in terms of love rather than of justice, and which has a particular application in the field of human reproduction. This is based on the perception that God's motivation in creating life in the first place is above all one of benevolent love and generosity within a universal divine plan of self-giving, insofar as this is possible between uncreated being and created being. And, within such a design of creative love, God has invited his human creatures, men and women, to co-operate with him, not just in reproducing themselves, but in transmitting his gift of life to new human beings and of thus acting as co-creators with God in a total cosmic enterprise of loving creation. In this view, the initiative of love remains with God, but the channel which he has chosen to express it is the human love of man and woman, as this is expressed in a covenant of life and love between them. In this perspective their physical and emotional intercourse issues in the creation of a new unique person who is at the same time both literally the personal embodiment of their mutual giving of self to each other, and at the same time a further expression in human history, and through human agency, of the divine enterprise of creative love and divine self-giving.

Those are the broad lines of a religious interpretation of human reproduction which views it above all as the embodiment of love, principally that of God, but as expressed and articulated in the loving behaviour and attitudes of human parents as chosen and necessary collaborators with God. And this perspective on human creation and procreation in terms of human love as the agent of divine love provides an ethical structure within which humans are viewed as designed and expected to formulate and exercise their power and potential for procreation. In reality, and in the working out of human history, of course, such an interpretation regularly encounters a series of situations where every-thing does not appear to be going according to plan. And the most obvious of these apparent obstacles to the co-operation of humans in the divine enterprise of creative love is the phenomenon of human infertility and the incapacity of individuals for this or other reasons to act as the loving agents of the divine creativity. How does religion react to what is for many a humanly tragic situation and, in religious terms, an apparent frustration of the call to be co-creators with God?

Broadly speaking, until comparatively recently the only solution open was to consider such a situation of infertility as irremediable and in some sense or other divinely ordained so far as the individuals affected by infertility were concerned. When the sublime religious novel on human bewilderment, the Book of Job, relates how Job tragically lost his family by the inscrutable design of God, his first resigned and trusting reaction was, 'The Lord gave, and the Lord has taken away. Blessed be the name of the Lord'. And in the case of those who were incapable of producing a family, the traditional religious attitude and interpretation in the face of such a human tragedy could be summed up in the sentiment, 'The Lord has pleased not to give. Blessed be the name of the Lord'. But it is this traditional religious attitude of a trusting acceptance of divine providence which has been profoundly challenged in modern times by the development of procedures and techniques designed to remedy human infertility and to give to infertile and frustrated couples the child for whom they long. For such developments raise, within a religious context, not just the question of morally evaluating the means and methods being tried and adopted in order to achieve successful fertilisation but, at a deeper level, the whole rationale of assisted conception and artificial reproduction and, of course, at base the entire enterprise of medicine and of medical therapy. It is here that we encounter fundamental religious attitudes of ambivalence towards human enterprise, human initiative and human ingenuity. For some their religious perspective on life and human history can find expression in a whole-hearted welcoming of any scientific or medical advance which will overcome existing human limitations and expand the range of human options and choices in the face of hitherto insoluble situations. Such a positive and encouraging attitude will find religious warrant in a theology of creation which views it as a continuing process of collaboration between God and the human creatures whom he has endowed with intelligence and freedom. For Christians it will find confirmation in the once-for-all victory of Christ himself in overcoming death and dissolution and in commissioning his followers to continue to spread even now in human history what St Paul termed 'the power of his resurrection'. And this religious perspective is, of course, one which readily recognises the privileged and honourable calling of medicine in the history and destiny of the human race.

For others, however, such human attitudes of enterprise and remedial ingenuity will tend to be seen not as a collaboration with a divine continuing and loving initiative but as a challenge to the power and decrees of an almighty God, expressed occasionally in the accusation of 'playing at God with people's lives'. This is not intended to be a theological paper, but perhaps it will help us to understand many of the underlying and unspoken religious attitudes which motivate and fuel many current scientific and medical controversies if we realise that they spring from very different ways of perceiving the archetypal relationship between God and his human creatures as one of collaboration or as one of confrontation; or to what degree God has, or has not, delegated to human creatures a positive share in the divine initiative and in divine providence for the human future.

In the history of Western religion there can be discerned a marked suspicion of any bids to stress the positive resources of humanity and of creation, and a reaction that regards these bids as so many further expressions of the original sin of humanity in reaching above itself to grasp at the knowledge and power which rightly belong only to God. Such a continuing concern to draw a circle around humans, outside which they step only at their peril, appears to point to what might be called an underlying 'theology of inverse proportionality', which can be discerned in much of the Christian tradition, in the viewing of humanity's relationship in general with God as a continual demarcation dispute. What is gained by humans is snatched from God in a promethean rewriting of the judaeo-christian gospel of creation. As the 'secular' expands among the society of men and women, the 'sacred' is marginalised to the limits of life in a re-enactment of the proud defiance of Adam. But the basic weakness in all such theologies of inverse proportionality is that they are not only bad theology; they also run counter to the historical record of God's dealings with his human creatures. They unwittingly depict God and humans as engaged in a continuing territorial dispute over the field of knowledge and of power. And in so doing they actually bring God down to the level of humans, as a knower like any human knower, a cause like any human cause, a power like any other power. Moreover, by the very fact of his generous creation of humans God has revealed that he is not by temperament a jealous or grudging God, and that he is best appreciated by acknowledging the inherent dignity and powers for action with which he has graced us, and of which humanity has today become so conscious. It was such positive considerations of the relationship between God and his creatures which led the Second Vatican Council of the Roman Catholic Church 20 years ago to conclude that: 'far from thinking that the achievements of human enterprise and ability are in opposition to the power of God, or that the rational creature is a rival to God, Christians are of the view that the successes of the human race are a sign of God's greatness and a result of his marvellous design'.

There is one further religious consideration which may be mentioned about the relationship between humans and God which may throw light on the developments in assisted conception and artificial reproduction. If it is true that religion, as I have suggested, can take a positive attitude to human enterprise and ingenuity in its remedying of human deficiencies, such as infertility or the incapacity to reproduce itself, it can also locate the phenomenon of fertility in a wider context and de-absolutise it. By providing a religious context of ultimate trust in a loving creator, it can remove the psychological burden of considering that fertility and having a child are a human and social absolute which must be achieved at all costs, or that infertility is somehow a stigma or a reproach. It can offer other satisfactions of the parental urge through acceptance and through its channelling into the service of others. And it can place a radical question mark against the idea of individuals, whether women or men, somehow possessing a natural, or God-given 'right' to have a child.

The parents

And that brings us to the second major topic of the contribution of religious reflection to the assistance of conception, that of the relationships between the potential parents. I suggested earlier that the perspective offered by religion on human creation and procreation, in terms of human love as the agent of divine creative love, provides an ethical structure within which humans are viewed as designed and expected to formulate and exercise their power and potential for procreation. What shape might this ethical structure take in considering the modern and increasing possibilities for assisting conception? Religion has traditionally considered the basic structure created by God for human love and reproduction to indicate that every child should be the fruit of interpersonal sexual love between a man and a woman. And it appears, then, that whatever contribution technology can offer should be resorted to only within such a basic structural context of interpersonal sexual love.

For religion this raises two particular issues with regard to assisted conception: the connection between assisted conception and sexual intercourse; and the resorting to donor material or services. And here again there is a diversity of religious views. So far as concerns the connection between assisted conception and physical intercourse, one radical view takes the form of insisting that assisted conception cannot be considered a substitute for intercourse between the parents, so central is the total loving union between them to expressing their unity as a couple and to producing a new human being as the embodiment of their loving and life-giving congress. Only in this way, this view insists, can justice be done to God as the ultimate personal creator of life and to the contribution of the man and woman who are his chosen collaborators in that life-giving enterprise. In other words, this religious attitude discerns within the structure of sexual intercourse two values which are interconnected and which call for equal respect if such intercourse between humans is to be properly appreciated: the value of interpersonal loving unity and the value of life-giving fruitfulness, as expressive of that unity and in turn reinforcing it. And for some of a religious frame of mind the ethical consequence of this close connection between the values of love and life as inherent in the human sexual relationship is that neither may be deliberately sought to the exclusion of the other. Hence the moral objection to masturbation as a source of semen for artificial insemina- tion or *in vitro* fertilisation, as an action which is no doubt in some sense life-giving but which is not an expression of mutual love between the partners. Hence also the disapproval of the subsequent action of inserting the semen into the vaginal tract or of implanting the embryo into the uterus, since this stage of reproduction also cannot be viewed as expressing the loving mutuality between the parents which is called for by the function of human sexuality in the production under God of a new living human being.

Such detailed and specific ethical conclusions, however, are not shared by others who would nevertheless subscribe to the importance of the values of love and life-giving fruitfulness in the production of a child. For one thing, to insist so scrupulously on such absolute respect for the co-presence and moral inseparability of the potential for love and the potential for life at every stage of sexual intercourse and human reproduction must lead logically to a morally negative judgement on any resort to contraception in order to express in- terpersonal love while excluding the possibility of its proving procreative. Indeed, the insistence in some religious quarters on maintaining the connection between the process of procreation and the expression of sexual love, in order to disapprove of assisted conception or artificial reproduction as in some sense non-loving, is a moral mirror-image aimed at reinforcing and confirming disapproval of any procedure which permits the expression of sexual love while rendering it designedly non-life-giving. And, naturally, those who can see no moral objection to contraception, or to expressing love in sexual intercourse while limiting its life-giving capacity, will view with equal approval the recourse to life-giving procedures which are not necessarily in themselves expressive of love between the parents. The most they might be prepared to concede is that any recourse to assisted conception or artificial reproduction on the part of individuals who could quite easily reproduce through loving sexual intercourse could call in question their motivation in resorting deliberately but unnecessarily to such a substitute for intercourse as a means of reproducing.

There is the further objection to the religious position which insists that reproduction ethically requires a context of intercourse on pain of its being evaluated as non-loving, that it presumes that intercourse between a couple is the only possible life-giving expression of their love for each other, a view which is quite simply mistaken. There are no grounds for asserting that the inconveniences, discomfort, self-sacrifice and frequent frustration involved in the procedures of assisting conception or of *in vitro* fertilisation cannot be the expression and vehicle of personal love between husbands and wives who long to give each other a child of their union and who long to produce a child as the ultimate expression of their love for one another. And to assert that only intercourse can be lovingly creative is either entirely gratuitous or else it betrays an underlying suspicion of anything other than the traditional process of reproduction and a clinging to so-called 'natural' processes of behaviour as the only possible ones ordained by God. In short, the ethical disapproval of assisted conception which concentrates in such questionable detail on the minute application of the values of loving and life-giving in the process of human reproduction is in grave danger of evoking the neglect or disregard of those very values along with the rejection of the detailed applications which are claimed for them.

The other major problem which arises from the religious attitude of viewing human reproduction within the basic created context of interpersonal sexual love concerns the use of donor material or services when the man or woman concerned are incapable of providing the reproductive resources by themselves and either semen or ova are obtained from other sources, or even the child-bearing capacity of another woman is resorted to. It is widely recognised that several religious bodies approach these possibilities with varying degrees of moral reservation, all more or less centred on the interpersonal nature of marriage and the family, and the intimate texture of the human relationships involved. Some would go so far as to label recourse to a third adult party to facilitate conception as 'adultery', thereby invoking by implication all the ethical connotations of that term. But this seems to me to be a simple abuse of language which confuses rather than clarifies the issue, and typically classifies new possibilities for action under older ethical terminology. In this case, it ethically equiparates the new human capacity for shared parenthood with the age-old phenomenon of sexual infidelity between partners. For, of course, the fact is that, with the development of donor-insemination, *in vitro* fertilisation and surrogate motherhood, our traditional simple concept of parenthood has become fragmented into genetic, physiological and social parenthood, in ways which call for careful ethical reflection and analysis rather than for a nostalgia for older simpler conditions cloaked in evaluative terminology.

However, the implications of third- and fourth-party assisted conception do raise fundamental questions about the relationships between the husband and wife resorting to them, and about the relationships between them and the male or female donors of genetic material or genetic function. It is partly a concern for the future well-being of the spouses and of their union which leads not a few religious bodies to view increasing recourse to donor-insemination as a remedy for an infertile marriage with considerable misgivings. But in this field, as in any other, it is not enough to predict future disastrous consequences of a course of action as warrant for ethical disapproval of embarking on that course of action, unless one has good reason for such gloomy prognostications. And it is here that society appears to have been remiss in the past in not making careful provision for follow-up studies on the effects of donor-insemination on the couples having recourse to it as a remedy for their infertility. One result of such studies might well be to show that donor-assisted conception actually proves beneficial to the couple, and consolidates their union in a way which attempts together to accept their infertile lot might not. The difficulties of adjustment on the part of the infertile partner may prove to be no greater than those of a step-parent towards the children of the other partner's previous marriage. And at the very least it might be shown that children born in this way are no more harmful to the quality of a marriage than children conceived and born in the traditional manner.

It is difficult, however, not to surmise that the rational arguments from predicted harmful consequences which are marshalled by some religious bodies against donor-assisted conception – arguments which, as I have suggested, are in principle susceptible of verification – do not express the basic underlying religious consideration, which is that of the religious nature of marriage as the God-given and exclusive matrix for human procreation, and of the couple as the chosen and indispensable sole agents of divine creative love. But again, as we have seen in examining homologous artificial insemination and IVF, what this may be in danger of neglecting is the enterprising and inventive nature of human interpersonal love seeking ways in which to express itself. What it would appear to require as a moral minimum is that the decision to invoke third-party donation should be a shared decision on the part of the husband and wife, and that the choice of such a loving initiative on their part should be an expression of their often self-sacrificing concern for each other.

Moreover, although in some religious interpretations of donor-insemination the shadowy figure of the donor is visited with considerable moral reserve as a continuing potentially divisive or recriminatory presence in the marriage, this does not need to apply in all instances, any more than the memory of a previous partner does. What, in fact, it may indicate is that the religious view of marriage which is being entertained exists in a social vacuum as what the French terms a sort of *égoïsme à deux*, which is not at all typical of the history of marriage as a social institution. And in a broader social context, it is not impossible to view the contribution of semen as at its best an act of social benevolence aimed at helping an infertile couple to have the family for which they long. What, however, such an attitude of benevolence would appear to preclude would be any financial considerations or financial inducement which would have the effect of reducing altruism to a marketable commodity.

For some religious views on assisted conception there are, of course, other shadowy or background figures who cannot be ignored in assessing the ethical quality of new technological procedures, and they are the medical and laboratory personnel often involved in the application of such procedures. The reaction towards such supplementary agents of conception sometimes takes the form of viewing them as invading the privacy of the extremely intimate texture of the marital and sexual relationship between the two partners, and as in this respect incurring a moral censure similar to that directed towards the donor of semen. Here again, however, while there must be clear and obvious canons of respect and delicacy, if the root objection to such contributions on the part of medical personnel is not again the old one of ethical suspicion of all that is branded as 'artificial' or 'contrived' or 'manipulative', then the contributions of technology can be ethically assessed much more positively within a richer socially corporate context of marriage and parenthood. And the enabling and helping of a couple in this way to have a family can be viewed rather more generously as the enterprising contribution of human and constructive benevolence towards fellow humans in their profoundly personal needs.

Before moving to my third part of considering the child who is the end result of all such human contributions, it may be relevant to consider here briefly some further conclusions which appear to follow ethically from my arguments so far. One is the provision of assisted conception for single parents. The entire thrust of the religious context which I have been portraying, of course, militates against such provision as seriously failing to fulfil the view of human procreation as the expression, in some degree or another, of a shared enterprise of mutual interpersonal love which serves as the human channel for the divine creative life-giving process, and which also views such procreation as in some sense a culmination of human loving. And this is without considering the interests of the child of such solitary conception. It also calls in question from a religious viewpoint any claim on the part of individuals to possess a natural, or God-given 'right' to have a child.

There are some commentators who view with impatience the contemporary proliferation of human rights. And at least such reactions compel us to scrutinise carefully a claim to a human or natural right to have a child. Presumably one important consideration is, against whom is this claim made? For, of course, rights are not asserted in a vacuum, but most frequently are involved, or discovered, or hammered out, in conflict situations. From the religious point of view, in the light of what I have been saying, it is difficult to make any sense of an individual claiming against God a natural right to have a child, since he is the author of life and, indeed, the ultimate warrant for all human rights. It is possible to envisage a spouse making such a claim in respect of his or her reluctant partner, either on the ground that the idea of having a family was inherent, or at least implicit, in their marriage agreement, or on the ground that their mutually shared view of marriage was one which included children as an intrinsic component. And it is equally possible to recognise such a right to have a child as a moral claim against the State should it attempt to impose any population or family policy on individual couples, as may be implied by the Universal Declaration on Human Rights of the right to found a family. But the moral claim to exercise such a human right, where it exists, cannot be absolute and must be hedged about by other considerations. And from the religious point of view, it is considerably easier to envisage it as a right not so much of individuals as of particular couples *vis-à-vis* society or the State; although even as a joint right, it need not necessarily imply a moral claim on the resources of society to supply all the means required for the exercise of the right.

The other conclusion relating to the couple, which I wish briefly to consider in the light of all these religious factors, is the vexed question of surrogacy as a means to assisted conception and artificial reproduction. Possibly the most obvious feature of surrogacy, as compared with semen or egg donation, is that the donor in this case is very much to the fore, both socially and financially, in the provision not only of genetic but also of physiological parenting. And indeed these are the two major reservations expressed in society today about the provision of surrogacy as an aid to parenthood: the possibilities for financial exploitation, whether of the commissioning parents or of the women acting as surrogates; and the enormous psychological complexity which is considered by some to result from recourse to this method of producing a child. It would be possible, as has been done in Britain, to legislate against the entire financial aspect of surrogate arrangements or agencies, and from the religious point of view this would appear an eminently desirable and ethical course of action. So far as concerns the psychological difficulties arising from surrogacy, it may be useful to distinguish, as is not always done in the ethical analysis of surrogacy, between what may be called partial surrogacy and total surrogacy, where the latter refers to the surrogate woman providing both the genetic material and the process of gestation, while the former – partial surrogacy – denotes only the gestation of an embryo produced from the ovum of the commissioning woman. Where surrogacy implies only, literally, 'womb-leasing', in the popular term – that is, receiving and carrying to term the embryo of a couple produced by *in vitro* fertilisation – there appears little difference in principle between the provision of such a service by another woman and the use of an artificial placenta, should such a development ever be successfully achieved. And if, for example, the organ donation of a kidney *inter vivos* is considered morally legitimate, it is not easy to see why function donation should be morally proscribed in comparable circumstances, as between relatives, particularly since such womb-leasing is a transitory gift and one which is much less perilous to the donor. Moreover, in such cases of what I have called partial surrogacy, where the surrogate has not conceived the child, the possible psychological (and contractual) complications involved in the relationship between the commissioning couple and the host-mother, and in the bonding between the host-mother and the genetic child of another woman which she is carrying, might be easier to handle than a situation where the surrogate woman is both the genetic and the physiological mother of the child. Indeed, although the parallel is admittedly a very weak one, there may be lessons to be learned from the social arrangement of surrogate breast-feeding of a child.

In total surrogacy there is, of course, the additional ethical factor arising from the use of donor material, and in this respect there are further parallels to be considered with the case of semen-donation in donor-insemination in assessing not only the obvious possible objections but also the possible stimulation arising from donor-material and services to our consideration of marriage and parenthood in a wider social context than has hitherto been the case. And here again, rather than religion rushing in with a moral veto on total surrogacy in all possible circumstances on largely *a priori* grounds, it might be more prudent to await what follow-up studies would have to show on the individual and social effects of surrogate parenthood, not only on the commissioning parents but also on the children born of such arrangements.

The child

I turn now to the third focus of ethical concern from the viewpoint of religion on recourse to assisted conception and artificial reproduction: the child resulting from such procedures, whose interests, I suggested at the beginning, provide the primary reality which should dominate all others. In discussing what meaning might be given to any claim to a natural or God-given right to have a child, I was careful to phrase this, not in terms of anyone having a right to a child, but in terms of possessing a right to have a child, or a right to parenthood. For, of course, claiming a right to a child appears almost tantamount to reducing a child to the status of property or of a possession of the parents. And this highlights the basic consideration which religion brings to bear from the child's point of view on the application of modern conceptive or reproductive procedures: to what extent they recognise, or enhance, or impair the human personal dignity of the end result of such procedures.

For one powerful religious tradition this question is first raised chronologically at the stage of the embryo, where an ontological and moral status of human personhood and corresponding respect are claimed for the embryo which are seriously offended by embryo experimentation involving the destruction of human embryos. This topic, however, has been given detailed treatment in an earlier contribution with whose conclusions I substantially concur, since, to put it no more strongly, I find it difficult to consider the early embryo prior to the emergence of the primitive streak as sufficiently developed and individualised to be anything more than a human entity possessed of astonishing promise or potential.

There is, however, another consideration of a more subtle nature which is raised in some quarters on religious grounds concerning the whole enterprise of resorting to advancing technology to enable a couple to have a child. It is the charge that such procedures, involving manipulation and the choice and rejection of various materials in order to produce an acceptable infant, are in effect treating the future child as a product, subject to quality control and various other scientific and social criteria, and that this is offensive to the human dignity, if not of a present person, at least of the future person who will result from such procedures. Such an objection is seen as having its greatest impact in what is considered its logical culmination: the genetic manipulation of embryos, not to remedy, but to modify or enhance some of the inherited characteristics of the child-in-the-making, so as to produce the best possible end-product. But it is an objection which is also directed in principle at the very prospect of any scientific attempt to improve on nature in the production of a child. And it claims that not only the contributions of medical personnel but even the decision by the couple to have resort to these contributions renders the resulting child inferior in terms of human dignity and human personal equality to all those who have conspired in its production.

Such a line of argument I find more impressive for its rhetoric than for its logic, and highly dependent on the terminology it invokes in order to describe what is going on. And even although it may claim not to be implicitly dependent on a facile distinction between what is, on the one hand, natural and therefore human and to be approved and, on the other hand, what is artificial and therefore inhuman and to be ethically deplored, I think it does in fact rely on such a distinction, and is implicitly based on an impoverished view of the human which it deploys in its argumentation. I also find it difficult, for example, to credit that parents going to great lengths to overcome their infertility or other incapacity in order to have a child will regard that child as somehow less than fully human or as somehow inferior to them, and the same can be said of the various other individuals who co-operate with the parents. Indeed, to the contrary, it can be argued that a child produced in such challenging and difficult circumstances will be prized and cherished all the more for itself. Nor can it plausibly be argued that children brought into existence in this way are somehow being treated simply as a means to an end, and as produced merely to satisfy the wants or needs of the couple, or even simply to meet the needs and ambitions of the medical team involved. Such oversimplifications of motives do not adequately correspond to the mixture of interersts, wishes and desires which may be in play in this human scenario, as they are in every context of options and moral choices. It is evident, of course, that the procedures being considered can be abused, but it by no means follows that they are inherently abusive of the interests of the child in question, any more than would be the case of a child produced through normal intercourse and pregnancy and as a result of the whole series of choices made by the parents and their medical attendants.

Nevertheless, what such lines of objection from one religious viewpoint can prompt is the regular need to scrutinise the various motives involved in resorting to and applying assisted conception and artificial reproduction, particularly in the light of the human dignity and natural rights of the child born of such procedures. And perhaps this is of more relevance in assessing the introduction of donated material and functions which we have already considered from the point of view of the adults involved. What invites examination here are the child's future relationships with its social parents in view of the biological imbalance by which it is more fully the child of one than the other, and its relationships with the donor who has made a vital contribution to its coming into existence, whether as semen or ovum donor or as surrogate mother. And the unique point at which all these relationships converge is the personal, emotional and psychosocial identity of this new human being.

It is this salient consideration of the child's and future adult's interests, for instance, which provides the primary ethical criterion for evaluating recourse to assisted conception or artificial reproduction on the part of single women and lesbian couples. There may be an argument, even on religious grounds, when a much-loved husband has died, for his widow to use banked semen or a banked embryo in order to have a child by him as a posthumous and abiding expression and continuation of their mutual love. But even such a decision would have to consider the future effects on the child of being the sole object of such emotional investment on the part of its mother. And, more generally, it would have to take into account the concern which society in general, and various bodies, including religious bodies, feel about one-parent families, which are not only socially disadvantaged in numerous ways, but in which there are also psychological and emotional disadvantages, particularly for the child. It appears to be the contemporary wisdom that children in such families are at risk of being emotionally and, in a broad sense, sexually disadvantaged or even harmed in their upbringing if both a mother and a father, or at least a mother and a father figure, are not to hand to co-operate in such a delicate task. No doubt there are individual instances, perhaps arising from force of circumstances, where such challenges meet with considerable success. Yet it scarcely seems to be in the best interests of the future child deliberately to set about creating such a situation. And here particularly is a case where the motivation of the adult contemplating the founding of a one-parent family calls for considerable ethical examination.

Similar considerations, concerning motivation and the best interests of the child, appear to weigh in assessing the ethics of lesbian couples wishing to have a child which they can somehow regard as their own, although here, of course, there is the added ethical factor of individual and social attitudes to homosexuality. In such cases, it seems fairly clear what kind of domestic environment and what attitudes to homosexual behaviour await the growing child. And even although the couple in question may consider this entirely defensible, and indeed desirable, society at large may have quite different views. While it would be wrong of society to express any sort of punitive attitude towards such a life-style being adopted or pursued by adults, it would, it appears, be within its rights and entirely justified in taking what it might consider protective measures concerning the deliberate introduction of a child of either sex to such a life-style. Nor, from the religious viewpoint we have been considering, would it be possible for adult couples in a lesbian relationship to claim that in some sense either one or both of them had any sort of natural right to have a child, since it is impossible to view such a child as in any sense the expression or fruit of their love for one another. What appears basically at issue here are the single-minded pursuit of self-fulfilment, and perhaps in some cases the desire of a couple to 'prove' something to themselves or to society. In either case the danger cannot be discounted that a child introduced into such an arrangement is at real risk of simply being used without much or any consideration for its own interests and its natural rights.

A final consideration which appears to emerge from the point of view of the child in assessing the ethics of assisted conception or artificial reproduction is a built-in preference for truth rather than for falsehood or concealment or subterfuge concerning the origins of the child and later adult. Of course, timing is all-important in the imparting of such literally vital information, so that the famous question, 'What is truth?', needs to be accompanied frequently by the rather more nuanced question, 'When is truth?' Nevertheless, if in religious terms it is the case that God is always in the truth, but never in falsehood, and if it is also the case that a house built on the shifting sands of deceit is in continual risk of collapse, then in the context of human origins, as for instance also in the context of dying, the motivation for withholding truth calls for careful evaluation in terms of the interests and rights of the individual most intimately affected, rather than in terms of an unacknowledged paternalism, or of embarrassment, or even of moral uneasiness. And the burden of proof and moral justification must be recognised to reside with those who would wish to withhold the true state of affairs, whether this be done by silence or by evasive replies to questions or surmises, or by the deliberate and systematic falsification of public and historical records.

It is, in other words, only by confronting the truths and implications of this, as of all the other aspects of assisted conception and artificial reproduction, that we as individuals and as society can adequately assess and appropriate the developing techniques of modern medicine and their possibilities for enhancing the quality of human life, including human reproduction. To do less is to incur the risk of colluding with perhaps uneasy consciences in what we shrink from exposing to the full scrutiny of ethical evaluation. But to confront such developments in the light of our philosophy of life is surely what characterises the human in us. And to do so in the light of religion, or of a theology of life, as many but not all religious believers attempt continually to do, is to make a bid for a wider and deeper context in which to situate the many moral options facing human beings. The point of religion in such cases is not to impose its beliefs on others. For its own adherents, religion is best expressed in attempting to make religious sense of human experience and at the same time to make experiential sense of religious beliefs. And this is a dialectic which is essential for any religion which claims to be both transcendent and at the same time rooted in human history and to present a destiny for a species composed of rational free individuals. The contribution of such a religion to others is to offer them perspectives, insights and evaluations on human phenomena and experiences which it hopes will strike human chords in those others, and which it also hopes will evoke genuinely human responses, to form a continuing dialogue from which religion has much to learn, as also a dialogue to which, in my view, religion also has much to contribute, as I have endeavoured to show.

Discussion   Chairman: David Bromham

H. Murray: I have heard comments about the early embryo prior to the primitive streak. If left alone would it remain not changing, inert, or is it, in fact a thing which has an impetus: growing and subdividing, reproducing its own cells, which is the biological definition of a living being? There seems to be an arrogance on the part of embryologists who say that because they cannot interpret which destiny these particular cells have, be it placenta, be it embryo, these cells have no significance. Is what is there prior to the primitive streak a human being or not?

Mahoney: That is not the question – the question is, is it a human individual person in more traditional philosophical terms. No-one can deny that it is human but when we use the phrase human being, we are referring to adults. We say: You wouldn't treat a human being like that'; we mean a human person. That is why I prefer to call it, and I am not alone in this, a human entity. It is human genetically. It is not yet individualised in the sense of irreversibly taking a shape beyond reduplication. Therefore, it is at some identifiable stage, before which, one can say of it, it is not yet a human individual. If that is the case, it cannot have the right to life.

Page: The early embryo cells would have to be regarded as a human organism. However, when you say human being, it carries so much moral weight. The very early embryo does not have the moral status of the later fetus, never mind the full person or human being.

Snowden: What we are doing is trying to find 'how many angels fit on the head of a pin'. We have found the primitive streak, and in one sense it means that we can do things before that happens that we would not allow ourselves to do after. If we are to agree that what happens before the primitive streak at 14 to 15 days permits certain types of behaviour, we will in due course be having these same discussions about the next point on in embryonic development.

For this reason, my advice to the Department of Health and Social Security, on their most recent White Paper, has been that experimentation on embryos is something that we should consider banning. Development is a process and we are trying to find a compromise in that process. As an individual I come to the conclusion that the slippery slope is not so gentle. It is so steep that we will require quite a considerable amount of equipment to ensure that we do not go all the way. That worries me more than the actual philosophical argument as to when does individual life start.

Lee: People have talked about the Warnock Committee's reasoning on embryo experimentation. Warnock was split three ways on this. It is by no means clear that the final legislation will reflect the majority's reasoning. On surrogacy there were two distinguished people who dissented from the general conclusion. The White Paper has really adopted the dissent rather than the majority approach. These kinds of exercises set out arguments for us, but it is up to society to decide. Warnock was an interim stage in a long process.

Serr: A little was mentioned about the question of donor anonymity. In Sweden anonymity had been declared an absolute wrong and registration must take place. With all the computer viruses of today the question of anonymity is both a data control problem and a moral problem. In Sweden, donors have disappeared completely. I would like to know what your thoughts were?

Snowden: They have not disappeared completely; some people still want to be donors. Evidence was given to the Warnock Committee and recommendations in the White Paper, that certain information should be allowable to the child and to the parents as to the genetic health aspects of the donor. We have been arguing that a description of the sort of person this man was, short of his actual name and address, is necessary. The Swedish situation is that donors must accept that, at the age of 18 years, the child will have access to a name and address. This is a step in advance of our own. Within a period of 18 years the public climate will be different than it is now. But with the adoption situation this came along at a time when we were ready for that. Maybe in 18 years time, we will be thinking differently about donor insemination. The British approach of a step at a time is the right one. The ultimate objective should be that the child, in order to have truth about its own origins, should have access to this information in a non-hurtful way. To say we should maintain anonymity so we can keep these donors is the wrong argument. If we lose some of our donors, so be it. This is the risk that we have to take.

Gorovitz: I would be interested in Mr Page's views about the case in which the commissioning couple declines to accept the child after it is born. This is a precedented situation.

Page: If you are allowing the commissioning parents to have the status of legal parents then they have to take the full consequences of that and they would be in the same position as ordinary parents who are refusing to take their child. It is a question for society – what is going to happen to that child? But I do not think we should assume that it is to be dumped on the surrogate mother.

Gorovitz: Hypothesising that there are grounds for refusing the child, it could be that the child is in some significant way defective as a result of the irresponsible behaviour of the surrogate mother so that the commissioning couple now claim that they have good grounds for calling the deal off.

Page: This is the kind of problem that could arise at some stage. If you have a framework within which the surrogate mother is doing a favour, then one's view of that woman must be charitable, rather than that the commissioning parents are paying for a service and are going to get good value for money. We have got to have some kind of structures for taking care of this rather than saying: 'This is your responsibility so we are not taking it, here it comes back to you'.

Jackson: Dr Snowden talked about the childless couple who have the alternatives of either the wife being artificially inseminated because the husband is infertile or of adoption. There are many difficulties with the first possibility, that is artificial insemination, the distressing inadequacy that the husband feels in this situation, and the difficulties about how the child eventually comes to terms with what it is told. All these are doubly applicable to the other alternative of adopting because that is not just one parent who is genetically unrelated and has ambivalent feelings. You might see adoption as worse than artificial reproduction from insemination of the mother. On the other hand, something enormously important in the case of adoption is that one is dealing with a child who already exists and needs parents, whereas in the other case it is a question about bringing something into being which presents these problems if it crops up.

Snowden: With adoption the husband and the wife are going in on equal terms. When you go in for artificial insemination, you have 'her' child but 'not his' and that is where distress is.

Jackson: In the artificial reproduction case, one parent is inadequate, to put it rather unkindly, and so with adoption neither can have the joy of being genetically connected to the child. Is this equality? This equality is important?

Snowden: I am not suggesting that one is inadequate, they are unequally yoked. Where you have artificial insemination by an anonymous donor the wife is able to fulfil her motherly role, whereas the husband is having to find a way of adjusting to his fatherhood. In adoption both of them are supporting each other to deal with a child that already exists, that requires, love, housing, nurturing and all other things. With donor insemination one is planning for this situation to actually happen. This choice between potential child and a living child is between going into a delicate situation, deliberately planned, versus responding to a difficult situation, childlessness, on equal terms. The societal responsibility is also not really towards the couple which is having a particular difficulty in their life but towards the child itself.

Braude: I am concerned with this question of truth and the identity of donors from the point of practical enforcement. In the majority of cases, the husband is oligo-, that is too few, rather than azospermic, that is no sperm. Therefore, unless you enforce abstinence on that couple, we do not know the identity of that child without typing the child, the donor and the husband. This becomes impractical because you have to keep enormous records, and if you are going to allow this right to a child of donor insemination, presumably the law must also apply to any child who wishes to know the identity of its father.

Snowden: But the state does not set up adultery centres! The number of children born as a result of extramarital affairs is much greater than the number of children born by these procedures. But this is no argument for suggesting that the state should be providing scientific and medical help for this to take place in a planned way. The mixing of a husband's sperm with donor sperm is a step in the process of deceitfulness which does not do anybody credit. In a situation where oligospermia is present, we ought to be putting resources into helping that husband to use his sperm to have a child by his wife. When the donor does come into it, there ought to be some recognition. I do not believe that a gynaecologist would provide donor's sperm in order to help the husband and then inform the husband, "Well it could have been your sperm anyway, let us pretend that it is in order that you can have psychological comfort."

Braude: Ten per cent of couples, when the husband has oligospermia, will conceive their own child. How are you going to explain to this child that they are definitely not the child of the union. You are going to have to type everyone. We have been in a situation where we have had couples who are undergoing *in vitro* fertilisation and have had terrible sperm. Having made two attempts at IVF, perhaps one egg out of 10 will fertilise. We could say to them that they could have a further attempt but would they like to have the back-up of donor sperm, half the eggs being put to donor sperm. We have been in the situation where some of each are fertilised and the patient has requested that embryos from both groups come back. Now, do we enforce typing onto children who are born?

Mahoney: The bias should be towards truth rather than falseness. I find very alarming the provision both in Warnock and the White Paper for falsifying public records. That seems to be a systematic social injustice. Of the particular problems that you raise, one might be justified in discussing it with the couple saying: 'Do you think it would be better for the child to remain in ignorance, to be unsure or would it be better for the child to be taught a possible falsehood?', and to try and elicit the ethical decision from the parents and the doctor. The optimum would be to invite them to abstinence in the interests of truth and the psychosocial identity of the child. On the provision of sperm, although the number of donors had fallen dramatically in Sweden there has now been a slight rise and the profile of the donor is significantly different. Now it is the secure married man who wants to be able to help infertile couples. I do want the children to know but it will inevitably result in fewer donors. Nevertheless I think the right of the child to the truth prevails.

McWhinnie: I feel very uneasy about the Warnock recommendation that children should have access to knowledge about their genetic origin and ethnic origin. I cannot understand why they would do that to a child and not tell them all.

Snowden: I agree. It is saying, 'We know all about it but we are going to let you have this information only'. Over a period of 18 years maybe we will be in a position to be more relaxed about this than we are now. The genetic and the health information, plus a pen picture of the donor, is automatically going to lead to a demand for more information which will have to be available so that a child will be told the truth – at least those who wish to avail themselves of that information.

Cohen: Dr Snowden said that only from 1844 has sex been separable from reproduction. Among women having a normal reproductive cycle, that is pregnancy, lactation, pregnancy, lactation, a mere 2% of acts of intercourse, if they are doing it two and a half times a week, are potentially reproductive. Nearly all are for recreation and loving rather than procreation. You set up a distinction in order to reinforce the conjunction of loving and productive sexuality: sex on the one hand and procreation on the other. We should look at this as recreational sex that is part of the procreative system, in biology as well as in the ethical circumstances. Most acts of intercourse are necessarily infertile and for loving and recreation rather than procreation.

Snowden: Society at all time and all places wanted to regulate reproduction. It was not a question of regulating sexual activity but regulating the circumstances in which sexual activity would take place. Until fairly recently the idea of sexual intercourse was something which was maintained within marriage itself; people did not have sex outside marriage. Sexual intercourse in marriage was for the purpose of reproduction. These were the sorts of values that were placed upon it. All of that changed in 1844 when Goodyear vulcanised rubber and condoms became much more generally available than they had been before. This changed the whole approach to sexual activity amongst people. You are denying that – you do not believe that?

Cohen: I could not disagree with you more. I think that non-fertile sexual practices were used and the difference that Goodyear made was trivial, bringing technical possibilities into something that people had arranged in their own lives, in all kinds of other circumstances such as anal intercourse and oral sex.

Mott: Relating to quality control of the products of conception, I would like to give a particular case for Professor Mahoney to go to the general. The particular case is the one that is hardest in our society which is trisomy 21 or Down's syndrome.

Mahoney: I presented the argument, which I do not share, that in principle assisted conception and artificial reproduction is manipulative, is a merchandising activity in terms of quality control and so on. Those are perfectly human types of activity. I do not see the point of you mentioning Down's syndrome in that context. Presumably those who say that this is manipulative, this is quality control, would want to say, 'However, if this is to prevent handicap and have a normal child it is all right'. So there is inconsistency within the argument that was put forward, that when it is to prevent having defective children, then this is good and desirable and human, but when it is just normal procedure to remedy infertility, then it is bad, it is inhuman, it is artificial.

Mott: Where are you with regards to this concept of what is normal and what can, therefore, be defined as abnormal?

Mahoney: The concept of normal, like that of health, is a totally open-ended concept. For instance, in genetic medicine, there is a standard distinction which is made by some religious authorities and others that genetic intervention for therapeutic purposes is good, but for enhancement purposes, it is bad. The difficulty is what one means by remedy and enhancement. If one's concept of life and quality of life is one which becomes richer all the time, then in a sense 'par' is being moved and more and more people, as it were, are going to be born 'under par'. It is extremely relative and difficult and something which the White Paper simply avoids.

Solbakk: In your definition of human being as an entity your argument is from a biological perspective. When you are speaking about a human being as an individual, you are using the metaphysical or ontological way of argumentation.

I think you could be trapped in the argument as this kind of distinction is very problematic from a logical point of view.

Mahoney: If this is confusion between a biological description and an ontological interpretation, the ontological interpretation of the idea of the individual requires a biological component, because we are talking not about angels but about humans. The Warnock Report itself, which would not claim to be a major piece of philosophical reason but of medical reasoning, talks about the primitive streak and the 14th day as the beginning of individuation. Now that term is used biologically, therefore I think the ambiguity that you raise does not actually hold.

Gillon: One of the things that seems to emerge is the notion that artificial reproduction of one sort or another ought to be controlled in the interests of the children. The alternatives that we are considering, insofar as those children are concerned, are between non-existence altogether and existence in the situations you refer to. Can we really be so certain that it would be preferable for them not to exist at all than to exist with these various problems?

Snowden: The children do not exist. Your argument makes it sound as though they are waiting and being denied their existence by actions that are taken or not . . .

Gillon: No. The argument is based on your presupposition that you are trying to argue from their interests. It is based on the notion that if they existed then it would be in their interests not to have existed. I would argue that actually that is not the case. In most cases it would probably still be in their interests to exist as surrogate children, as having problems of identity, as having one parent or another.

Part 3
The neonate

Withholding neonatal care 1.
A paediatrician's view

Introduction

Care is essential to the ethos of any organisation dedicated to help patients. Care is as much part of the philosophy of a high technology intensive care facility for newborn infants as it is for a low technology long stay institution for the elderly. We talk about newborn intensive *'care'* in intensive *care* units or nurseries. In no way should care in this widest sense of comfort, concern and compassion be withheld or withdrawn from newborn infants. What is sometimes withheld or withdrawn are certain intensive treatments or procedures that while valuable, indeed life-saving for some infants, may be painful, cruel, meddlesome and futile for others.

As background I will sketch the historical development of newborn intensive care and describe how the withholding or withdrawing of intensive treatments has become a major issue in medical ethics. I will indicate what I see as the justification for this practice and will suggest a process for making a decision. These difficult and troubling decisions require us to recognise and respect the obligations that parents, doctors and other 'carers' have towards small babies. Through some mechanism we must ensure that the interests or, as some would say, the 'rights' of infants are protected while at the same time recognising the family and social realities of each individual circumstance.

The status of infants

Conferring rights on infants, including the right to life is a relatively recent development. Premature infants, known as 'congenital weaklings', and infants with congenital abnormalities did not excite much interest or sympathy in ancient times. A child had no intrinsic right to life or protection by virtue of being born. Value and rights were acquired perhaps only after several years, either by the development of intelligence or by acceptance into society (Rist, 1982).

Ancient philosophers like Aristotle and Plato regarded infanticide as desirable in certain situations and even normal mature infants were regarded initially as 'non-persons'. Although Christianity and Judaism are credited with raising the status of children and outlawing infanticide, for centuries neither the law nor public opinion paid much attention. In this country infanticide remained a major problem until relatively recently, as is obvious from the frequent references in *The British Medical Journal* and *The Lancet* during the last century. In 1863, on the occasion of the inauguration of the National Society and Asylum for the Prevention of Infanticide, a leading article described infanticide as 'the crime ... which has prevailed so long without any attempt being made to check it by any adequate or organised means' (Editorial, 1863). Later a commentary entitled 'British Infanticide' began: 'We are approaching that indifference to child-murder which we are accustomed to think confined to un-Christian nations!' (Commentary, 1884). It is important to keep the infanticide of unwanted and abandoned infants in perspective. Contemporary infant and childhood mortality rates were appalling even in the best of circumstances. Of Queen Anne's 17 pregnancies only 12 infants were born alive and only one survived to 11 years. Gibbon, the historian tells how his birth was 'succeeded by five brothers and one sister all of whom were snatched away in their infancy'. As regards premature infants at the turn of the century, Ransom writes: 'most are quickly laid away with ... little if any effort being made for their rescue' (Ransom, 1900).

Although isolated reports of the survival of tiny premature infants appeared from time to time in literature and in the medical press it is hardly surprising that their needs were largely ignored. For centuries it had been appreciated that they needed warmth to survive. There is reference in the novel Tristram Shandy to one such infant who 'all the world knows was born a fetus .... He was no larger than the palm of a hand, but the father having examined it in his medical capacity and having found that it was scarcely more than a mere embryo, brought it living to Rapallo where it was seen by Jerome Bardi and other doctors of the place. They found it was not deficient in anything essential to life, and the father, in order to show his skill, undertook to finish the work of nature and to perfect the formation of the infant by the same artifice as is used in Egypt for the hatching of chickens'. In 19th century British medical literature there were a number of reports each claiming a new record for survival. In *The Edinburgh Medical and Surgical Journal*, Dr Rodman of Paisley describes the 'Case of a Child Born Between the Fourth and Fifth Month and Brought Up' (Rodman, 1815). He credits the baby's survival to 'being kept regularly and comfortably warm by the mother and two other females alternately lying in bed with him for more than two months'. The rarity of such an event is reflected in Dr Rodman's opening sentence: 'The following case I confess is one which the sceptic will find little difficulty in contradicting'. Thus, given the right circumstances and no doubt a lot of luck a few very immature babies could survive –

some went on to become household names like Isaac Newton and Voltaire – but it is only relatively recently that the survival of all has been viewed as a desirable social goal (Silverman, 1981).

The evolution of neonatal intensive care

The modern organised care of premature, sick and abnormal newborn infants began in France through the pioneering work of two Paris obstetricians, Stephane Tarnier and Pierre Budin, who saw the potential of the incubator (or 'brooder' as it was originally called) for protecting infants against the fatal effects of cold. Tarnier and Budin also applied other principles, learned by the Ancient Egyptians in rearing chickens, to the incubation of human infants and achieved a remarkable reduction in infant mortality to an extent not emulated in this country or the United States for the next 20–30 years (Holt & Babbitt, 1915; Eden, 1921). Previous attempts at human incubation in various types of hot boxes had been less successful because doctors, unlike the Ancient Egyptian chicken farmers, did not appreciate the importance of reducing the environmental temperature *pari passu* with increasing endogenous heat production to protect these vulnerable infants from overheating and dangerous hyperpyrexia.

Budin deserves to be called the father of newborn special care. In his book *Le Nourisson* (The Nursling), considered a classic in paediatric literature, he was the first to outline basic principles that remain valid today (Budin, 1907). He organised a system of 'consultations for nurslings' that served as a model for the revolution of newborn care that followed. They were the prototypes of the newborn special care services as we know them today. Budin's success came to the attention of politicians appalled by the tragic loss of so many young men in the Franco-Prussion War and who, with an eye to France's future security, were anxious to reduce any wasteful mortality in early infancy. In 1907, the year of Budin's death, M. Clemenceau, the Prime Minister, issued a circular to Prefects throughout France 'calling on them to proceed with the least possible delay in the methodical organisation of consultations for infants' (Special Correspondence, 1907).

In other countries, including the UK, there were isolated reports to indicate that incubators were being used in some hospitals but it took some time for neonatal care to be organised in the way Budin had pioneered. *The Lancet*, in a leading article entitled 'Human Incubators,' considered that the results were 'most satisfactory' but quoted one user of the apparatus as attributing the good results 'largely to the fact that it saves the occupants from being overburdened by the weight of clothing which would otherwise be required for the purpose of retaining their body heat' (Editorial, 1897a).

Then occurred one of the most bizarre but important developments in the organised care of premature infants. As noted in *The Lancet*, 'On Monday members of the press were invited to a private view of the incubator for infants at the Victorian Era Exhibition, Earl's Court ... the public were admitted to the Central Room and here they can view the infants lying within the incubators and are shown how the apparatus was ventilated and warmed and the temperature automatically maintained' (Editorial, 1897b). Putting premature infants on show may now seem mercenary and distasteful, but there is little doubt that but for the efforts of Martin Couney, 'incubator doctor' and showman extraordinary, many of these infants would not have survived (Silverman, 1979). Concern was expressed about these incubator shows in these words: 'But if music hall proprietors, caterers for refreshments at exhibitions, and public showmen generally, who have no sort of scientific training, are going to start baby incubator shows in all parts of the country, the question arises whether the attention of the sanitary authorities should be directed to the dangers which may result'. (Editorial, 1898). Unquestionably Couney's shows were the special care units of the time and he deserves particular mention for demonstrating the essential role played by teams of skilled nurses.

For most of the first half of this century, in spite of attention to body temperature and meticulous attention to feeding, infant mortality and morbidity rates remained high. Increasingly, the importance of maternal health, the influences of maternal disease, and what are now called 'social factors', began to receive long overdue attention. The traditional killing diseases of childhood such as diphtheria, whooping cough and tuberculosis were controlled. More attention became focussed on the high mortality around birth. Here was one of the last remaining challenges. Childbirth, especially 'high risk childbirth', became increasingly centralised and became the responsibility of obstetricians based in hospitals and infant care from birth gradually became the responsibility of paediatricians, members of a relatively new specialty.

The stage was set for the rapid expansion of neonatal special care and the development of neonatal *intensive care*. Central to this evolution, and beginning in the 1950s, was a greater understanding of the pathophysiology of life and death and the explosion in knowledge, skills and medical technology which occurred in the years after World War II. Particularly noteworthy were:

(a) The realisation that death was a process and not an event. Cessation of breathing and stoppage of the heart were potentially reversible – for a time at least. It became necessary to develop new definitions of death.

(b) The development of electronic equipment for the monitoring and treatment of the critically ill – especially the introduction of respirators and other forms of life support.

(c) Advances in the surgical treatment of birth defects.

Major changes resulted from these developments over a relatively short time scale, including the birth of a new sub-specialty, neonatology, or perinatology as some prefer, and increasing investment in neonatal *intensive care units* – temples of high technology medicine.

There were enormous benefits. Neonatal mortality rates have fallen to levels hardly thought possible even 30 years ago. Original concepts of 'viability' are outmoded. In Budin's book he states 'we shall not discuss infants of less than 1000 g. They are seldom saved and only very rarely shall I need to allude to them'. Any contemporary newborn unit now proudly reports many infants of under 1000 g, and some not much over 500 g, who not only survive but are normal at follow-up. In the care of the tiny infant, optimism has replaced fatalism. Many infants with congenital abnormalities once thought to be untreatable now benefit from corrective surgery. In almost a hundred years, beginning with temperature control and incubators and culminating in organ transplantation and life-support technology, neonatal intensive care has come to epitomise the success of modern medicine.

The dilemmas of success

There is a darker side to this undoubted success story – a 'flip side' to the coin. Debate is now focussed not on our technical competence in overcoming so much death and disability but on the rights or wrongs of utilising these new powers over life and death. We agonise over the troubling ethical dilemmas thrown into sharp focus by the new medicine. We agonise because we know that for some families the outcome will not be a happy one. About some infants we ask the same questions once asked about all premature infants – are they worth saving? Worth, not in the sense of social utility or worth to others, or even in strictly economic terms of costs and benefits, but worth reflecting concern about the future quality of life that might be expected for the infant and the implications for the family.

New medical problems have been created by efforts to keep alive babies whose organs are immature and not yet ready for independence, or babies whose vital organs are so faulty that no surgery on earth can ensure a healthy future. An increasing prevalence of iatrogenic disease, a major problem in modern newborn nurseries is inevitable when immature organs are forced to function before their time, and the complexities of care increase the probability of medical and nursing mistakes (McClead & Menke, 1987). Neonatal intensive care has become so complex and so demanding, physically and emotionally, that it is an extremely fertile field for staff 'burn out' and errors of judgement. For babies, there are risks as well as benefits from each new development in intensive care.

At the same time the successes of neonatal care have been trumpeted far and wide by media eager for human interest stories and hospitals keen for publicity. Public expectations have reached a point that when the end results are less than perfect, there is an increasing tendency to seek fault and lay blame. There is need to temper excessive optimism and, while taking care not to destroy hope, introduce some realism into situations inevitably fraught with uncertainty.

Is it possible to strike a balance between the responsible and the irresponsible use of the skills and technologies inherent in intensive care? Should there be limits to neonatal rescue? Is it wise to promote a 'save all' policy for tinier and tinier infants and for infants with major abnormalities? Is it sensible to claim that without such an aggressive policy we are on the slippery slope to infanticide or that to restrict these pioneering efforts will impair medical progress? In other words, should life-saving intensive care be withheld or withdrawn when infants are at major risk of grievous and permanent handicap, especially involving the brain. I believe that it should.

There is nothing new in this. For generations doctors and parents have withheld treatment and have allowed babies to die when they believed that this course of action was in the infant's and in the family's best interests. As the ability to save and prolong life has increased so have the difficult moral questions raised by decisions to 'let nature take its course', decisions made more difficult when they increasingly involve others and are made not in the privacy of the home but in relatively public places like intensive care units. In the early 1970s greater awareness of these poignant and increasingly troubling dilemmas, and the plight of parents caught up in them, stimulated us to analyse and publish our experience in a large American newborn intensive care unit (Duff & Campbell, 1973). We found that 14% of the deaths in our nursery had resulted from deliberate decisions to withhold or withdraw life support. While this information did not surprise doctors or nurses familiar with neonatal units it disturbed others. As Jeff Lyon in his book *Playing God in the Nursery* puts it: 'An uproar followed publication of the article. Not that anyone in medical circles was very shocked that someone had let babies die. Generations of doctors have been doing the same thing on the sly. But here were two doctors openly admitting it.' (Lyon, 1985).

Since then the medical, moral, social, theological and legal debate has continued with increasing complexity and an unfortunate tendency for the arguments to become polarised to extremes, a trend that is unhelpful and disturbing to the doctors and nurses who have to face these problems every day. At one extreme, 'pro-life' groups insist that all infants no matter how small or however abnormal have an inherent and absolute 'right to life' and that all available treatments must be used in their rescue. At the other extreme there are those who believe that to withold intensive care and to allow an infant to die slowly and perhaps painfully or to allow severely compromised survival is cruel and inhumane. Following the 1981 trial of Leonard Arthur, a consultant paediatrician accused of the murder of an infant with Down's Syndrome, a Limitation of Treatment Bill was proposed which with appropriate safeguards would allow the withdrawal of life-saving treatment for severely abnormal infants within the first 28 days after birth without liability to criminal prosecution (Brahams & Brahams, 1983). Some go further. Surely, they say, it would be far better if these infants could be killed quickly and painlessly to minimise suffering (Kuhse & Singer, 1985). Thus the wheel has turned full circle. Some might claim that we have almost returned to the infanticide of earlier times.

The troubling nature of these difficult dilemmas was expressed most eloquently by Robert Morison: 'Decisions made on such grounds are difficult, if not impossible, to differentiate, in principle, from decisions made by the Spartans and other earlier societies to expose to nature those infants born with manifest anatomical defects. We are being driven towards the ethics of an earlier period by the inexorable logic of the situation and it may only increase our discomfort without changing our views to reflect that historians and moralists both agree that the abolition of infanticide is perhaps the greatest ethical achievement of early Christianity' (Morison, 1971).

Endlessly, philosophers, theologians, lawyers and armchair ethicists of all kinds debate these issues: the differences or lack of them between 'killing' and 'letting die'; between 'being alive' and 'having a life'; or between 'person' and 'non-person'. The irony that pervades so many of these dilemmas is heightened by the day-to-day advances in obstetrics and neonatology that make nonsense of laws that allow the abortion, 'the killing', of even normal fetuses at and even beyond the stage of real viability but protect all infants born alive whatever their gestational age or condition. Unless one believes in pointless vitalism, decisions to stop treatment are likely to become more rather than less frequent in future years. A review of recent experience during the years 1981–85 reveals that 82% of neonatal deaths followed decisions to withhold or withdraw life-support. As the neonatal mortality rate is now very low this apparently dramatic increase (from the 14% reported from the USA in 1973) does not mean that more infants are being denied intensive care, but reflects the increasing number of tiny infants who now survive birth under 28 weeks gestation. There must be some limits to the prolongation of dying, and limits to the application of intensive care, if it is not to become a new and pointlessly cruel form of child abuse. Apart from the human costs, the enormous financial burdens of such treatments are becoming all too apparent, especially in a country like the United States where there seems to be even less willingness than in the United Kingdom to provide adequate resources for long-term care (Gustaitis & Young, 1986). This problem was recognised by the President's Commission for the Study of Ethical Problems in Medicine: 'Furthermore, to the extent that society fails to ensure that seriously ill newborns have the opportunity for an adequate level of continuing care, its moral authority to intervene on behalf of a newborn whose life is in jeopardy is compromised.' (US Government, 1983).

Ethical basis for non-treatment decisions

We talk of infants' best interests as being paramount in the judgement of doctors and parents when making decisions for and against intensive care. From the doctor's moral obligation of beneficence, if the treatment is for the benefit of the infant it should be used. The absolute duty to use it may be modified if the price is too high and will be weighed against the duty of non-maleficence – 'doing no harm'. For infants, decisions are further complicated by the need for proxy decision-making. While a competent adult can exercise autonomy, someone else must decide for an infant. To decide that an infant would be 'better off dead' is indeed an awesome decision but one that must be faced if we believe it and wish to act in the child's interests.

Some might ask how it is possible to say that death is for a child's benefit at the threshold of life. Surely 'where there is life there is hope' so that treatment to save or prolong life must be started or continued? This is the position taken up by 'pro-life' organisations who have been vigorous critics of 'selective non-treatment' or as I prefer, 'selective treatment'. 'Sanctity of life' proponents, especially those who hold the most extreme position, 'vitalism', believe that all withholding or withdrawing of treatment is wrong unless the patient has been declared dead. A moment's reflection will indicate that to take this position may be needlessly cruel and virtually untenable when applied to children who are obviously dying or to infants afflicted with the worst injustices of abnormal birth, e.g. anencephaly and other gross abnormalities of brain development – who used to be called 'monsters'. Even the late Paul Ramsey, the noted theologian, who was prominent in opposing selective non-treatment, believed that the appropriate response to a dying child is kind and respectful care designed to ease the child's passing (Ramsey, 1978). At the opposite extreme of the 'sanctity of life' position at birth would be one which considers treatment or non-treatment, survival or death, in strictly utilitarian terms, someting akin to the farmer who chooses from a litter the strongest and least flawed and who eliminates the rest, the runts. His decision would be based on what was best for him and his herd as regards future productivity and economic yield.

In practice, all decisions are made somewhere in between these two extremes. We all draw lines at some point between absolute adherence to the 'sanctity of life' ethic, on the one hand, and culling by killing on the other. We draw lines according to an infant-based best interests standard using the future quality-of-life of the infant as a major consideration. According to some we do this not on a line but on a slippery slope to infanticide. Perhaps we do play on slippery slopes, but with well defined and reasonably secure footholds based on personal professional and societal standards of acceptable moral behaviour.

Quality of life

It is important to establish what is meant by quality-of-life in this context. In their opposition to selective non-treatment, various individuals and groups have distorted and misrepresented this to mean 'worth' in utilitarian terms of costs or benefits to others – lives 'worth saving' or 'not worth saving'. They have also interpreted selective non-treatment for seriously abnormal infants as implying a general policy of discrimination against all individuals with disability or handicap. This hyperbolic propaganda has been distressing to many families and has been influential in causing quality-of-life judgements in complex neonatal treatment dilemmas to be seen as unacceptable or at least inadmissable in many hospitals in the United States. Rigid rules to prohibit such considerations represent a naive oversimplification of a very complex problem and ignore the practical realities of abnormal birth by implying that disability or potential handicap is irrelevant to medical decision making. When parents and doctors consider quality-of-life for an infant they do not weigh up an infant's future social utility or worth. Parents have high hopes for their children. They know the kind of life that they want for their child, *in their child's own interests.* They wish for physical and mental health; freedom from pain and suffering; brain function sufficient to allow sentience and cognition; the potential to develop human relationships, and the ability to achieve independence. In other words parents wish their child to 'have a life' and not merely 'be alive'; or, as Father Richard McCormick tells it, 'granted that we can easily save the life, what kind of life are we saving?' (McCormick, 1974).

As autonomous adults we would insist on our right to choose to die once all hope of meaningful life has gone. Recently courts have provided guidelines to protect adults' rights to do just that. Why should infants not have the same 'right to die' or 'right to be allowed to die'? (Campbell, 1983). Why should they be treated aggressively in the face of parental choice and professional judgement to the contrary?

Withholding or withdrawing: Is there a difference?

A recent review of treatment practises in several countries revealed interesting differences in approach to these dilemmas (Rhoden, 1986). In the United Kingdom an 'intermediate' approach is taken compared to those adopted in Sweden and the United States although there is a great variation within each country. In Sweden doctors seem more willing to withhold treatment but are reluctant to withdraw it once started. In the US there is a much more aggressive initiation of treatment on almost all viable infants and its continuation until death is certain. In the UK, for most infants, treatment, even aggressive intensive care, may be initiated but British paediatricians seem more willing to withdraw treatment if further information and subsequent developments indicate that death or severe brain damage are likely outcomes. To me this seems the appropriate approach. I do not see any moral distinction whatsoever between withholding treatment and withdrawing it. If something is not indicated for the patient's benefit, not starting it or stopping it are of equal moral weight. Put another way, if a treatment like Intermittent Positive Pressure Ventilation (IPPV) is indicated it is equally wrong to withhold it or withdraw it. Indeed, if there is any difference it could be argued that withdrawing is preferable to withholding. Withdrawing gives doctors and parents more time for discussion and reflection on the likely consequences for the infant with or without treatment and, as more and perhaps better information will be available, decisions will often be based on firmer grounds than earlier and perhaps premature decisions to withhold. The aim must be to reduce to the minimum the small but inevitable degree of uncertainty that remains with all these difficult decisions.

Recent legal interventions have undoubtedly influenced American doctors towards more aggressive treatment out of fear of being reported to the State Child Abuse Agency for 'medical neglect'. Sadly, the legal interests of the doctors and the hospitals may now take precedence over the interests of the infant and family. The philosophical confusion over withholding and withdrawing can also influence decision-making in another potentially dangerous way. If it is psychologically or medico-legally more difficult to withdraw treatment than to withhold it, doctors may withhold treatment simply out of fear that once treatment is started they may not be able to stop it. Even in circumstances of considerable uncertainty, e.g. the birth of a very low birth weight infant, IPPV may be denied when it could be to the infant's considerable benefit. Thus we should consider withholding and withdrawing together. If treatment is not believed to be in the infant's best interests or may cause harm it should not be given and may be withdrawn.

Withholding care at birth

A particular dilemma about withholding intensive treatments such as IPPV relates to the increasing number of tinier and tinier infants born at the very limits of viability (22–26 weeks gestation age). Occasionally such an infant will do remarkably well but resuscitation at birth may result in only a brief period of intensive care until death or will ensure prolonged survival but with severe disability. It is in such situations that withholding immediate intensive care at birth may be wrong simply because of the degree of uncertainty involved. The delivery room is no place to make 'snap judgements' on inadequate information. As it is junior doctors who are most often faced with these decisions at delivery, and they must be given clear instructions about their responsibilities, I would argue that whatever the gestation age or condition, an infant born alive should receive standard resuscitation including IPPV if necessary. At this stage life-saving measures should not be withheld. Any subsequent decision to continue, withdraw or introduce further intensive treatment is the responsibility of a senior doctor or doctors after careful consideration of the facts and discussion with the parents.

Previously I have suggested a flexible 'cut-off' birthweight of 750 g (at appropriate gestation age) below which IPPV and other intensive care treatments should not be continued *routinely* without discussing the implications with the parents (Campbell, 1982). Although criteria will change, I remain convinced that such apparently harsh decisions are necessary.

There are circumstances when withholding intensive treatment like resuscitation may be justified at birth. One could list examples of congenital abnormalities for which resuscitation is inappropriate but there is so much variation in complexity, severity and prognosis quite apart from the varying attitudes of parents and staff that considerable latitude in decision making is necessary in individual circumstances. Anencephaly and similar gross abnormalities are obvious examples where aggressive resuscitation and other forms of intensive care are not indicated. With modern techniques of pre-natal diagnosis many of these infants are now detected before birth and discussions with the parents prenatally should include consideration of the appropriate care to be given at birth. In this situation there is no justification for employing various intensive treatments in futile attempts to prolong life. Nevertheless, as human beings, these infants deserve our respect and should be given ordinary care with relief of any apparent discomfort or distress until death. Recent suggestions that they might be kept alive *solely* as valuable sources of organs for transplantation are disturbing. Such a practice conflicts with the infant's best interests standard and would have disturbing implications if applied to other areas of clinical practice (Capron, 1987).

In this context, I might also mention the plight of fetuses born with signs of life after attempted terminations of pregnancy. This has been called 'the new neonatal dilemma' (Rhoden, 1984). Increasingly, paediatricians are being asked to resuscitate and treat one of these tiny abortuses minutes after a colleague in gynaecology has been trying to kill it. At present the law confers protection on every infant born alive. We have a duty to care for these infants but they may have been damaged during the abortion procedure itself and are likely to be hypoxic, acidotic and hypothermic by the time help is sought from an adjacent neonatal unit. It is also most unlikely that their mothers will wish to care for them. I believe that aggressive resuscitation and intensive care should be withheld from these infants.

Taking the decision

In the UK, as far as can be judged, most people and most doctors prefer decisions about withholding and withdrawing life support to be determined by individual case-by-case analysis and sensitive informed discussions by responsible doctors and the parents. It has been said that good ethics should begin with good facts. The primarily responsible doctors, in co-operation with specialist colleagues, must take all necessary steps to establish the diagnosis and estimate the prognosis as accurately as possible. They are most likely to be knowledgeable about the medical problems and the outlook for the infant's future health. In spite of all too frequent examples of parental exploitation and abuse of children, parents are still generally viewed as the most appropriate decision-makers for children. To deny them this role and to infringe this obligation and duty of care might further erode the family as the most desirable social unit in which to rear our young. Compared to others, parents are more likely to make concerned and loving decisions for the welfare of their child if given the facts and options accurately, sensitively and objectively, and are given time for reflection and perhaps for consultation with other family members, their family doctor, clergyman or others. Parents are the ones who usually must assume the responsibility of caring in the future, perhaps for a lifetime, certainly long after the doctors and others involved have withdrawn or turned to other problems.

There will be occasions when even loving parents may make choices that conflict with the infant's best interests. They may be so emotionally overwhelmed by the 'bereavement' of abnormal birth that their judgement is affected. Their joy is suddenly replaced by grief. They may be unable to understand the clinical complexities of the condition, or its treatment, so that they may view the future either unduly pessimistically or excessively optimistically. Very occasionally they may put their interests and those of other family members first. It is in these situations that doctors may have to intervene and take decisions contrary to parental wishes and with or without the authority of another agency such as the courts. Court action in such circumstances is distressing for parents and should be used as a last resort and on good grounds. In most circumstances, where there is doubt about the benefits of treatment or where it seems likely that the infant's quality of life will be seriously impaired, the doctors usually will support the family and decide against treatment. Moreover, doctors should usually assume the *primary* responsibility to relieve the family of any guilt they may feel later if left to take the decision on their own. Occasionally, when, because of eccentric personal or extreme religious views (perhaps acceptable for decisions affecting themselves), parents refuse clearly efficacious treatment for their infant, e.g. blood transfusion in Jehovah's Witnesses, doctors will sometimes give treatment with parental knowledge but without parental consent and put the onus of taking futher legal action on the parents. Very occasionally it may be necessary to withhold or withdraw intensive care against the parents' wishes when it is clear to everyone concerned that it is futile, pointless and inhumane. Apart from being of no benefit to the infants concerned, indefinite intensive care of this kind, in an understaffed and overcrowed intensive care nursery, may have a detrimental affect on the care that can be given to other infants.

Role of legislation

In 1973, we ended our paper with these words: 'If working out these dilemmas in ways such as those we suggest is in violation of the law we believe the law should be changed'. Ten years later, the US government sought to change the law, but in the opposite direction to what we had hoped – it sought to compel doctors to treat severely abnormal infants. After a controversial case in Indiana in 1982, 'pro-life' lobbyists persuaded the Reagan administration, which was sympathetic to their views, to attempt the enactment of legislation which would prevent doctors and parents from exercising any discretion in deciding for or against treatment (Annas, 1984). The original rules issued by the Department of Health and Human Services (DHHS) came to be known as the Baby Doe Directives and were coupled with warning notices for neonatal units and a telephone 'hot line' to report offenders anonymously. (In the US, to protect anonymity, a boy or girl subject to court order is known as John Doe or Jane Doe respectively.)

As originally drafted under Section 504 of the Rehabilitation Act of 1973, these directives were rejected by successive courts, including the Supreme Court, but in 1984 the US Government achieved much the same purpose by requiring individual States if they wished to qualify for Federal funding to bring withholding or withdrawing of treatment under existing Child Abuse legislation as 'medical neglect'. Apart from this categorisation being deeply offensive to parents and paediatricians acting sincerely and compassionately in the interests of infant and family, this legislative move caused great concern to State Child Protection agencies already swamped with abused, neglected and abandoned children.

This probably unique example of government interference in family tragedies has not fundamentally altered the law relating to abnormal infants nor the careful and considered practice of many paediatricians. Nevertheless there is evidence that it has created an unfortunate climate of compulsion towards aggressive treatment for all newborn infants and has inhibited some paediatricians and parents from seeking the 'least-worst' of several unsatisfactory options. The legislation was aimed at the problem of infants with potentially handicapping congenital abnormalities. It did not address the much larger and ever increasing problem of extreme prematurity at the very limits of viability or the implications of treating all infants resuscitated successfully by modern techniques but seriously damaged by asphyxia. For many infants determining the prognosis with complete certainty is impossible. Undoubtedly a few abuses of infant 'rights' to full treatment may have been prevented by this intervention but many more infants are now being kept alive by State or hospital directive against the wishes of parents or hospital staff. Thus this vague and ill-focussed legislation has been detrimental to the interests of many more infants than it has protected. It has influenced doctors, in their own interests, to err on the side of over-treatment.

In 1973, we sought to stimulate open debate on these issues because we had become concerned that high technology medicine, its excitements and triumphs notwithstanding, increasingly was being applied relentlessly and indiscriminately to newborn babies whatever their gestation age or condition. We believed that we were paying too little attention to the dilemmas of 'human ambiguity', too little attention to parental views and their hopes for the future of infant and family, too little attention to pain and suffering and quality of life, and too little attention to the realities of family living in individual circumstances. Recent developments have greatly increased that concern.

Infant ethics committees

In attempts to defuse the confrontation between paediatricians and government that resulted from the Baby Doe Directives it was suggested by the American Academy of Pediatrics and others that committees be set up to review these medical non-treatment decisions for infants somewhat similar to the Ethics Committees that had been in operation in some American hospitals since the early seventies to deal with 'do not resuscitate' (DNR) decisions and other issues affecting those at the other 'edge of life', the elderly. Infant Care Review Committees (ICRC) or Infant Ethics Committees (IEC) have a broad inter-disciplinary and lay membership and a wide remit to review cases, to recommend policies and practices within the hospital, and to educate. Good IECs should attempt to clarify the medical and ethical issues and ensure that the infant's best interests have been properly considered. They may also provide some ethical 'comfort' for the doctors and staff who have to struggle with these complex problems (Fleischman, 1986). In particular their role should be advisory – committees like these should not make decisions. Occasionally they may refer particularly difficult problems to the courts. Unfortunately, in the current climate of legislative interference and with the notorious tendency to litigation now current in the United States, in some hospitals the ethics committees have taken on, or have been seen to take on, a decision-making role and many doctors, understandably, have been happy to 'pass the buck' of difficult decision-making to the committees. As they are institutionally based, and may contain lawyers and hospital administrators as members, their decisions may have less to do with the welfare of the infant and family than with the interests of the institution. Often, no decision is taken and the situation is allowed to 'drift' – to nobody's benefit. Unfortunately, parents, in spite of the fact that they will be the ones most affected by any decision, may not be invited to participate in the discussions.

In the UK, we have not yet formalised such a committee structure although there is often wide consultation with many individuals similar to those included in American committees. They include specialist colleagues, nurses, social workers, and clergymen but not lay persons outside the family and certainly not hospital administrators or lawyers. I believe that infant ethics committees properly constituted can serve a useful purpose in guiding medical staff towards decisions that are sound in ethics as well as in medicine, but I remain sceptical that most ethics committees, as currently constituted, can improve the quality of decision-making in individual cases.

Lawyers have criticised the lack of due process in decisions to allow infants to die and what they see as our profession's unwillingness to establish rules of conduct. To me rules imply rigidity. Individual doctors have suggested guidelines or criteria for such decisions but have emphasised the importance of flexibility and pointed out that as the individual circumstances are so varied much latitude in decision-making should be tolerated (Duff & Campbell, 1976; Milligan & Shennan, 1984; Whitelaw, 1986). Paediatricians working in neonatal units have widely varying personal views on the appropriate use of intensive care. How selectively or how indiscriminately they use their skills and technology will be the subject of continuing debate both inside and outside these units. Inevitably the criteria will continue to change but we must always keep in mind the effects of our current policies on the infants themselves and the families who must bear the consequences. I believe that it would be folly to remove the responsibilty, the obligation, the duty and the agony of final decision-making from the doctors primarily responsible for the care of patients and the appropriate next of kin, in this case the parents. The welfare of the infant comes first but in an increasingly pluralistic society there must be room for discretion based not only on technical considerations but on personal religious and cultural values affecting and cherished by individual families.

References

Annas, G. J. (1984). The Baby Doe regulations: governmental intervention in neonatal rescue medicine. *American Journal of Public Health*, 74, 618–20.

Brahams, D. & Brahams, M. (1983). The Arthur case: A proposal for legislation. *Journal of Medical Ethics*, 9, 12–15.

Budin, P. (1907). *The Nursling: The Feeding and Hygiene of Premature and Full-Term Infants*. Caxton Publishing Co., London.

Campbell, A. G. M. (1982). Which infants should not receive intensive care? *Archives of Disease in Childhood*, 57, 569–71.

Campbell, A. G. M. (1983). The right to be allowed to die. *Journal of Medical Ethics*, **9**, 136–40.

Capron, A. M. (1987). Anencephalic donors: separate the dead from the dying. *Hastings Center Report*, 17, **1**, 5–9.

Commentary (1884). British infanticide. *Lancet*, **1**, 266.

Duff, R. S. & Campbell, A. G. M. (1973). Moral and ethical dilemmas in the special care nursery. *New England Journal of Medicine*, **289**, 890–4.

Duff, R. S. & Campbell A. G. M. (1976). On deciding the care of severely handicapped or dying persons: with particular reference to infants. *Pediatrics*, **57**, 487–93.

Eden, T. W. E. (1921). A note on the mortality of premature infants. *Lancet*, **2**, 127–8.

Editorial (1863). National Society and Asylum for Prevention of Infanticide. *British Medical Journal*, **2**, 348.

Editorial (1897a). Human incubators. *British Medical Journal*, **1**, 813–4.

Editorial (1897b). The Victorian Era Exhibition at Earl's Court. *Lancet*, **1**, 161–2.

Editorial (1898). The danger of making a public show of incubators for babies. *Lancet*, **1**, 390.

Fleischman, A. R. (1986). An infant bioethical review committee in an urban medical center. *Hastings Center Report*, **16**, 16–18.

Gustaitis, R. & Young, E. W. D. (1986). *A Time to be Born, a Time to Die: Conflicts and Ethics in an Intensive Care Nursery*. Addison-Wesley, Reading, Mass., USA.

Holt, L. E. & Babbitt, E. C. (1915). Institutional mortality of newborns. A report of 10,000 consecutive cases at the Sloane Hospital for Women. *Journal of the American Medical Association*, **64**, 287–90.

Kuhse, H. & Singer, P. (1985). *Should the Baby Live? The Problem of Handicapped Infants*. Oxford University Press, Oxford.

Lyon, J. (1985). *Playing God in the Nursery*. W. W. Norton & Co., New York and London.

McClead, R. E. & Menke, J. A. (1987). Neonatal iatrogenesis. *Advances in Pediatrics*, **34**, 335–56.

McCormick, R. A. (1974). To save or let die: the dilemma of modern medicine. *Journal of the American Medical Association*, **229**, 172–6.

Milligan, J. E. & Shennan, A. T. (1984). Perinatal intensive care: where and how to draw the line. *American Journal of Obstetrics and Gynecology*, **148**, 499–503.

Morison, R. S. (1971). Death: Process or event? *Science*, **173**, 694–8.

Ramsey, P. (1978). *Ethics at the Edges of Life: Medical and Legal Intersections*. Yale University Press. New Haven and London.

Ransom, S. W. (1900). The care of premature and feeble infants. *Pediatrics* (NY), **9**, 321.

Rhoden, N. K. (1984). The new neonatal dilemma: live births from late abortions. *Georgetown Law Journal*, **72**, 1451–509.

Rhoden, N. K. (1986). Treating Baby Doe: the ethics of uncertainty. *Hastings Center Report*, **16**, 34–42.

Rist, J. M. (1982). *Human Value: A Study in Ancient Philosophical Ethics*. E. J. Brill, Leiden, Netherlands.

Rodman, I. (1815). Case of a child born between the fourth and fifth month and brought up. *Edinburgh Medical and Surgical Journal*, **11**, 455–8.

Silverman, W. A. (1979). Incubator – baby side shows. *Pediatrics*, **64**, 127–41.

Silverman, W. A. (1981). Mismatched attitudes about neonatal death. *Hastings Center Report*, **11**, 12–16.

Special Correspondence (1907). The organisation of consultations for nurslings. *British Medical Journal*, **1**, 1089.

US Government (1983). Deciding to forego life-sustaining treatment: ethical, medical and legal issues in treatment decisions. *President's Commission for the Study of Ethical Problems in Medicine and Biomedical and Behavioural Research*. US Government Printing Office, Washington DC.

Whitelaw, A. (1986). Death as an option in neonatal intensive care. *Lancet*, **2**, 328–31.

Withholding neonatal care 2.
A philosopher's view

Introduction

As Professor Campbell has observed in the foregoing chapter, there is no question but that doctors must provide care for their patients whereas the necessity of their administering intensive treatment, even life-saving treatment, does deserve questioning. May not the obligation to provide care in some circumstances itself dictate the withholding of intensive treatment?

At the heart of the debate about ethical criteria for selective neonatal treatment are two conflicting considerations: on the one hand considerations of humanity which seem to tell in favour of withholding treatment from very severely handicapped infants, on the other, considerations of justice which seem to tell against so doing. In what follows we will assume that a defence for withholding treatment does not succeed if it simply brushes aside considerations of justice in the interests of humanity. The constraints of justice are supposed to set limits on how we may pursue our aims, however noble, however humanely motivated. Therefore, a legitimate defence for withholding treatment has to be one which does not involve the infringing of rights.

Is there ever a case for withholding neonatal treatment? Sometimes we have no choice; resources are scarce, treating one infant necessitates delaying treatment of another. If neither infant can survive waiting, we are obliged to let one die. As we cannot be obliged to do the impossible, non-treatment in such a case is uncontroversially defensible.

Such triage situations apart, how else might the withholding of treatment be justified? Let us briefly dispose of two unconvincing lines of defence for withholding treatment before we turn to a more studied discussion of some more credible lines of defence.

Letting nature take its course

A doctor is never entitled to excuse withholding treatment on this ground. He has a duty of care towards his patients; letting nature take its course is just what he is employed to prevent if he can. That said, it does not follow that he is obliged to do all in his power to save or sustain a particular patient's life. There are other patients with claims on him and he has a right to time off. Apart from these qualifications upon his duty of care to any particular patient how else might he legitimately defend a decision not to treat?

Normal standards

Doctors might appeal to normal standards of care in defence of decisions to withhold treatment, the idea being that provided these decisions are in line with normal practice, it is all that their patients are entitled to expect. But normality is a poor measure of justice. Even if we are complacent about the rectitude of what is normal practice in our own hospital services we can easily cite disquieting instances of traditions of malpractice elsewhere. An unjust practice is not made innocent by becoming widespread or by being accepted without qualms by its practitioners. In some areas it may be normal practice to put Down's Syndrome infants born with intestinal blockage on 'nursing care only' or to allow friends and relatives of staff colleagues to jump queues for hip replacements. Whether either policy is morally defensible cannot be settled merely by appeal to the prevailing convention.

In law, to be sure, a doctor's duty of care is assessed partly in the light of prevailing medical practice, i.e. normal standards, along with the proviso, though, that these standards are themselves consistent with moral and legal norms. The New Jersey Supreme Court, in permitting the disconnecting of Karen Quinlan's respiration, notwithstanding that so to do was acknowledged to be contrary to prevailing medical practice and that a doctor's duties in law are related to the practices prevailing in the profession, maintained that the Court had a 'non-delegable judicial responsibility' to be responsive to the 'common moral judgement of the community at large'; in this case, to uphold the patient's right of privacy. Justice Hughes suggested, moreover, that prevailing standards might be somewhat corrupted because of the understandable anxiety of members of the medical profession to avoid charges of malpractice – 'But, in the question of whether the doctor was in breach of his duty of care in allowing the patient to die, evidence of a professional consensus should not be treated as conclusive.' (Skegg, 1984).

Let us turn now to certain more credible lines of defence for withholding treatment. We will examine two, each of which has been invoked in USA courtrooms, both of which are cited in the *President's Commission for the Study of Ethical Problems in Medicine and Biomedical and Behavioural Research* (US Government, 1983).

The principle of substituted justice

This principle invokes a right of self-determination according to which doctors must seek valid consent and patients are entitled to refuse treatment. It is argued that this patient-right may be exercised by proxy on an incompetent patient's behalf; a guardian may substitute his judgement to ensure that treatment is not imposed contrary to what he knows the patient's wishes would be. In such a case it is not merely permissible for a doctor to withhold treatment, it is obligatory. Treatment, where consent was withheld, would be unjust, would constitute battery.

In order to appraise this line of defence for withholding treatment where appeal is made to the principle of substituted judgement, we need first to clarify the principle of self-determination which underpins a patient's alleged right to refuse treatment and, secondly, to discuss how this right is to be qualified (even its keenest champions accept that some qualification is necessary).

The principle of self-determination appeals to what is widely perceived to be a basic right of choice each of us, *qua* autonomous agent, has concerning what we do and have done to us. It is important to understand that this right is not derivative from a presumption that each of us is best judge in his own interests. Rather the right is claimed in recognition of the crucial importance we attach to being able to exercise control over our own lives. The right safeguards personal freedom not personal welfare.

The right of choice is not, then, merely a right to choose sensibly – a puny right that would be. Assuming then that patients *qua* autonomous agents have this right, they may exercise it by refusing treatment, even treatment that is obviously in their interests. They are not obliged to be rational or reasonable; not obliged to give up smoking, drinking or eating unwholesome foods even though their doctors urging them to do so do know best. Doctors may advise but must not compel.

But this right of choice, precious though it is, is not absolute. J. S. Mill (Priestley & Robson, 1963), its eloquent advocate, himself admits it must be qualified. How?

Harm to others

All sorts of choices which we generally consider we are entitled to make concerning our personal lives would become morally problematic if we were obliged to avoid harm of any kind to others, e.g. a woman's (or even, these days, a man's) right to say 'No'. The sense in which harm to others constitutes a legitimate constraint upon our choices needs to be defined.

Let us say, then, that the right of choice is circumscribed by other people's rights. We are free to choose for ourselves provided we do no wrong, provided we do not invade other people's rights. That said, there may be occasions where rights conflict and another person's right is legitimately over-ridden.

One way, then, in which a patient's right to refuse treatment may be challenged is on the ground that non-treatment would injure the rights of others. This is one of the grounds regularly treated as relevant in court cases in

America in determining if a patient's right of refusal of life-saving treatment is
to be upheld. It was on this ground that American courts over-rode a Jehovah's
Witness patient's right to refuse a blood transfusion when she was in her eighth
month of pregnancy, in Raleigh Fitkin-Paul Morgan Hospital v. Anderson (42
N.J. 421, 201 A.2d 537; 1964), but upheld the right of another Jehovah's
Witness patient who had no minor dependants in re Brooks (32 Ill. 2d 361 N.E.
2d 345; 1965).

Self harm

It may be argued that while a person has a right to make choices, foolish choices
even, provided others are not wronged thereby, there is one form of self-abuse
that is not permissible, *viz.* suicide. If so, a doctor is not obliged to withhold
life-saving treatment from an unwilling patient. One cannot have a right to do
wrong. If suicide is wrong one's right of self-determination cannot include it as
a choice one is entitled to make and which others must respect. In that case a
doctor who frustrates one's making of it is not infringing the right of choice.

Not that we should assume that whenever a patient refuses life- saving
treatment he is attempting suicide. As is common knowledge some suicide bids
are not genuine, are recognised as 'cries for help'. These sorts of bids aside,
whether a patient's refusal is a suicide bid or not depends on his underlying
intentions. It all depends why the patient refuses; on whether he is aiming at his
own death (e.g. by allowing his disease to kill him). The Jehovah's Witness who
refuses a blood transfusion has no suicidal intent. He does not want to die and if
he recovers in spite of non-treatment he will celebrate.

In a minimal sense of 'wanting' it is true that even he 'wants' to die *viz.* he
consents to that outcome though it is in his power to prevent it. But he does not
'want' in the sense 'intend' that outcome – he does not reject the transfusion *in
order that* he may die.

A suicidal patient, on the other hand, may be expected to look for *other* ways
and means to end his life if non-treatment proves to be insufficient (unless of
course he changes his mind meanwhile). The patient who is caught surrepti-
tiously unplugging himself from life-support apparatus is likely to find himself
under surveillance just because it is assumed he will make further attempts to
'do himself in' if the opportunity arises (Bartling v. Glendale Adventist Medical
Center, Case No. C500735, June 22, 1984, Superior Court, Los Angeles Ca.,
Dept. 86, Waddington J.).

Consider now the plight of a patient terminally ill, let us say, but whose life is
immediately threatened by some remediable condition the treatment for which
is painful and which will leave him an invalid for the remainder of his life, e.g.
amputation of both legs. The patient is faced with a choice between treatment
and death: if he rejects the former he is choosing the latter. Is it correct then to

say that if he refuses treatment he is attempting to kill himself by allowing the disease to kill him?

The answer surely depends upon his intent in rejecting the treatment. Suppose, miraculously, he survives in spite of non-treatment. Are we to assume that he will look for some other way to cut short his remaining life? Surely not. Even if he *hopes* for death he may not be minded to kill himself. Indeed he might dismiss the thought believing perhaps that were he to do so his family would lose the benefits of his life insurance. This hypothetical case illustrates the possibility of a patient refusing life-saving treatment on the grounds that it will not be of net benefit to him yet without suicidal intent.

Now if a patient's refusal of life-saving treatment on the grounds that the treatment would do him more harm than good is not necessarily an attempted suicide, neither is a doctor's decision to withhold life-saving treatment from an incompetent patient on those grounds necessarily attempted murder. The 'necessarily's are necessary since the decision (to refuse or) to withhold could be based on several reasons including the intent to (die or) kill. Even supposing the doctor hopes for the patient's death and believes that without the life-saving treatment the patient will die, it does not follow that the doctor intends to kill him. If miraculously the patient survives we need not assume that the doctor will resort to other means to cut short the patient's life, e.g. removing the patient's blankets.

But suppose a patient's refusal is quite unmistakably a suicide bid, is a doctor who permits the patient to die, withholding treatment, not an accomplice? To be an accomplice is not only to assist but to assist in wrong-doing. The doctor is an accomplice only if the patient acts unjustly in choosing suicide – only if suicide is tantamount to self-murder.

'Wrongness' of suicide

There are two matters of fact about suicide which, taken together, constitute a very good reason for regarding suicide as strictly taboo:

(1) it is irrevocable; if one takes this step in error there is no going back;

(2) it is a step which one is most prone to contemplate when one's powers of detached judgement and self-awareness are highly unreliable.

That is why to avoid this drastic folly it is necessary to resolve *in advance* that suicide is never an option. Unless we form a firm resolution that suicide is 'unthinkable' we may be vulnerable to the temptation at a moment of weakness.

Yet while most suicides are tragic mistakes and the victims are mostly young persons who are overwhelmed by troubles that in truth are temporary and surmountable, it has to be admitted that, in some situations, conditions of living may be exceedingly grim and there may be no prospect of respite. Furthermore, people who are so sadly circumstanced may be poignantly aware of this and may correctly judge that they'd be better off dead. The problem here is that there seems to be no self-applicable test they could employ to confirm if they are judging correctly.

For the journey of life it is rationally necessary to equip ourselves (and those we care for) with whatever attitudes, dispositions, rules are most likely to stand us in good stead. Once we are well embarked on that journey we may not, though, be able to re-equip ourselves at will should the unexpected turn out to be our lot. It would not follow that the original choice of equipment must have been ill-judged nor that it would have been more rational to travel unequipped. It would seem then that the strategy of not allowing suicide onto one's agenda of practical options is prudentially necessary.

But so far I have been talking as if the only reason anyone might have for contemplating suicide stems from an adverse calculation of what life has in store for oneself. That is, after all, typically the motivation of suicidal patients. There are other reasons, though, why a person (who might be a patient) might consider killing himself: heroic suicides are performed for the sake of others, e.g. Captain Oates walking out into the blizzard so that his friends, who refused to abandon him alive, would themselves have a chance to survive. But did Captain Oates commit suicide? Certainly he was not 'giving up' on life, and he was dying anyway. Should we not say: 'He did not choose to die, but to die one way rather than another'? Yet he chose as he did in order to hasten his death in order that his friends could continue on their journey before time ran out for them. There is no justification for supposing that because he chose to hasten his death by allowing or, more accurately, inviting, the blizzard to kill him that his *hastened* death was any the less intentional than it would have been had he shot himself (Holland, 1980).

Now the prudential argument I have sketched for treating suicide as some-thing not to be contemplated does not apply against heroically motivated suicide, only against contemplating suicide as an escape from the ills of life – 'defeatist' suicides, let us call them. To be sure one would hardly describe a heroic suicide as a manifestation of prudence. But it does not follow that such an act must be a manifestation of imprudence. At least, such a deed may be rational – granted, that is, that a person can clear-headedly and informedly attach more importance to the good of another than to his own personal advantage. Captain Oates, surely, was acting rationally when he stepped out into the blizzard.

Now granted that it is prudentially necessary to refuse to contemplate defeatest suicide, is it also morally necessary? Are defeatist suicides not only (for the most part) disastrous mistakes but also unjust?

Can one, literally speaking, do oneself an injustice or is such talk merely metaphorical? Rights imply constraints. If A has a right against B, B is obliged not to infringe it. If A has a right against A, A is obliged not to infringe it. But to be obliged is to be bound and in this case A is both binder and bound (both gaoler and prisoner). In that case he can release himself at will which is to say that he is not really bound at all. Suicide then is not in itself unjust. It may yet be unjust if it invades the rights of others – God, say, or minor dependants. We have already allowed for this possibility (that the right of choice is qualified by the claims others have on us).

A doctor then has no general right to over-rule a suicidal patient's refusal of treatment even if he rightly regards the patient's choice as unreasonable. After all, when we discover our friends or colleagues to be making disastrous personal choices, e.g. in marrying someone unsuitable (or unmarrying someone suitable), we do not feel entitled to go beyond advising. Why then should the patient status deprive someone of autonomy and therewith the right to be a fool?

We have so far proceeded on the assumption that those asserting the right to refuse life-saving treatment are clear-headed and relevantly informed and thus competent to exercise autonomy, to give or withhold consent. What though is a doctor's responsibility towards incompetents – do they have a right to refuse treatment, a right which would, of course, have to be exercised on their behalf by proxy?

Competence and proxy consent

Only those who are competent can exercise a right of choice. However, might it not be exercised by proxy on behalf of those who are not competent? Some things you can either do for yourself or have done for you. You can feed yourself or be fed by another, keep yourself warm or be kept warm by others. But how can an incompetent incapable of making choices regarding his own destiny have his autonomy exercised by others who decide his destiny on his behalf?

Surely this is only a possibility where the person who is incompetent has formerly been competent and revealed enough of his ambitions, attitudes, preferences then for us to be able to say that he would now want us to choose for him. Ideally, he would have indicated his settled wishes regarding his own destiny in a 'Living Will'. But in the absence of any such document, it might still be obvious enough to his intimates what his wishes in the circumstances would be, e.g. that an unconscious patient, known to be a long-standing dedicated Jehovah's Witness, would not want us to consent on his behalf to a blood transfusion.

We would, in such a case, be applying the principle (or test) of substituted judgement. While such a test makes sense in relation to persons whose wills are known and can therefore be represented and respected by others, it cannot intelligibly be applied to strangers or to infants. In the one case we could have no knowledge of their wishes, in the other they would be too young to have developed wills of their own. Thus, while it is legitimate for a wife, applying the principle of substituted judgement, to refuse proxy consent to a life-saving blood transfusion for a Jehovah's Witness patient who is her husband, it is not so for a Jehovah's Witness parent to appeal to this principal as justification for refusing proxy consent on behalf of his newborn infant (Kleinig, 1985).

We must conclude, then, that while one legitimate reason for doctors withholding treatment, even life-saving treatment, from a patient is that patients have a right of choice, hence a right to refuse treatment, and further that such refusals can be made by proxy, this reason cannot be used to defend with-holding treatment from infants since firstly they are incompetent and, secondly, the conditions under which the right of choice can be met by proxy (employing the principle of substituted judgement) cannot be satisfied in their case.

The principle of best interests

Let us consider next the line of defence for non-treatment which appeals to the principle of best interests, the argument being simply that in some cases withholding life-saving treatment can be in a patient's best interests. With this line of defence for withholding neonatal treatment we are not obliged to postulate that infants have wills, only that they have interests, that we can harm or benefit them by what we do or omit to do to them.

If a treatment would do more harm than good, a doctor not only may not, he must not, administer it. Why? Doctors are obliged to do no harm to their patients in just the same sense that we are all obliged to do no harm to those with whom we have dealings. As we have already remarked, a general prohibition on harming others would debar us from all sorts of things we consider ourselves entitled to do. It is harming only in the sense of wronging that we are all plausibly obliged to avoid.

But doctors have a duty of care towards their patients; they are obliged to look after them, and that necessity puts them in a special position *vis-à-vis* their patients. It entitles them to inflict suffering (pain, indignities, incapacities) on them provided that:

(1) the benefits of the treatment in question are anticipated to be com-pensatory (for the said patient);

(2) there are no less disagreeable forms of treatment as effective;

(3) the patients, if competent, give valid consent.

Let us call treatment which satisfies these conditions 'therapeutic' treatment, that is, where its aim and the form it takes are to be explained solely in terms of net benefit to the patient (not necessarily a health benefit, though; we may include other benefits accessible only via medical technology, e.g. cosmetic surgery).

Are there any circumstances in which the withholding of life-saving treat-ment could be justified on purely therapeutic grounds? We should not instance here so called 'futile' treatments, i.e. the treating of some remediable life-threatening condition in a patient who cannot survive owing to other irremediable conditions. By definition, such treatments are not 'life-saving'. But suppose it is indeed possible to administer life-prolonging treatment to a patient yet the prognosis for what the extra life would be like is so bleak that its benefits do not compensate for the ills of the treatment, e.g. resuscitating a patient in the final stages of bone cancer. In that case, by our definition of therapeutic treatment, the treatment could not qualify as such.

Now anyone who decides that a life-saving treatment is not therapeutically justified is employing the highly controversial quality of life test; he is allowing that some lives if salvaged are predictably so ghastly as to be not worth saving, that their possessors would be better off dead.

Well, maybe no-one really wants to deny that sad truth. What is questionable, though, is if the doctor who humanely wishes (and devoutly prays perhaps) for a patient's quick death, is entitled to act on the wish by withholding life-saving treatment. We have already allowed that he may, indeed must, if a competent patient refuses the treatment. What, though, about incompetents?

Slippery slopes

Is reliance on quality of life assessments, by those engaged in making decisions whether or not to withhold life-saving treatment from patients, corrupting both to those who use them and to the society at large which permits their use in this way? Even though we can cite clear cases, where patients' life prospects are so grim that they would be better off dead and would benefit if life-saving treatment were withheld, is it not still necessary to uphold a strict prohibition against use of such calculations? Once we begin to qualify the prohibition will not the pressure and temptation to further quality become irresistible? Surely the power of such life and death decisions should reside with God alone.

This slippery slope type of objection is made where:

(1) there is on the one hand some practice 'A' presumed to be morally permissible in itself and on the other hand some practice 'Z' presumed to be morally impermissible;

(2) the practice 'A' is the first of a series of steps which if taken would inevitably lead to the rest being traversed one after the other leading ultimately to the impermissible practice 'Z' as the final step.

Consequently, it is argued, the first step must not be taken.

In what circumstances is it reasonable to maintain that allowing one practice inevitably leads to allowing another? When, in other words, is firm and stable line-drawing impossible? Two conditions must apply: The circumstances have to be such that:

(1) any line that is drawn is bound to be somewhat arbitrary;

(2) there is a one-way pressure on any line that is drawn to redraw it more permissively.

Arbitrary line-drawing

Line drawing is bound to be somewhat arbitrary in the sense that wherever the line is drawn there is equally good reason for drawing it slightly to one side or the other, wherever, that is, the line is being drawn between adjacent steps that are not significantly different from each other though steps some distance apart on the same scale are.

In many areas of life we adopt workable rules that are based on somewhat arbitrary line-drawing; rules which rightly command respect, nonetheless, e.g. fixing an age criterion for voting rights. In fixing on 18 years, say, we do not pretend that upon reaching his 18th birthday a young person undergoes a sudden metamorphosis into maturity. Nor need we be uneasy if we hear of other countries which have a slightly different age criterion from our own. Black and white are clearly distinguishable though there be indistinguishable shades of grey in between. We do not prohibit white for fear of black provided we can draw a line somewhere or other in the grey area and it may not matter much precisely where in that area the line is fixed.

One-way pressure

Descent down a slippery slope is inevitable only if besides there being no particular intermediate step on the way which has to be seen as a non-arbitrary halting point, there is a predictable substantial one-way pressure to readjust the line downwards (Williams, 1985). Unless this second condition applies, the slippery slope objection has no force. That is why it has no force against the practice of fixing on a precise age criterion for voting rights. We do not anticipate the day when 12-year olds will have the vote, then 6-year olds, then toddlers be on the march for their enfranchisement. In some cases stability may be preserved because pressure on one side of the line is counterbalanced by pressure on the other side, e.g. in the fixing of speed limits or public house opening hours there are pressure or interested groups on both sides of the line.

Does the slippery slope objection apply against the permissibility of withholding life-saving treatment on therapeutic grounds? Let us concede straightaway that whereas there are some clear cases of devastating handicap where, considered in themselves, withholding life-saving treatment appears to be therapeutically justified, e.g. anencephalics, there are other cases where the handicaps sustained by infants do not warrant at all the judgement that lives so handicapped are not worth living, e.g. a child born blind or with cleft palate or club foot, who might also happen to be born with an intestinal blockage necessitating immediate surgery. Between such extremes let us further admit that any line that might be drawn to separate handicaps that are such as to make life not worth living from those not so serious is bound to be somewhat arbitrary. The first condition, then, for the slippery slope objection to have force, applies.

But the second? From whom is the one-way pressure towards withholding treatment for decreasingly serious handicaps supposed to come? From doctors? On the contrary they might be suspected of putting pressure in the opposite direction, there being many things for them to learn, techniques to develop from which to cull research publications, in the course of neonatal treatment. From parents? Might not their disappointment over not having produced a perfect baby or their apprehensiveness over the burdens of care, distort their judgement regarding what would be therapeutically justified? Neither doctors nor parents can be presumed to be disinterested in their handling of the therapeutic question. But possibly in so far as their interests are opposed, stability may be preserved.

In any case we need not leave the doctors and parents to shoulder the burden of judgement on their own. Why should not this responsibility rest with bodies such as Ethics Committees – to issue guidelines as to what degree of handicap might therapeutically justify or even require withholding treatment? I conclude that it is unreasonable to apply the Slippery Slope Objection against the permissibility of withholding life-saving treatment on therapeutic grounds. Ethics Committees should be able disinterestedly to represent the interests of neonatal patients.

Therapeutic assessment

A brief comment on therapeutic assessment in relation to withholding treatment from neonates is desirable.

Do we give enough weight to the ills of treatment as against the benefits of treatment in calculating net benefits? Treatment of neonates with a precarious hold on life, e.g. premature infants too young even to manifest a sucking instinct, may involve measures which impose acute suffering. It is easy to underrate this suffering since the victims at the time (and for a good long time after) are not able to protest.

When David Alton dwells on the horror of what is done to the fetus in the course of late termination (head crushed, body dismembered, etc.) is he wanting to make the (pertinent) point that the fetus already has all the limbs of a newborn baby and looks very like a newborn baby and so should be regarded and treated as already a baby albeit unborn, or is his point (also) that the procedure of termination inflicts appalling suffering on the fetus? If his point is (in part) the latter, it might be argued that the protracted sufferings of some premature infants, in intensive care units undergoing repeated intubations, is incomparably worse than the brief sufferings of fetuses in late termination.

In his study of the attitudes of parents, doctors and nurses to the plight of infants in an intensive care unit, Frohock (1986) remarks how the pain endured by infants is discounted both by doctors and parents on the grounds that they are too young to remember it subsequently. Would we be willing to endure pain provided only we had the assurance that afterwards we would not remember it? Only, surely, if we thought it necessary to endure the pain, e.g. as part of a life-saving treatment for a life worth prolonging. Even then we might not be willing, especially if the pain were severe and would last some considerable time.

People are impressed to hear from severely handicapped adult survivors how thankful they are that they were treated. But their evident present satisfaction does not necessarily vindicate the judgement of whoever treated them. They may be extraordinarily lucky that things have turned out as well as they have; it may have been contrary to all reasonable expectations. If someone, in response to a wager, sprints across a busy motorway and survives to tell the tale and collect his winnings, it does not follow it was wisely done.

In any case, by what right does an adult affect to legitimate with retrospective consent, so to speak, what was done to the infant he was? Does one's later self necessarily have the right to speak on behalf of one's former self? How little the later self may be able to recall (mercifully) of his tortuous beginnings.

Thus far, it has been argued that doctors are not obliged to initiate or persist in life-saving treatment that is not of net benefit to the patient. Let us note that in such circumstances doctors are obliged not to treat. For what business can a doctor have in treating (at least if the treatment involves substantial discomfort to the patient) if the treatment is not therapeutic? None whatsoever, except if the patient has consented, e.g. to be an experimental subject. Proxy consent on an infant's behalf is neither morally nor legally admissible (Re D. (A Minor) (Wardship = Sterilisation), Fam. 185, 1976). It is somewhat disquieting to hear Magdi Yacoub commenting after the infant Hollie Roffey failed to survive heart transplant surgery that: 'Hollie has answered some unknowns for us' and that her parents were 'very keen' that Hollie should undergo surgery, observing that 'if Hollie didn't make it, she would at least benefit others' (Byrne, 1986). The thought that 'no treatment is in vain' is legitimate consolation to the bereaved but no vindication of a decision to treat.

So far we have defended the justification for withholding neonatal treatment which is based on the principle of best interests. Not every condition which is medically treatable ought to be treated. Treatments, even if life-saving or life-prolonging are not always beneficial to patients. In regard to infant incompetents the over-riding consideration in respect of any treatment is whether it is expected to benefit the patient. To treat on any other basis would not only be uncharitable, it would be unjust.

But in defending this basis for withholding treatment are we not endorsing passive euthanasia – arguing that it is permissible to allow seriously handicapped infants to die where that is clearly for their own good? If so, such a defence, it may be said, is morally questionable and surely illegal.

Euthanasia or 'mercy killing'

One often hears it said that doctors already practise euthanasia although it is illicit to do so. Three types of practice are instanced as measures of 'indirect euthanasia' which doctors are said to employ:

(1) administering a death-dealing pain killer;

(2) ceasing treatments that prolong life – 'pulling the plug';

(3) withholding life-saving treatments.

But doctors who follow any of these measures need not do so with *intent* to kill, albeit they *foresee* as a consequence of their so doing their patient's death. If then euthanasia, passive or active, necessarily involves the *intent to kill* it does not follow that doctors who bring about their patients' deaths in these ways are practising euthanasia.

This point is forcibly made by Steinbock (1980) in her article 'The intentional termination of life', wherein she takes issue with Michael Tooley and James Rachels over their interpretation of the 1973 statement from the House of Delegates of the American Medical Association (AMA). This statement begins by condemning the intentional termination of life and proceeds to defend 'cessation of the employment of extraordinary means' to prolong life. Tooley and Rachels both interpret this statement as a condemnation of active euthanasia and endorsement of passive euthanasia. They assume, thus, that ceasing to administer life-saving treatment amounts to passive euthanasia. It does not – though if it did, as Steinbock remarks, the AMA statement would be self-contradictory, both condemning and permitting the intentional termination of human life. To be sure, doctors who cease to administer life-saving treatment are allowing their patients to die and allowing someone to die can be an intentional termination of life; as such it may be as bad as, or worse than, killing someone. But allowing to die is not necessarily intentionally terminating. Steinbock proceeds to describe two types of situation in which ceasing to administer life-saving treatment does not amount to intentional termination:

(1) where the doctor merely complies with a patient's refusal to be treated;

(2) where the doctor judges that the treatment itself is not a net benefit to the patient.

Doctors who cease to administer (or who withhold) life-saving treatment on either of these grounds are not practising passive euthanasia.

Nor, therefore, was the New Jersey Supreme Court's decision in regard to Karen Quinlan, permitting that she be taken off a respirator, an endorsement of passive euthanasia since, as Steinbock notes, the decision was based on the first of the above grounds. I think myself that the Court should have justified cessation of treatment for Quinlan by appealing not to the right of autonomy but rather to the doctor's duty not to impose treatment which is not of net benefit to the patient. In fact, the court followed the regrettable practice of referring to what I have been calling the right of self-determination as the 'right to privacy'. Is it not more perspicuous to relate the latter alleged right more specifically to protection against prying, spying, snooping and the like, into one's personal activities?

I have already argued against extending proxy consent based on a patient's right of autonomy to incompetents whose preferences are unknown. If, as happened in the Quinlan case, this is excused with the argument that any reasonable person in that situation would prefer cessation, this is really an appeal to what is obviously in the interests of the patient masquerading as an appeal to the patient's right of autonomy. Significantly Justice Hughes declares not that 'the preferences' or 'will' of the patient, but that the 'interests' of the patient 'as seen by her surrogate, the guardian, must be evaluated by the court as predominant . . .'.

Whether the traditional teaching, according to which it is sometimes permissible to bring about another's death, as a foreseen consequence, though never permissible to do so intentionally, is a teaching which deserves to be taken seriously, is not a subject which we can settle briskly here. Suffice it to say that the defence for withholding life-saving treatment from neonates upheld in this chapter does not offend against that teaching.

But do those who follow that teaching, then, have to stand by once they have decided to withhold life-saving treatment on therapeutic grounds, unable to make a quick end of a patient's pointless misery, 'letting nature take its course'?

Surely they do not. Firstly, there can be no justification in continuing or initiating other life-prolonging measures which in the circumstances would necessarily be inadequate, e.g. no justification for continuing or initiating artificial feeding – or any other form of invasive treatment which cannot in the circumstances prevent death and in itself involves additional discomfort. Withholding bottle feeds from a newborn baby able to suck is another matter. In these circumstances feeding does not in itself cause more discomfort than relief. Withholding the bottle would not be therapeutically justified; it would constitute neglect.

Secondly, whatever dosage of sedation is necessary to relieve discomfort is defensible even if it is life-shortening – granted the patient is dying anyway.

Whether a doctor who follows these measures on therapeutic grounds and without intent to kill is safe from prosecution is another matter. While there is some dispute among learned judges over the interpretation of intention in relation to homicide, whether the appropriate *mens rea* requires merely that death be foreseen (as a probable consequence) or actually intended, by the accused, they seem generally agreed that intention in law should include at least consequences foreseen as virtually certain: 'A consequence should normally be taken as intended although it was not desired, if it was foreseen by the actor as the virtually certain accompaniment of what he intended' (Williams, 1983).

Now we are concerned here with the plight of a doctor who contemplates ceasing to administer, or withholding, life-saving treatment in situations including those where it is virtually certain the patient will die in consequence. If 'intent to kill' in law includes consequences foreseen as virtually certain, it would appear that this doctor would run the risk of a murder charge.

Williams (1983) suggests three lines of defence whereby doctors might be exempted from liability notwithstanding. Let us consider these.

(1) The patient, it may be argued, was already dead when the doctor ceased to treat. Such a plea is most likely to succeed in regard to the 'brain stem dead' where talk of a beating heart in a dead environment seems apposite enough. More controversial is the condition of patients who, like Karen Quinlan, are irretrievably comatose. Anyhow, as severely handicapped neonates rarely fall into either category, we need not pursue this line of defence further here.

(2) It may be argued that the doctor, in ceasing to treat, is merely permitting death to occur, the death being caused by the patient's illness or injury. This seems to me to be a specious line of defence for a doctor to adopt. Surely, it is the doctor's job to intervene to offset the consequences of injury or illness to patients, so far as that is possible.

J. Farquharson, in directing the jury in R. *v.* Arthur (1981), observed that no-one would say that a doctor was committing an act of murder by failing to operate on a mongol who has a physical defect from which he will die if not operated on. Similarly, if the mongol child gets pneumonia and, the parents not wishing him to be kept alive, the doctor decides not to administer antibiotics, and 'by a merciful dispensation of providence he dies, once again it would be very unlikely, I would suggest, that you (or any other jury) would say that the doctor was committing murder' (Williams, 1983).

This sounds like an invitation to the jury to apply the second line of defence to this case, deeming the cause of the mongol infant's death to be its organic defect (or, in the other example, its illness, pneumonia). But, if so, why is the same line of defence not available if a doctor fails to operate (or administer antibiotic) to a normal child in corresponding circumstances? The latter child would as surely be killed by its organic defect (or illness) if the doctor did not treat. If a doctor would be negligent in the one case and not the other there must be more explanation forthcoming. Farquharson's advice was unsatisfactory; it gave no guidance as to what is a doctor's positive duty (unless there was a tacit reliance on prevailing custom). Not only 'right-to-lifers' should be dissatisfied with this judgement.

While, in the law of homicide, a person who is not under a duty to act to save or protect life will not be regarded as the cause of someone's death even if he has deliberately omitted to succour in order that the person should die, where there is a duty to save or protect life, as with a patient's doctor, an omission resulting in death can be regarded as the cause (Skegg, 1984).

How then should courts decide whether a doctor's omission constitutes a breach of duty? Two tests suggest themselves, one phrased in terms of the distinction between ordinary and extraordinary means of prolonging life, the other according to whether a doctor has failed to do what any reasonable doctor would do in the circumstances.

The former test is less likely to be invoked by the courts partly because it is beset with confusion between whether 'ordinary' treatment is to be construed as treatment which is 'established' or, as treatment which is 'appropriate', i.e. of net benefit for the particular patient.

But confusion dogs the latter more favoured test too. If distinguished and experienced doctors can be found to testify that they do the same as the accused (as happened with Dr Arthur), is the court entitled to presume (as Farquharson seems to have done) that these doctors are being reasonable? May we assume that a practice which is common and approved by eminent practitioners is reasonable?

A more reliable, because more direct measure of reasonableness in the matter is, I submit, whether in the circumstances an omission is defensible on therapeutic grounds – is in the best interests of the patient. This brings us to Williams' third line of defence:

> (3) He raises the question as to what is a doctor's duty *vis-à-vis* his patient: 'A doctor must never do anything actively to kill his patient, but he is not bound to fight for his patient's life for ever. His duty in this respect is to make reasonable efforts, having regard to customary practice and expectations, and in particular having regard to the benefit to the patient to be expected from further exertions.' (Williams, 1983). Does not this amount to a legal endorsement of the defence for withholding, or ceasing to administer life-saving treatment to severely handicapped infants upheld in this paper where the ground for so doing is the patient's best interests.

In re B (A Minor) (Wardship: Medical Treatment) 1 W.L.R. 1421 (1981) the Court of Appeal over-rode parents' wishes that their mongoloid child should not undergo life-saving surgery, L. J. Templeman conceded in principle the legitimacy of withholding life-saving treatment if it is not therapeutically justified but held *that* defence had not been shown to apply in the case of this mongoloid infant whose life prospects if treated were not 'demonstrably awful'.

Granted that treatment of infants (life-saving or otherwise) is not justified morally or legally unless it is therapeutic, compassionate doctors may continue to do what it is rumoured they already do both with a clear conscience and without fear of legal reprisal – provided, that is, that they are exercising their compassion on behalf of their infant patients and not on behalf of the beleaguered parents or families of such infants.

Does there remain a need for legislation to permit euthanasia? Maybe so. But many instances cited as proof of the need are of patients whose sufferings result from life-prolonging treatments that are patently not therapeutically justified. See, for instance, Dr Christiaan Barnard's account of the sufferings endured by his own mother in her terminal illness and of another patient, a Mr Kahn. He instances their plight as evidence of the need for euthanasia. But neither would have suffered had their doctors confined treatment to what was therapeutically justified (Barnard, 1986).

References

Barnard, C. (1986). The need for euthanasia. In: *Voluntary Euthanasia*, eds. A. Downing & B. Smoker. Peter Owen, London.
Byrne, P. (ed.) (1986), *Rights and Wrongs in Medicine.* Oxford University Press, Oxford.
Frohock, F. (1986). *Special Care.* The University of Chicago Press, Chicago and London.
Holland, R. (1980). *Against Empiricism.* Blackwell, Oxford.
Kleinig, J. (1985). *Ethical Issues in Psychosurgery.* George Allen & Unwin, London.
Priestley, F. E. L. & Robson, J. L. (eds.) (1963). *J. S. Mill. The Collected Works*, Vol. XVIII. Toronto University Press, Toronto & London.
US Government (1983). Deciding to forego life-sustaining treatment: ethical, medical and legal issues in treatment decisions. *President's Commission for the Study of Ethical Problems in Medicine and Biomedical and Behavioural Research.* US Government Printing Office, Washington, DC.
Skegg, P. D. G. (1984). *Law, Ethics and Medicine.* Clarendon Press, Oxford.
Steinbock, B. (ed.) (1980). *Killing and Letting Die.* Prentice-Hall, New Jersey.
Williams, B. (1985). Which slopes are slippery? In: *Moral Dilemmas in Medicine*, ed. M. Lockwood. Oxford University Press, Oxford.
Williams, G. (1983). *Text Book of Criminal Law*, 2nd edn. Stevens & Sons, London.

Discussion   Chairman: Dr Raanan Gillon

Harris: Miss Jackson seemed to be arguing that you can act on the patient's best interests but only so long as you do not intend to do so. A lot of the moral impetus was that you should protect patients from suffering but not intend their deaths. She concedes that we may hope for their deaths or know their deaths will result from what you do, but you must not intend their death. It seems to me that If you ought to do all of those things then you ought to bring about their deaths. The one caveat entered was that if a patient miraculously survives, the doctor would not then kill him by other means. That is not plausible because if the doctor is still of a mind that their continuing existence is not in their best interest, causing them terrible distress, then that doctor ought to find another means of bringing about their deaths. If on the other hand the suffering has ceased the situation is different. Professor Campbell mentioned that he was in favour of recommending the law be changed and one of the examples he cited was that he was against the aggressive resuscitation of aborted fetuses. Why not recommend that those fetuses should be killed rather than merely 'not aggressively resuscitated', if that secures their death and avoidance of their suffering?

Jackson: Is this moral traditional teaching, that there is a significant difference between what you do intentionally and what you bring about as a foreseen consequence, something that can be defended? Granted many people think this is an important distinction. Within the restrictions on what a doctor can do, he is still justified in withholding, not initiating, or ceasing treatment when he knows the consequence would be the patient's death. He is not offending against that teaching. If he is really bound by a restriction not to do anything that is not therapeutically justified, this will enable him to manage the caring of a patient in a way which will not prolong their suffering.

Campbell: The difference between a foreseen consequence and an intention is a bit of a smoke screen. While it might be used as a legal nicety of distinction it really is of no practical value whatsoever. As for why one does not kill fetuses where the abortion has not been successful, and this relates also to other infants in prolonged and lingering distress, there is in neonatal units a very important difference between actually killing and allowing to die. This may be of no significance philosophically but is very important psychologically.

Levy: This points to the importance of prevention. We have genetically subnormal infants who could have been spared the agony of being born to die by treatment and biopsies which necessitate experimentation. This would be an outstanding achievement, and it should put considerable weight on the decision to continue experimenting and researching, to prevent such cases coming to life.

Campbell: Of course, one of the major problems of neonatal intensive care units would be solved if somebody could discover the cause of premature onset of labour. One of the anxieties about *in vitro* fertilisation is the production of multiple pregnancies at very low birth rate. If that could be prevented it would be a much more appropriate intervention than at the point of birth.

Pickup: Although there may not be a moral difference between withdrawing and withholding treatment, there is certainly a legal difference because there is a legal difference between an act and an omission. To simply withhold treatment may not be a legal liability but if you withdraw treatment then there will be. There may be a need for legislation, not to interfere with your decision as to whether the baby should be treated or not, but simply to protect you when making that decision and to provide you with a specific statutory defence to the charge of murder.

Campbell: The suggestion has been made, after the Leonard Arthur case, that there would be legislation. The Limitation of Treatment Bill would allow 28 days for the withdrawal of life-saving treatment under an appropriate safeguard.

Pickup: That Bill actually also dealt with the criteria for the decision-making. Is that restrictive?

Campbell: Whereas 15 or 16 years ago we thought the Law should be changed, it may be better without the law getting too involved in this. The law is very conservative and hates setting precedents. It may be more restrictive than appropriate.

Macdonald: I would like to reinforce this crucial watershed between passive and active intervention. It is sensible to withhold treatment where it does not seem helpful but if we were once to take active steps to terminate life then that would be against society as a whole. Future patients would then be afraid of what we were going to do. This debate is absolutely crucial.

A. Murray: I am not sure where this dividing line between active and passive lies. For example, I am mindful of a case where a spina bifida hydrocephalic baby was allowed to deliver vaginally by the breech, controlled at a slow enough rate to ensure that cord pulsation had ceased before the baby was delivered, so that the baby was stillborn. Is that active or passive?

Gillon: One of the things that has emerged is the difference between philosophers, who tend to go very strongly for there being no moral difference between acts and omissions, and the medical profession who feel a very definite moral difference is possible in some circumstances.

Kluge: Decision-making procedure, where it is primarily focused on physicians, runs into serious difficulty. There is agreement, by the Canadian Medical Association and the Canadian Bar Association, that the primary decision-making structure is the parents. If there is any query on the part of the physician, it has to go through the social legislation resources. There is a rather famous case from Alberta, of a doctor who administered a rather large dose of morphine to a radically defective neonate and, although that was legally pursued to some extent the action stopped but was not perceived as painless by the medical profession or those involved in the nursery because life would have been an agonising slow dying process. There are these cases where the distinction, active or passive, is not merely unacceptable philosophically but also as a matter of practice ought to be ignored.

Campbell: The balance of decision-making between parents and the doctors varies according to individual circumstances, and markedly on each side of the Atlantic. In this country the onus of decision-making goes on the doctors. In the USA, many parents now demand to be involved, Here, there is still a tendency for a semi-paternalistic approach where the doctor knows best and is almost required to know best. The parents wish to take no part in the decision-making and still trust the doctor.

Kluge: My experience is Canadian which is closer to the British context than the American both in law and practice. Joseph Magnet and I looked at the sort of situation where it was said the parents do not want to make the decision, and we found this was frequently a professional perception which was not born out when actually analysed.

Jackson: The distinction between the traditional teaching, that it matters whether you bring about a consequence intentionally or as a foreseen result, is not to be confused with the distinction between bringing something about by a doing or by a not doing, by the active or passive. Thus you can bring about someone's death intentionally just as surely by starving them deliberately as by shooting them. Both defenders of the traditional teaching and its critics are misled by this other distinction between doing and not doing.

H. Murray: One of the thoughts coming out is the difference between saving life, which I would have said is obligatory, and prolonging a death, where it is not unethical to withhold useless treatment as long as the child is fed, kept warm, pain-controlled and given affection until death, and not experimented on. Also the future of the child should not entirely be dependent on the reaction of the parents to the child's condition. I would cite the Rochdale case. Here a middle-aged couple gave birth to a child who had Down's syndrome and also a convoluted bowel, which is not uncommon in such children. The operation for a convoluted bowel is a fairly simple one without which the child would pretty soon die. The parents would not give consent for this because they wanted the child to die. The child was made a Ward of Court and operated on and came to foster care. Social Services were absolutely flooded with offers to adopt that child. It is certainly a thing worthy of consideration when one puts such weight on the wishes of the natural parents.

Botros: Miss Jackson said that withholding treatment is not euthanasia, based on the distinction between foreseeing and intending. Then she says that it is all right not to treat where treating would not be a net benefit and that is not euthanasia. With any case of euthanasia, there still has to be some justification for not treating.

Botros: I am still not too pleased with the idea of treatment, 'which is not of net benefit', because underlying that is the 'quality of life' judgement. It is very difficult not to argue that the object is to procure death.

Gillon: Where the probability of an outcome is high, even if it is the undesired outcome, then the distinction is specious. At the same time it does not seem to be a problem where the probability is very low.

   Therefore it seems to be another of these fuzzy border problems; at one end of the spectrum it becomes a bit peculiar, morally speaking, to say, 'I did not intend it but I knew 100% that it was going to happen'. If, on the other hand, the probability of a death is 1% and the treatment that is being given is quite clearly beneficial, then to say, if death occurs, 'Yes I'm sorry, I did not intend it and it was rather unlikely that it was going to occur', seems to be of considerable moral distinction. Perhaps the problems arise because of not considering probability issues.

Singer: Although there is certainly a difference between action and omission in law, where there is a duty to care, an omission can certainly lead to criminal charges, the charge of murder. Certainly a doctor has a duty to care and is not safe from murder charges simply because death results from omission. Professor Campbell thought it was the best interest of the child that ought to be the standard that prevailed. Sometimes he referred to the best interests of the child and family. In the case of the fetus from the abortion, it could be argued that the best interests of the fetus are to live although it is not in the interests of the mother. I do not see the reason for taking only the interests of the child involved. The interests of others affected should be considered.

Campbell: I agree. I do not see why the interests of the child necessarily should over-ride all other interests in a family, for example with a severely handicapped infant.

Jackson: You said that overwhelmingly you found it the case that properly counselled parents gave a very considered and careful judgement of what is in the best interests of the child. Ultimately the question is: 'What is in the best interest of the child?' The reason you attach weight to the parents is that they are the best people to assess that. Does the decision whether to treat or not depend simply on the interests of the child, or if they happen to be in conflict with the family's interests should they be over-ridden?

Campbell: I think it is a matter of weighting.

Smith: A great deal of the practices within the units are affected by the Ethics Committees. Professor Campbell was quite sceptical about the present constitution of these committees.

Campbell: I was talking about the USA where these committees are in being in over half the hospitals. In this country Ethics Committees devote their time to problems of research. Similar committees to those in the USA can be helpful in certain circumstances. As constituted in some American hospitals they involve fiscal, administrative and legal interests of the institution that are not necessarily related to the child and the family.

Lilford: The philosophical objection to the difference between active and passive killing ignores the *symbolic* importance of that distinction. This has an immensely powerful influence. There is a moral force to symbolic actions.

Millican: If there is an obligation to treat extreme prematurity and if the moral status of the fetus is acquired at conception then we ought to do everything we can to prevent spontaneous abortion. This particular combination of views is untenable, the consequences would be immense. Miss Jackson was saying that where somebody had not had the opportunity to express interest and desires we could not bring in considerations of autonomy. What about a case where we are pretty sure that a child, when it grows up, is going to have certain views, for example, if it were born into a particular religious community?

Jackson: Enthusiasts for autonomy and the right of self determination will not agree that you can predict attitudes from the kind of society that someone is born into. The importance of autonomy in our context is that you are respecting the wishes of the patient by withholding treatment. I do not see how you can project ahead for an individual.

Spillane: 'Hi-tech' treatment does not necessarily equal good health care and these treatments themselves are creating moral dilemmas. It is something that we have to consider when discussing other things. The presumption that more research is going to give us answers to moral problems we are creating with other technologies is not good logic. For example with infertility problems the questions 'Why do they happen?' and 'What about prevention?' should be brought into the debates on *in vitro* work.

Part 4

Termination of pregnancy

The notion of the potential human being

The question of the moral status of human embryos has already been treated here by Professor Dunstan. The present chapter, adapted from a longer French essay (Fagot-Largeault & Delaisi de Parseval, 1987), tackles the same question again from another perspective. How should we conceive the status of embryos, in order to allow ourselves the possibility of making thoughtful ethical decisions about termination of pregnancy?

Termination is undoubtedly intended killing of beings who undoubtedly belong to the human species.

In many countries nowadays *early* abortion has been made legal (though the notion of 'early' varies considerably: up to the tenth week in France, up to viability in England). This means that early fetuses are less protected than later ones. Very early (pre-implantation) human embryos get no legal protection at all. Implanted embryos, within the legal delay for abortion, are weakly protected, to the extent that abortion laws set weakly dissuasive conditions on the right to terminate. Later fetuses are protected, except in the case of a 'therapeutic' problem certified by the medical profession.

Protection, however, does not mean 'rights'. In no country, so far, have human fetuses been granted the full constitutional rights attributed to persons.

Saying that abortion is legal does not amount to saying that it is ethical. However, the legal distinctions are in agreement with common intuitions such as the intuition that late abortions are morally worse than early ones. Should this not be a deep conviction we would not strive to improve the techniques of prenatal diagnosis, so as to make them available earlier and earlier during pregnancy. Legal distinctions are also in agreement with the common intuition that the termination of a defective fetus is morally more acceptable than the termination of a healthy fetus of the same age.

We do have some intuitions about not every abortion being morally the same, and not every reason for abortion being equal (*cf.* Sowle Cahill, 1987). We also have conflicting intuitions, for example about letting some frozen spare embryos evaporate or keeping them frozen indefinitely, or about contragestion. When the 'abortion pill' (mifepristone), a progesterone antagonist that prevents gestation (if taken before implantation), or induces chemical abortion (if taken later) was marketed in France, some people worried (CCNE, 1987) that this was going to make abortion decisions too easy (implying that an easy chemical abortion would be morally worse than a surgical abortion), whereas the women who were on the drug trial felt that this chemical abortion was preferable to surgical abortion and probably not much worse than oral contraception (Couzinet *et al.*, 1986). Finally, in some cases we have ambiguous feelings, as with respect to the selective termination of one or a few of too many fetuses successfully implanted in the course of an *in vitro* fertilisation (IVF) programme.

The point I want to make is that the notion that the fetus is a potential *human being*, as the Warnock Report (1984) suggested, or a potential *person*, as was stated by the French National Ethics Committee (CCNE, 1984) is a useful philosophical notion to give a rationale to our intuitions and decisions about termination of pregnancy.

The European Parliament has expressed the view that human embryos are endowed with human dignity, even though the respect due to them may not encompass the full rights of persons (Recommendation 1046, 1986). Why do we think that the human person is entitled to respect? What do we reckon is the source of human dignity? There is no philosophical consensus on this. There are roughly two kinds of answers, using two kinds of criteria for personhood: biological (natural) criteria, or ethical (cultural) criteria. They characterise positions at both ends of a spectrum of intermediate positions. I shall first contrast them, and show that neither allows us to make the moral distinctions I suggested we need to make.

Take the biological criterion. Assume that a *sufficient* condition for human dignity is human organic life of an individual being. Such a life is there from the moment of conception. So, the early human embryo has exactly the same human dignity as the late fetus, or the newborn infant, or any adult.

This is the position advocated by the Roman Catholic Church: 'From the moment of its conception, the life of any human being must be absolutely respected' (*Donum vitae*, 1987). It implies that termination of pregnancy is murder, exactly like infanticide, or like using means of contraception (such as the IUD) which inferfere with implantation. It also implies that selectively terminating a defective fetus, when a serious anomaly (such as major thalassae-mia) has been diagnosed, is as indefensible as terminating a healthy fetus, and that terminating a defective fetus, however severe the defect may be, is always morally worse than letting it come to term. Furthermore, it implies that no scientific research aimed at the acquisition of new knowledge should be carried out on human embryos or fetuses. Indeed, the Roman Catholic Church declared that one should only experiment on animals. That is a very coherent

position, even though one is not sure why the respect for life should not extend
to all forms of life (it takes a theological argument to make this point). At any
rate, here we have a clear universal rule: 'do not terminate' and a firm limit:
'from conception on'.

Take now the ethical criterion. Assume that a *necessary* condition for human
dignity is moral autonomy. Further, assume that what constitutes the human
person is his/her capacity to be responsible for his/her own decisions.

This was Kant's criterion and it is substantially the criterion of personhood
used by neo-Kantian philosophers, such as Engelhardt (1986). In that perspective, obviously a fetus or embryo is not a person. Even a newborn infant is
not yet a person. You become a person during your childhood, as you become
conscious of your own identity and start acting as a subject, with his/her own
sense of what you want (or do not want) to do (or be done to you). Such a
position implies that terminating a late fetus, or even a newborn infant (a point
forcefully made by Tooley, 1983), is no more objectionable than using any
means of contraception, or contragestion, or than terminating animals. It also
implies that any kind of research on human embryos, or fetuses, or fetal tissues,
is permissible.

However, in this perspective, you owe an absolute respect to actual or future
persons. It means that you should not interfere with the parents' decision to
terminate or not, as you should not interfere with the decisions of responsible
researchers using fetal tissues with the consent of the aborting woman (unless
you pay for the research, which may entail a right of control that nothing is done
that you do not want done). On the other hand, if you choose to let a fetus
develop and be born, you are responsible towards the person it will become.
Letting a defective fetus come to term, at the risk that the future person will not
want what you wanted for him/her, may therefore be morally worse than
terminating the defective fetus.

Here the general rule for termination decisions is: 'the choice is with the
pregnant woman', for no actual person should be coerced to act against her own
will.

Such a position has the advantage of being tolerant of a wide variety of moral
choices. It emphasises the moral obligation we have to respect the choices of
other persons. The main difficulty, as I see it, is that it does not make clear *when*
exactly a human being is, or is not, a full person, nor *who* is entitled to decide
that someone is, or is not, capable of acting as a responsible subject. Yet for the
termination problem this difficulty does not arise so long as the mother is
presumed to be an autonomous adult. Of course, there is the question of the
extent to which the community should provide the facilities for abortion, but if
there are safe methods at a reasonable cost (as may be the case for
contragestion), they certainly should be available.

What the two positions just sketched have in common is that, although they
have different ontologies for personhood and yield different rules of action,

they end up saying that from the point of view of the respect due to persons, all the options we mentioned about terminations of pregnancy are morally equivalent (be they all bad or all acceptable): taking the pill, or taking mifepristone at the end of each cycle, or having an early or late surgical abortion, or letting a healthy or handicapped newborn infant die before it has been registered as a legal person. This makes one feel uneasy, because it goes against our common intuition that these are not morally equivalent and because we are left without any reason to discriminate between options.

Of course, tentative propositions have been made from either point of view to move the limit and make the implications less rigid.

Some Christian theologians have argued that conception may not be the relevant threshold, for a condition necessary to be a human subject is to be one individual, and since until the end of the second week one embryo can become two or more individuals, the person proper might not be there until biological individuation is irreversible (Bondeson *et al.*, 1983, Section V). This would make the use of IUDs, or of mifepristone early after conception, tolerable within the first perspective.

On the other hand, some pychoanalysts have speculated that late fetuses do make decisions (to terminate themselves or to be born). This would justify extending human rights to newborns and late fetuses, from the second point of view.

But, in order to make carefully thought-out termination decisions, it is of little use to move a threshold forward or backward. We need to recognise that the progressive development of an embryo and fetus from one cell to a full human person is a continuous process and that (as in all biological processes of growth) there are identifiable cases of 'abnormal' development. Given this evidence, any attempt at setting a general threshold must be arguable.

Warnock (1987) advocated taking a pragmatic line. We do not need, she said, to decide when exactly the embryo or fetus becomes a person, or what we mean by a person. We need to put limits on what may be done to human embryos. Our limits will always be arbitrary. But is is important to appreciate that we can set limits, even though arbitrary. As is well known, the Warnock Report (1984) proposed that experimenting on embryos should be permissible up to the 14th day. There are other examples of pragmatic rules. Thus, the French association of obstetricians has defined a professional ethics for late abortions of defective fetuses. Roughly, 'therapeutic' abortions are acceptable in cases where the defect is severe and not curable; they are not acceptable in cases where the defect is light or curable (Maroteaux *et al.*, 1984).

Is there a rationale behind such pragmatic rules? Far from being merely pragmatic and arbitrary, Warnock (1987) referred to some kind of ontology, for the 14 days limits were justified by saying that, at that stage, the embryo is 'only a bunch of cells'. So, she took into account what she thinks *is there*.

When the French National Ethics Committee came up with the notion that the human embryo is a 'potential human being' (CCNE, 1984), the Roman

Catholic bishops retorted, as they did in England to Warnock, that the embryo is not a 'potential human being', but a 'human being with a potential' (cf. La Documentation Catholique, 07 04 1985, pp. 392–401). The CCNE maintained its notion of a potential human being (CCNE, 1986). One might be sceptical that an old philosophical concept like the concept of potentiality could help resolve the issue. (This is discussed in detail in *Bioethics*, Special issue: Human Embryo Experimentation Vol. 2 No. 3, pp. 187–253, 1988). The concept of potentiality takes us back to Aristotle. Aristotle used it as a rather descriptive notion to mean that when a living entity develops, although it is the same entity (organism) developing throughout, in the process of development some things are actualised at some point, that were not there before. Take for example the heart of the embryo: first, it is not there (it is only potential), then it is there (it is actual).

How is this relevant to our ethical discussion of termination? Kuhse & Singer (1985) said in a rather crude way, somehow reminiscent of Aristotle, that in its early development the human embryo has the moral status of a lettuce or other vegetable, then with organic differentiation it takes the moral status of an animal and, later on, finally it acquires the status of a rational being. The CCNE (1986) had a more cautious approach, perhaps unconsciously reminiscent of Thomas Aquinas. It views our moral obligations towards fetuses from two sides.

Our moral obligations towards this individual fetus can only be obligations towards what is actually there. There is no moral duty not to inflict suffering when the capacity to feel pain is not there. There is no moral duty to respect autonomy when the capacity to make autonomous decisions is not there.

Is there a moral obligation toward the potentials? Yes. However, we do not know the particular potentials of this individual; we can only estimate in some cases the reduction of potential deriving from a diagnosed actual defect. This may justify (or not justify) the selective termination of a particular defective fetus. Otherwise we know the potential *only generically*. We know that it is a human potential. We do not necessarily want every human potential to actualise (we do not want every ovum to be fertilised). What we may want is the human potential to be respected as human. What can this mean? We know that no person can develop properly without a proper human environment. So we may want this particular fetus to be treated in a way that inspires a respect for the idea and dignity of the human race, so that no person will live in an environment where human dignity is offended. That does not imply that termination decisions should be prohibited. What it implies is a humane way of acting: we shall not throw the embryo away with the garbage, because is it *not* just a bunch of cells, these are human cells, and the way we treat human cells is symbolic of the way our culture goes and of how we treat humanity.

This has been an outline of a tentative analysis of what respect for a potential human being may mean. This position implies that we do not have a general moral rule for termination decisions. Our decisions should be sensitive to what we know scientifically and medically about the biological development of embryos and they should be informed of the particulars of each situation. Thus, we cannot *a priori* state that termination is right or wrong. Of course, from a number of particular choices we will be able to generalise and say that as a rule we shall tend to act this way or that. We must, however, accept the possibility that such generalisations be only provisional and may change with time, a point made by the CCNE (1985), and a disquieting one. This position implies (an implication again reminiscent of Aristotle) that expert judgement may be a better moral judgement, to the extent that it is better informed, which may warrant a certain amount of paternalism.

One difficulty of an Aristotelian type of ethics is that it is open to a confusion between what is normative (ethical) and what is normal, or that it tends to see our moral wisdom as possibly inspired by the wisdom of nature. That seems to be the theoretical price to pay, if we want a rationale for the selective termination of some embryos or fetuses.

References

Bondeson, W. B., Engelhardt Jr, H. T., Spicker, S. F. & Winship, D. H. (1983). *Abortion and the Status of the Fetus*. Reidel, Dordrecht.
Comité Consultatif National d'Ethique pour les sciences de la vie et de la santé (CCNE) (1984). Avis sur les prélèvements de tissus d'embryons ou de foetus humains morts à des fins thérapeutiques, diagnostiques et scientifiques & Avis sur les problèmes éthiques nés des techniques de reproduction artificielle. *Rapport 1984*. La Documentation Française, Paris.
Comité Consultatif National d'Ethique pour les sciences de la vie et de la santé (CCNE) (1985). Avis sur les problèmes posés par le diagnostic prénatal et périnatal. *Rapport 1985*. La Documentation Française, Paris.
Comité Consultatif National d'Ethique pour les sciences de la vie et de la santé (CCNE) (1986). Avis relatif aux recherches sur les embryons humains *in vitro* et à leur utilisation à des fins médicales et scientifiques, suivi d'un Rapport scientifique et d'un Rapport éthique. *Rapport 1986*. La Documentation Française, Paris.
Comité Consultatif National d'Ethique pour les sciences de la vie et de la santé (CCNE) (1987). Avis sur l'utilisation de la mifépristone (RU 486). *Rapport 1987*. La Documentation Française, Paris.
Couzinet, B., LeStrat, N., Ulman, A., Baulieu, E. & Schaison, G. (1986). Termination of early pregnancy by the progesterone antagonist RU 486 (mifepristone). *New England Journal of Medicine*, **315**, 1565–70.
Donum vitae (1987). *Instruction sur le respect de la vie humaine naissante et la dignité de la procréation*. Editions du Cerf, Paris.
Engelhardt Jr, H. T. (1986). *The Foundations of Bioethics*. Oxford University Press, Oxford.
Fagot-Largeault, A. & Delaisi de Parseval, G. (1987). Les droits de l'embryon (foetus) humain et la notion de personne humaine potentielle. *Revue de métaphysique et de morale*, **3**, 361–85.

Kuhse, H. & Singer, P. (1985). *Should the baby live? The problem of handicapped infants.* Oxford University Press, Oxford.

Maroteaux, P. *et al.* (1984). A propos de l'Avis du CCNE sur le diagnostic prénatal et périnatal. *Archives Françaises de Pédiatrie*, **41**, 445–8.

Sowle Cahill, L. (1987). Abortion pill RU 486: Ethics, rhetoric and social practice. *Hastings Center Report*, **17**, 5–8.

Tooley, M. (1983). *Abortion and Infanticide.* Clarendon Press, Oxford.

Warnock, M. (chairperson) (1984). *Report of the Committee of Inquiry into Human Fertilisation and Embryology.* HMSO, London.

Warnock, M. (1987). Do human cells have rights? *Bioethics*, **1**, 1–14.

Wrongful birth

Introduction

The ethical problems surrounding prenatal screening and termination of pregnancy can be approached from two very different perspectives. One of these involves establishing the moral status of the human embryo which is a necessary precondition to understanding what one might be entitled to do to, or with it. This problem I will not address here, both because I have examined it extensively elsewhere (Harris, 1985) and because it forms the subject of other contributions to the present proceedings (Chapters 1.1 and 4.1).

The other perspective involves examining the question, not of whether or not we might be entitled to kill the fetus, or indeed experiment on it, but rather that of whether or not we are sometimes morally justified in bringing it into existence or in allowing it to continue in existence.

This problem also has two distinct dimensions. The first involves examination of potential children for their adequacy as children; and the second involves examining potential parents for their adequacy as parents. Or, to put the point another way, one dimension of the problem involves asking the question as to whether we might do wrong by bringing particular children into existence because of problems relating to what one might call the constitution of those children and in virtue of which we might expect them to have less than adequate or satisfactory lives. The second concerns the question of whether we might do wrong by permitting children to be brought into existence who will suffer from less than adequate parenting.

So the issue of prenatal screening has two distinct dimensions. There is the issue of prenatal screening of potential children and there is the practice of prenatal screening of potential parents.

The prenatal screening of potential children is becoming more and more common and more and more effective. We can now screen for all sorts of disorders from Down's syndrome and spina bifida to Huntingdon's chorea and AIDS. This process will often result in termination of pregnancy where screening gives warning that a child will, or will probably, be handicapped or be at substantial risk of developing a disorder. In what follows, I will say something about whether and why such practices are ethical, if they are. Certainly, these practices presuppose a view about what is a reasonable quality of life for a child to be born with, or to expect, or a view about what quality of life it is reasonable to inflict on a child when we can avoid so doing by terminating pregnancy.

But it is not only embryos or indeed potential embryos that are screened. As I have suggested, there is another and equally important dimension of prenatal screening – it involves very often the screening of parents.

The recent House of Lords decision on sterilisation is a case in point (Re B, 1987, 2, [All Eng.] p. 207 & T. v. T. 1988, 1 [All Eng.] p. 613.). In this case, Jeanette, who was described as having a mental age of about 5, was sterilised at the instance of her mother on the grounds (among others) that she was unsuitable as a parent. Now this decision, and other recent cases in which mentally handicapped young girls have been sterilised or have had abortions ordered by the courts, have all involved judgements about the fitness of those girls to be parents.

Judgements to the same effect (though of course far from similar) are made when candidates, for example, for *in vitro* fertilisation are turned away on grounds that take into consideration concern about their quality as potential parents.

These and other cases challenge the supposed right to found a family, a right which is protected by Article 12 of the European Convention on Human Rights and by Article 16 of the Universal Declaration of Human Rights. I will be returning to these issues later.

Our question then is: Are there any constraints upon who should be allowed to be a child and who should be allowed to be a parent? In what follows I will try briefly to say something in answer to both these questions.

I should add that I shall not try simply to set out the arguments on all sides and leave the question open. I shall try to argue towards a conclusion. If you do not like or accept the conclusion that I reach so much the better – for my hope is that you will be provoked to find different and better answers on the basis of different and better arguments.

But even the arguments towards the conclusions that I reach will be sketchy at best – my priority is to show the ways in which the problems surrounding selective termination are really instances of a much larger and broader problem, that of who should determine the fitness of children to be children and of parents to be parents and of what might even approach respectability as grounds for so doing.

I shall begin by considering the problems associated with prenatal screening and try to say something about the underlying principles that might justify such screening and one of its consequences: namely the abortion of embryos found to be defective in some way. I shall then briefly consider the question of screening parents for their suitability as parents.

Prenatal screening

Can we do wrong by bringing children into the world?
It is usually assumed in discussions of abortion that the only moral issue is
whether or not it is justifiable to abort a viable fetus – whether that justification
is seen in terms of women's rights, or in terms of protecting the health of the
mother, or in terms of what is sometimes called the moral status of the fetus. It
is not usually thought that the person who decides not to have an abortion, who
decides to go ahead and have a child, might be doing something culpable.

One reason for this is the great attraction of having children. Without
commenting on the rationality or indeed on any other element in the cogency of
such a desire, there can be no doubt that having children is almost universally
acknowledged to be one of the most worthwhile experiences and important
benefits of life. This is perhaps why people do not usually think that there might
be any necessity to justify their decision to have children or to explain why they
have chosen to have an abortion. This is also perhaps why it is the case that, if
someone wants to have a child, we usually think that they ought to have every
assistance; and perhaps also why people have sometimes thought in terms of the
right to found a family. But might we do wrong in founding a family? Let us
pursue this a bit further.

Mill's argument
A classic formulation of the strongest argument against the freedom to reproduce is perhaps still that of John Stuart Mill (1972).

> It still remains unrecognised that to bring a child into existence without a fair prospect
> of being able, not only to provide food for its body but instruction for its mind, is a
> moral crime, both against the unfortunate offspring and against society.

Now of course the crimes to which Mill refers are relatively easily remedied, as
Mill is himself aware, for he continues:

> if the parent does not fulfill this obligation, the State ought to see that it is fulfilled, at
> the charge, as far as possible, of the parent.

So that we need not prevent people from reproducing themselves but merely
ensure that their children are properly educated and cared for. However, the
powerful argument that Mill introduces involves the idea that on can harm
people by bringing them into existence under adverse conditions. And this leads
us on to the question of just how, precisely, are we to characterise the moral
crime that we might commit by bringing children into the world in less than
favourable circumstances?

What is the wrong that we do?
To consider this question we will have to do an experiment. Not perhaps
the sort of experiment that one might expect from medical science. This
involves an experimental technique familiar in philosophy since at least the time

of Plato. It is a thought experiment. This technique involves inventing, some-times annoyingly fantastical, examples in which we can so manage the variables as to enable us to concentrate on just the question at issue. It is the problem of managing the variables that sometimes makes the examples seem so fantastical – so called 'desert island' examples – but our present thought experiment is fantastical only in the sense that the examples presuppose unknown medical conditions and undeveloped medical science. They derive from the philosopher Derek Parfit (1976).

Parfit's argument
Parfit invites us to consider the actions of two different women:

> The first is one month pregnant and is told by her doctor that, unless she takes a simple treatment, the child she is carrying will develop a certain handicap. We suppose again that life with this handicap would probably be worth living, but less so than normal life. It would obviously be wrong for the mother not to take the treatment, for this will handicap her child . . .
>
> We next suppose that there is a second woman, who is about to stop taking contraceptive pills so that she can have another child. She is told that she has a temporary condition such that any child she conceives now will have the same handicap; but that if she waits three months she will then conceive a normal child. And it seems (at least to me) clear that this would be just as wrong as it would be for the first woman to deliberately handicap her child.

Now, we can describe the actions of the first woman as acting in the best interests of her child, what she does prevents *that child* from becoming handicapped. To fail to take the treatment would be to deliberately handicap her child, to take the treatment is in her child's best interests.

However, the same seems not to be true of the second woman. For either there is no child whom she benefits by her action, because, when she takes the treatment, no child exists that she can thereby benefit, or, it is in the interests of the child that she can conceive this month that she does so and that it thereby comes into being. If she postpones pregnancy and takes the treatment she damages the interests of this child for she removes its only chance of existence.

There is a considerable and important philosophical problem as to how precisely to characterise what's going on here. For clearly the second woman can and does benefit her child by taking the treatment.

The first alternative – that because no child exists at the time she takes the treatment the mother does nothing that benefits her subsequent child – is false. Both women can have healthy children as a result of their decisions, both women take steps which result in their having healthy children, two healthy children consequently exist. The actions of the two women are therefore morally equivalent and both have children each of whom have benefitted from their mothers' decisions (*cf.* Parfit, 1984).

The second argument raises more problematic issues. The suggestion is that the second woman injures (or damages the interests of, or acts maleficently towards) her child by postponing conception and pregnancy and thereby causing the child not to exist. But, since the child is as yet unconceived it does not exist anyway. Moreover, and more importantly, it never will exist, and for both these reasons cannot be harmed. Therefore, like the first women, this mother acts in the best interests of her child – the child that will exist as a consequence of the actions she takes.

However, this explanation seems to be to be suspect. As Parfit (1984, p. 489) persuasively argues: 'Unlike never existing, starting to exist and ceasing to exist both happen to actual people. This is why we can claim that they can be either good or bad for these people.' This raises the question of when someone can properly be said to start to exist. Thomas Nagel, whom Parfit quotes with approval says: 'All of us . . . are fortunate to have been born. But . . . it cannot be said that not to have been is a misfortune'. However, the second set of dots in this quotation provided by Parfit are significant for they indicate a missing proviso. Nagel (1970) added the qualification that: 'unless good or ill can be assigned to an embryo, or even to an unconnected pair of gametes, it cannot be said not to have been (born) is a misfortune.'

Now Nagel clearly thinks that embryos and unconnected gametes do not mark the start of a person. If we take a rich conception of what it is to be a person this is of course true. By 'rich' I mean a conception of the person which sees persons not merely as co-extensive with humans but rather which attempts to understand what makes for personhood, what makes persons distinct sorts of individuals. On such a conception it will also be implausible to think of the person starting at birth (Tooley, 1983; Harris, 1985). But, in the sense in which it might begin to make sense to talk of one's actions benefiting a particular person, it is surely implausible not to think of the egg which eventually becomes a person as the start of that person.

There are now over 1000 babies, who will, or will have become persons, who will have cause to thank Robert Edwards and Patrick Steptoe for their beneficial interventions. The gathering of the particular egg and its fertilisation *in vitro* marks the start of the life of Louise Brown and the things that were done prior to conception, to the egg that became Louise Brown, were actions which she has good cause to regard as having been beneficial to her. So that, while Nagel was correct to be doubtful as to whether good or ill can be assigned to an embryo or even to an unconnected pair of gametes, good or ill can be done to the person those gametes will become and that good or evil is done while that person is at the gametes stage.

Starting to be a person

There is an important theoretical point at issue here which also, as we shall see, may have some practical importance too. To explain this point we must go back to Nagel. The point of saying that: 'all of us ... are fortunate to have been born. But ... it cannot be said that not to have been born is a misfortune' is simply that while those of us who were born, exist to be fortunate and to benefit from coming into existence, those who are not born do not exist to suffer the misfortune of non-existence. So that to cause someone to exist is to benefit that person, but to cause someone not to exist by failing to bring them into existence, harms no-one: for the simple and sufficient reason that there is no-one who suffers this misfortune. Again as Parfit (1984, p. 489) says:

> When we claim that it was good for someone that he was caused to exist, we do not imply that, if he had not been caused to exist, this would have been bad for him. And our claims apply only to people who are or would be actual. We make no claims about people who would always remain merely possible. We are not claiming that it is bad for possible people if they do not become actual.

But of course once someone has started to exist, then it might be bad for them to be caused not to eixst. I say 'might' be, for to understand what this might mean we need to say more about the idea of some things being bad for someone, and also more about the nature of the someone that it is bad for.

Briefly, either a person starts to exist in the sense of starting to be capable of benefiting from things done or not done to her, when the egg is first identifiable (I do not beg the question as to whether an individual's life literally begins at all, or rather whether it is more correct to say that life is a continuous process with the individual gradually emerging) or a person starts to exist at the point at which the developing (human in this case) individual becomes a person in some rich conception of the person.

It looks very much as though Parfit is committed to the first conception of the start of an individual's existence, although he is ambivalent to say the least as to when to date the start. Immediately following his approving quotation from Nagel which seems to date the start of life at birth, Parfit continues:

> ... if it benefited me to have had my life saved just after it started, I am not forced to deny that it benefited me to have had it started. From my present point of view there is no deep distinction between these two. It might be denied that it benefited me to have had my life saved. But, if this is claimed, it becomes irrelevant whether causing someone to exist can benefit this person. I ought to save a drowning child's life. If I do not thereby benefit this child, this part of morality cannot be explained in person affecting terms.

It seems clear that Parfit believes that it does benefit me to have my life saved immediately after it started and he insists, rightly it seems to me, that if this is so, then it would be strange to say that it did not benefit me to have had it started. And this is consistent with my denying that it would have harmed me had my life not started at all – for there would then have been no-one who suffered this harm. But, on this view one should date the start of *a life* (as opposed to *life*) at the first point at which one can identify an individual whose life can be saved.

To return for a moment to Louise Brown, if the egg that became Louise Brown would have died had it not been 'harvested', then Louise Brown benefited, in person, from that harvesting and from the subsequent fertilisation *in vitro*. In person-affecting terms, Louise Brown was favourably affected by those acts. both in the sense that they were acts done to her and in the sense that the person who developed from that egg also benefited.

Now, if this seems strained, we have to identify the strain. One possibility is of course the strangeness of calling an unfertilised human egg in a laboratory dish, 'Louise Brown'. Of course we identify a particular egg as 'Louise Brown' with the benefit of hindsight. But so far from being a disadvantage, it is notorious that hindsight is the most accurate vision of all – 20/20 every time. But the point is this. If Louise Brown did not start to exist as an egg, then when did she start to exist? This is not the place to rehearse all the possibilities. Birth is clearly a non-starter. Nagel talks about a brief period of premature labour as being the only period before birth that one could sensibly claim the same person to have started to exist, but, unusually for Nagel, this is a hopelessly primitive view. There can be no significance in birth as the start of the individual person – her life can have been saved a thousand times prior to birth and we are on the verge of an era in which individuals will grow to maturity without every having been 'of woman born'. If we regress from birth, through the development of the embryonic brain, past the formation of the primitive streak and past conception towards the identification of the individual egg, we cannot avoid the problems of morally significant person-affecting actions and omissions at every stage.

One alternative is to try to identify criteria for personhood in a rich sense, and argue that person-affecting only begins when we have a person properly so called (Tooley, 1983; Harris, 1985). The problem here is that the person obviously benefits from things done and omitted to be done to the potential person.

Harming and benefiting actual people

If we distinguish between human individuals who are potential persons and human individuals who are actual persons then we may find a defensible asymmetry between the various benefits and harms that may befall such individuals. Failures to benefit a potential person, or harms done to such an individual which result in its death, are harms to that potential person but are not harms to the person he might have become because that person does not exist at the time the harm is done and will in fact never exist. In this respect causing the death of a potential person is morally on a par with failing to bring a person into existence. Whereas benefits done to the potential person which save her life are benefits to the actual person she will become if and when that person starts to exist.

This may sound just a trifle like sophistry, but it is an approach which solves a number of problems and at the same time can be defended by at least one plausible approach to the question of what constitutes a person properly so called? Firstly, it solves the problem which so concerned Parfit, that of how to explain why causing someone to start to exist benefited them while failing so to do did not harm them. And of course it solves that problem in a way precisely parallel to the way Parfit solves the related problem. Secondly it performs the further task which Parfit's account looked as though it could not perform. That is the task of explaining our different reactions to abortion and perhaps also to infanticide on the one hand, and to murder on the other (Singer, 1976; Tooley, 1983; Harris, 1985). It also allows us to explain the moral symmetry between the actions of the two women considered earlier and indeed permits the drawing of distinctions and conclusions that are to come. Finally it does not simply rely on an appeal to intuition or on the utility of the account in solving certain problems, but more significantly, it is an account that can be defended.

What sort of beings are persons?

I cannot attempt a complete defence here but I can sketch the lines of such a defence. Most current accounts of the criteria for personhood follow John Locke in identifying self-consciousness coupled with fairly rudimentary intelligence as the most important features. My own account (Harris, 1985) uses these but argues that they are important because they permit the individual to value her own existence. The important feature of this account of what it takes to be a person, namely that *a person is a creature capable of valuing its own existence*, is that it also makes plausible an explanation of the nature of the wrong done to such a being when it is deprived of existence. Persons who want to live are wronged by being killed because they are thereby deprived of something they value. Non-persons or potential persons cannot be wronged in this way because death does not deprive them of anthing they can value. If they cannot wish to live, they cannot have that wish frustrated by being killed. So that creatures other than persons can be wronged in other ways, by being caused gratuitous suffering, for example, but not by being painlessly killed. This explains the difference between abortion, infanticide and murder, and allows us to account for how we benefit persons by saving the lives of the human potential persons they once were, but at the same time shows why we do not wrong the potential person by ending that life, whether it be an unfertilised egg or a newborn infant.

On this account, the life-cycle of a given individual passes through a number of stages of different moral significance. The individual can be said to have come into existence when the egg is first differentiated. This individual will gradually move from being a potential person into an actual person when she becomes capable of valuing her own existence. And if eventually, she permanently loses this capacity, she will have ceased to be a person.

We can now return to the two women in Parfit's example and to the issue of the ethics of prenatal screening.

The avoidance of needless suffering

Consider now a third woman. She is 18 weeks pregnant and has an amnio-centesis test. The results show that her fetus has spina bifida and she is offered a termination. She decides to terminate her pregnancy and try again for a healthy baby.

According to the arguments so far developed this woman acts in a way which is morally equivalent to the actions of the other two women. Like the second woman she decides not to actualise a potential person who will be handicapped, in order to have a healthy child at a later date. Both choose adversely to affect a potential person in being, for the sake of a future person. If we assume that all three women eventually have healthy children then the moral consequences of the policies adopted by all three women are the same. I am assuming the moral and causal isomorphism of acts and omissions, for which I have argued elsewhere (Harris, 1980).

If we want to say that the three women considered so far have all acted rightly and, indeed, that the courses of action chosen by each are morally equivalent must we also say that they would be wrong not to have acted as they did? Clearly the answer must be 'yes'.

If each of the three women has acted rightly, how do we characterise the actions of the three women? Each and all of them have chosen to try to bring into the world a healthy rather than a handicapped child when it *appeared* (the second and third women may have failed) to them that they had a choice. What then is the wrong of bringing a handicapped child into the world that these women and countless real counterparts choose to avoid doing so if they can, and regard themselves as acting for the best?

I want to suggest that the wrong they all try to avoid is the wrong of bringing needless suffering into the world. Each decided that when faced with the choice between having a healthy or a handicapped child they should choose to have a healthy child. Each could satisfy their desire to have a child without bringing into the world a child that would necessarily suffer. None wronged anyone, all benefited someone.

But when is suffering needless? Consider now the case of a fourth woman.

The fourth woman

The fourth woman is pregnant and is told that the child she is carrying will be born handicapped. Moreover, that unfortunately any future children she has will also be born with the same handicap. If she is to have children at all they will be handicapped and no prenatal nor postnatal treatments are available to ameliorate the handicap. We deliberately do not specify the severity of the handicap.

Are our intuitions the same? Do the good arguments that the mothers in Parfit's first two cases had for taking steps to avoid bringing a handicapped child into the world still hold for the mother who can only have handicapped children?

First we should notice that this woman cannot claim that an abortion would be in the best interests either of the child she is carrying or of any child that she will have in the future. For so long as the handicap is not so great or so terrible that it would be better for this potential person or indeed anyone with such a handicap that she had never been born, then it is in the interests of the child she is carrying to be born.

So that if this fourth woman decides to go ahead and have her child even though it will be handicapped, she is acting in the best interests of that child. Moreover, unlike the other three women, she would not be doing wrong in bringing avoidable suffering into the world. Any suffering that her child experiences due to its handicap is unavoidable just in the sense that she can have no child that will not be subject to such a handicap and whatever suffering goes along with it. This fourth mother wrongs no-one in having a handicapped child because it is in that child's interests to be born, she benefits that child by continuing her pregnancy and although the child will inevitably suffer, it will have a life worth living and such suffering as it will experience is unavoidable. Like the first three women she wrongs no-one and benefits someone.

We have one final case to consider, that of the woman who chooses to abort her pregnancy but not to have further children.

The morality of abortion

This case is easily dealt with. We do not need to consider why this woman wants an abortion. There is no risk of handicap, and she will not 'replace' her aborted child with another at a later date. This mother wrongs no-one and benefits no-one. She wrongs no-one because in ending the life of the fetus she deprives the fetus of nothing that it can value and she benefits no-one by bringing them into existence. I am ignoring the various people, other than the fetus or potential person, that the mother might wrong in having an abortion, for example, the father of the fetus who wants to have a child or members of the Society for the Protection of the Unborn Child, who may be outraged.

Interim conclusion

We can then come to an interim conclusion about the morality of selective termination and more generally about the morality of bringing individuals into the world.

I want to suggest that the rationale that unites and explains our intuitions about the various cases we have considered is that it is wrong to bring avoidable suffering into the world. One consequence of this conclusion is, of course, that the decision to go ahead and have a child requires as much and as careful justification as the decision to terminate a pregnancy and that it can also be wrong not to terminate a pregnancy.

We have recognised the powerful desire and the strong interest that people generally have in having children. Just as this desire should be exercised responsibly we should also be careful not to frustrate it without good reasons.

If children are wanted, it is better to have healthy children than to have handicapped children where these are alternatives, and it is better to have handicapped children than to have no children at all.

In suggesting that it is wrong to bring avoidable suffering into the world and in indicating that suffering is avoidable where an individual who is or will be handicapped can be replaced with an individual who is not handicapped I have assumed that replaceability is unproblematic. That is to say, I have assumed that if a woman delays conception or terminates one pregnancy in order to initate another pregnancy later, that this course of action will be successful. Now clearly many things can and do go wrong with pregnancy. Miscarriage is common and a host of other problems are more or less probable in any pregnancy. If, for good reason, it appears to a particular woman, perhaps because she is nearing the end of her childbearing years, that she is unlikely to be able, for example, to replace an established pregnancy with any reasonable probability of success, then in such a case if the child she is carrying will be handicapped she is entitled to regard that handicap as unavoidable.

Existential value

Before continuing I must make one point very clear. None of this means that healthy, or unimpaired, or non-handicapped or non-disabled children are better in any existential sense than those with disability or handicap.

If I say, as indeed I would, that I would prefer not to lose say a hand, that it would be better for me if I did not lose one of my hands, that I would be better off with both hands, and so on, I am not committing myself to the view that if I did in fact lose a hand that I would therefore and automatically become less morally important, less valuable in what I am calling the existential sense, more dispensable or disposable than you.

I have a rational preference not to lose any of my limbs, I have a rational preference to remain unhandicapped and I have that preference for any children I may have. But to have a rational preference not to be disabled is not the same as having a rational preference for the non-disabled persons.

Screening would-be parents

We have looked at the circumstances in which children or potential children are screened when questions arise as to whether it would be ethical to bring them into the world or to allow them to continue in the world. We must now look briefly at a parallel case in which it is the parents who are screened for their adequacy as parents. But as in prenatal screening the parents are screened not, so to speak, for their fitness to exist or continue to exist as persons but simply as parents. The concern here, as in prenatal screening, is with the quality of life of the children who are or may be in their care.

There are a number of different sorts of cases in which such screening takes place. There are the sorts of cases that have come before the courts in which very often it is mentally handicapped girls who are subjected to compulsory sterilisation or even compulsory abortion. These cases raise difficult issues, some of which have to do with autonomy and consent, some of which have to do with the rights of the handicapped and some of which turn on the question of what constitutes reasonable circumstances into which a child might be permitted to be born. All of these are too difficult to discuss in any detail in the space and time remaining, and many of these issues have been addressed at length elsewhere (Hirsch & Harris, 1988).

There are of course also the cases of routine screening of adoptive and foster parents which are far from unproblematic and raise fundamental issues of principle which are seldom discussed. And which again will not be discussed in their peculiar detail now.

Equally, those whom one might term 'established parents', those who have had children, are often screened by social services and other individuals and agencies with the possibility of losing custody of their own children. And recently there has been at least one case where such screening by social services has been carried out on a woman of eight months gestation who was at that stage judged unfit as a potential parent and warned that her child would be taken into custody when it was born.

All of these cases raise fundamental issues about the right to found a family and the criteria for adequate parenting. However one increasingly common form of prenatal screening of parents has been little discussed and it is to this that I would like to devote rather more attention in the remainder of this chapter before trying to draw some general, and I am afraid very swift, conclusions about the legitimacy of screening parents and selective termination of the right to found a family.

It is common for those administering *in vitro* fertilisation (IVF) programmes to screen parents as to their suitability. Not only as to their suitability to benefit medically from the procedures, but as to their suitability as parents *per se*, and as to their moral claims on a scarce resource. It is instructive to look at the criteria

employed by one major centre for IVF. This centre was the first National
Health Service clinic providing IVF and was established at St Mary's Hospital,
Manchester. The following criteria (Lieberman, 1988) are those employed at
this clinic and there are points in common with those in use at other centres
around the country. I should make clear that these are the criteria for being
admitted onto the waiting list for IVF, and it is of course not certain that those
admitted to a waiting list will eventually be treated.

(1) Women must be less than 36, men less than 46.

(2) Couples must have lived together for 3 years.

(3) No children living with the couple.

(4) No major physical or psychiatric illness.

(5) Evidence of regular ovulation.

(6) Couples not accepted if a male factor is the sole cause of infertility.

(7) Ovaries accessible to laporoscopy or ultrasound.

(8) Live in North West Health Authority Region.

(9) Female close to ideal body weight for height.

(10) Must not have had more than two complete courses of IVF or 'GIFT'
     treatment elsewhere.

(11) Must fulfill adoption criteria.

I should make clear that only heterosexual couples are considered but of course
by no means all of these. Excluded are heterosexual and even married couples,
couples who may have reached the far edge of their fertility, single parents, and
gay couples, and of course couples who have children living with them, even if
those children are not their own genetically.

Each of these criteria is worthy of detailed examination and each raises many
interesting issues of principle. However, it is clear both from the criteria
themselves and from the gloss that has been offered on them, that they are all
designed to achieve three separate aims. First there is the aim of selecting
among superabundant candidates for a scarce resource. Second is the aim of
gaining maximum benefit in terms of successful outcomes (children) from the
use of that resource, and finally there is a concern with the quality of parenting
that would result.

While it may seem on the face of it that each of these are legitimate and even
worthy aims, let alone essential ones in the case of allocating a scarce resource, I
believe that they are either illegitimate as aims or as means of achieving
legitimate aims.

Having made these extravagant claims, I am going to attempt to substantiate only one of them. I have discussed resource allocation elsewhere (Harris, 1987).

Should we screen parents?

The 11 criteria used for selection of candidates for IVF reveal a number of assumptions about adequate parenting. These can be separately identified as follows:

(1) Adequate parenting requires two parents, one of each gender.

(2) Adequate parenting requires parents to be under 65 years of age while the children are still at home.

(3) Adequate parenting requires that neither parent have major physical or psychiatric illness.

(4) Adequate parenting requires stable relationships between the parents, evidenced by three years cohabitation.

I know of no evidence for the truth of any of these criteria, indeed I know of no reliable evidence for any criteria of adequate parenting that can be applied to potential parents rather than to actual parents who have proved their inadequacy in objective ways. Indeed some of these criteria are scarcely plausible.

But suppose for a moment that there was sufficient evidence in favour of these criteria to make their use defensible. If this were the case then we should certainly not only apply them when candidates for a scarce resource come forward. We should apply them to any and all candidates for medical assistance with reproduction. General practitioner advice is probably the commonest form of medical assistance with procreation and it should certainly be withheld from anyone not meeting defensible criteria. As should the prescription of drugs such as clomiphene and other methods of assistance with ovulation or fertility. The use of drugs to support established pregnancies should be withheld from unsuitable candidates for parenting and so on.

It is irrelevant that these resources are cheap and plentiful, when compared with IVF, for if the grounds of selecting candidates are their adequacy as potential parents, this does not improve in proportion to the cheapness of the treatment.

But, more significant still, if we had any confidence at all in this, or indeed in any other prospective criteria of adequate parenting, we would be criminal to apply them only in these marginal cases. If we were at all serious about preventing inadequate parenting and permitting only sound potential parents to procreate, we would not, as we do, let any Thomasina, Dorothea or Harriet go out and have children without so much as a 'by your leave'. Remember that screening candidates for IVF let alone adoptive or foster parents is a tiny and numerically insignificant proportion of the population of parents.

The alternatives seem to be these. Either we believe that we have adequate and defensible criteria for adequate and inadequate parenting and it matters that people demonstrate their suitability for parenthood in advance, or it does not. If it does, then we should licence parents, all parents. If it does not, then we should not do what amounts to victimisation and apply indefensible criteria to the few unfortunates that need assistance with procreation.

The reason we do not in fact attempt to licence all parents is not because we could not, but because there are good reasons not to. Some of these good reasons have to do with the inadequacy of speculative criteria about good parenting. But more importantly they have to do with the importance and value that most people attach to the freedom to have children coupled with our reluctance to place the comprehensive powers that licensing would involve in the hands of anyone at all, whether that person be some central authority or an individual doctor or social worker.

But these powers would be unnecessary for we already have the only reliable method of protecting children from inadequate parenting. We simply remove children from the custody of parents who have palpably illtreated or placed in danger their children, and disqualify potential parents who have proved their unfitness by a history of damaging or mistreating their children.

In short there is only one reliable criterion for inadequate parenting and it is easy to apply – you just count the bruises or their equivalent. I do not pretend that this solves the problem of curelty to particular children, because it may not be the parents who are responsible for the harm and it may be extremely difficult to find out just who is responsible.

Conclusion

Just as in the case of screening potential children for their adequacy as children we found that while happy and healthy children were better than unhappy or handicapped ones, handicapped children were better than no children at all, so in the case of screening parents. After all, the justification for screening parents is the same as the justification for screening children. It is that we ought not to bring avoidable suffering into the world.

New parents can very often choose to replace the child who would have been born handicapped with one who will not, whereas children cannot replace defective parents so easily – not at least when those children are not yet in existence.

The important differences between prenatal screening of children and prenatal screening of parents seem to be these:

(1) There are no reliable predictive criteria for inadequate parenting.

(2) While there is evidence that children do suffer disadvantage from suboptimal parenting when that is defined in socioeconomic terms, the therapy of choice would be to work on the socioeconomic conditions rather than depopulate the world. For this reason I will say no more here about this type of suboptimality.

(3) Even if there were reliable predictive criteria of good parenting, the moral consequences of denying parents equal opportunities to reproduce are worse than the consequences of allowing some less than optimal parents to reproduce.

If parents want children of their own they should have every assistance with childbearing which is consistent with the like assistance for all other citizens. This means, where resources are scarce, distributing those resources in ways which do not discriminate against parents of the grounds of dubious allegations as to their adequacy as parents.

To fail to carry out prenatal screening and to decide to decline selective termination where the circumstances make it inevitable that avoidable suffering will thereby be brought into being, is to act wrongly precisely because it causes avoidable suffering. Similarly, if we screen parents for their adequacy as parents in advance of their being or becoming parents, then since there is no evidence that this prevents suffering to children and there is plenty of evidence that it causes suffering to the potential parents this is also wrong and for the same reasons, namely that it causes avoidable suffering.

References

Harris, J. (1980). *Violence & Responsibility.* Routledge & Kegan Paul, London.
Harris, J. (1985). *The Value of Life.* Routledge & Kegan Paul, London.
Harris, J. (1987). QALYfying the value of life. *Journal of Medical Ethics*, **13**, 117–23.
Hirsch, S. & Harris, J. (eds.). (1988). *Consent and the Incompetent Patient.* The Royal College of Psychiatrists, London.
Lieberman, B. (1988). Paper presented to the MA Health Care Ethics Course, University of Manchester.
Mill, J. S. (1972). On liberty. In: *Utilitarianism*, ed. M. Warnock. Fontana, London.
Nagel, T. (1970). *Mortal Questions.* Cambridge University Press, Cambridge.
Parfit, D. (1976). Rights interests and possible people. In: *Moral Problems in Medicine*, ed. S. Gorovitz. Prentice-Hall, Englewood Cliffs, NJ.
Parfit, D. (1984). *Reasons and Persons.* Oxford University Press, Oxford.
Singer, P. (1976). *Practical Ethics.* Oxford University Press, Oxford.
Tooley, M. (1983). *Abortion and Infanticide.* Oxford University Press, Oxford.

Discussion   Chairman: Simon Lee

Serr: The fertilised ovum as regards contragestion with prevention of implantation (this *may* be the mechanism of the intrauterine device but has been shown most probably not to be the case) is very similar to the spare embryo in an *in vitro* fertilisation programme. If they are either frozen or not used then they are in a similar position to the fertilised ovum going through the tube which is denied implantation. Therefore it is in a different regard that we should consider this as a life or potential or embryo.

Fagot-Largeault: What is not similar is the case of the embryos when too many implant successfully and you use fetal reduction. Our intuition is that it is not the same because we did not have to replace that many in the first place.

Holm: John Harris, we should not bring needless suffering into the world. If we make a small excursion into what Parfit calls moral mathematics, it could mean where there may be any needless suffering, for instance if this fetus were known to be myopic, the mother should be obliged to have it aborted.

Harris: If the child would be myopic unless the mother takes a simple form of therapy, she would be wrong to decline that therapy. To fail to do so would be to bring needless suffering into the world. I do not think there is a difference between that case and the women who aborts for that reason if she chooses. Of course conception is a problematic business and it may not be easy to replace this embryo with another one. If that is so that would make this suffering not avoidable.

Fagot-Largeault: If I choose to abort a fetus with Down's syndrome I am not sure it is to avoid putting into the world someone who will suffer. It is my suffering that is in question not his.

Harris: I was using 'suffering' as shorthand for a whole range of disadvantageous conditions. I do not mean literally being in pain or being in discomfort.

Spillane: I was not convinced that you were not making a moral heirarchy between lives worth living: 'the handicapped life was worth living but less so than if the handicap were not there'. The scenarios that you picked were based on a certainty that does not really exist. There have been examples in the States where women declined a Caesarean section recommended to avoid some serioius disability and the baby was normal.

Harris: I do not have to be committed to a view that if a person ought to take steps to avoid those things happening either to themselves or to those they care about that it follows that if those things do happen those persons are less existentially valuable.

Gillon: I wanted to pursue the difference between considering what an embryo *might* become and considering it as an embryo that 'will become'. That is quite a crucial distinction. If one divides the persons that will exist or do exist, and the persons that might exist, but will not exist, we have different moral obligations to the two. So far as the first is concerned we have obligations to them as persons even before they come into the world as persons. When you are intending that your embryo develops into a person you have obligations to it as if it already were a person. That is in no way to say that if you intend it not to become a person you have the same obligations as though it were, and therefore you can quite consistently abort an embryo before it becomes, or indeed experiment provided it actually ceases existence before it becomes a person.

Harris: If you are clear that you want this egg to develop into an embryo and then into a person, then you must not do things to the egg that would be bad for the person it will become.

Jackson: Dr Fagot-Largeault, commenting on the Warnock Report, suggested there was an inconsistency. First saying 'We were not going to be drawn by at what point does the developing human life become practically a human being?' and then referring to the embryo before 14 days as a mere clump of cells. That is not necessarily inconsistent. With a developing human life we may say quite definitely it is not actually a human being when it is only a clump of cells, obviously a human being at 18 months, and just not be drawn on the intermediate stage. You made remarks about the symbolic significance of how you treat an embryo or fetus aborted, putting it in the bin or flushing it down the drain or that sort of thing. These sorts of things are very culture-relative.

Hoyte: The gynaecologist may have to refuse a termination if he believes the request to be outside the existing law. The philosophers are not there to help him then and he makes that decision alone and as the appointed representative to society. What are the subsequent moral obligations of the doctor, and indeed of society, towards the parents and the child when they prove to have a less than ideal existence?

Harris: My views are that they should provide support in those circumstances. I think there will be agreement about that. There would not be agreement that since you do not wrong an embryo or fetus by ending its existence at any stage of its development, there is no wrong in abortion and therefore abortion ought to be permitted on demand. That is not to say that I approve of abortion – quite the reverse.

Somorjay: On the question of needless suffering, alarm bells started ringing for me at the early mention of the word 'adequacy'. Many decisions are now made on social and subjective criteria. The birth of a handicapped child might bring nothing but joy, whereas the birth of a normal child might bring nothing but sorrow because there are all sorts of outcomes both for normal children and handicapped children. Normal children might in fact bring much more sorrow than the handicapped child which you might have terminated.

Harris: That position is only tenable if you think this – you have this handicapped child and it is bringing you lots of joy, and somebody comes along with a complete cure – they can entirely remove the handicap and you say: 'No I'm not going to allow you to do that because it's bringing me too much joy'. Unless that is a defensible position, while what you say is true, it is not an argument against anything I have said.

Fetal brain cell transplants. The Ethical Committee decision

I shall be discussing the structure of an Ethical Committee and the factors it took into consideration over the matter of fetal brain cell transplantation.

As Chairman of The Medical Staff Committee at the Midlands Centre for Neurology and Neurosurgery since 1984, I was also the Chairman of the Ethical Committee which has considered a number of projects. Our Hospital Ethical Committee consists of three members of the consultant staff nominated by the division, a lay member appointed by the Community Health Council, a General Practitioner appointed by the Local Medical Committee, a Nursing Officer and an Administrator. We have never had a vote and what we have tried to achieve is consensus. If anybody had expressed a very strong view about any project then we would probably not have allowed it. There would have to be unanimous backing of any project, although there might be varying degrees of enthusiasm.

Ethical committees had a splendid birth. A book was published called *Human Guinea Pigs* (Pappworth, 1967) about outrageous human experiments conducted on both sides of the Atlantic, which caused considerable anxiety. The Royal College of Physicians set up a Sub-Committee and wrote a paper on The Ethics of Clinical Research in Institutions. In 1975, the Department of Health and Social Security (DHSS) published a document requiring every District Health Authority to set up an Ethics Committee.

The idea is not to form an authoritative ethical view but to get the feelings of those who work in the same institution. On the committee there is nobody who is particularly experienced in ethics. The general idea is to arrive at an opinion as to whether a project is sufficiently satisfactory to live with it.

In June 1987, Professor Hitchcock asked us about firstly adrenal and then fetal transplantation for the treatment of Parkinson's disease. Many of you know a great deal about the disease. It was only described in 1824 and its clinical manifestations are so gross that it is diffiuclt to believe that it was not around before. It may very well be a disease of pollution and the Industrial Revolution. It is caused by death of the dopamine-secreting cells in the brain stem and the manifestations are the 'shaking palsy' – tremor together with difficulty in moving and considerable rigidity of the mask-like face.

There are a number of drugs that can help a great deal but after a few years nearly everybody has breakthrough symptoms. The drug regime and proper advice about how to look after themselves enable most sufferers to cope reasonably well for at least ten years. After that there may be a lot of problems. These people may have a very difficult life in which they are unable to care for themselves, dress themselves or feed themselves, and may be very severely crippled. Many are old and it may be part of generalised cerebral atrophy. Some are young and may have single-system disease. For these we felt quite strongly that if any method could be found to help them we should support that method.

The New England Journal of Medicine published a report from Mexico about a successful adrenal transplant. This gland secretes dopamine but also secretes a number of other neurotransmitters. Implanted into the correct place it gave excellent results for two out of about ten patients. This is very impressive indeed. We gladly gave our permission for this to be approached on an investigative basis.

We are told that fetal cells in early pregnancy are not antigenically stimulating and in the brain seem not to have a rejection problem. This is the first advantage. The second is that they do not secrete the other neurotransmitters, such as adrenalin and noradrenalin, that adrenal cells do. There was a good deal of animal work to support these theoretical advantages. By the time we gave our permission for fetal brain cell transplants the procedure had already been carried out in China and Sweden as well as in Mexico.

In Wisconsin, work is done on the implantation of fetal pancreases into children with diabetes. This work is still going on despite the NIH withdrawal of governmental approval because apparently it is privately funded.

We felt strongly, therefore, that the use of fetal meterial in this way was entirely justifiable, as far as our patients were concerned, so long as there was informed consent. There was detailed informed consent and the patient understood perfectly that this was an investigative procedure and knew the pros and cons. I may say that such is the parlous state of the patients that there was a fair amount of enthusiasm for this technique. With regard to the use of fetal material for experimental purposes, the Peel Committee (1972) laid down recommendations: inspection of sources of fetal material, a licensing procedure and a fairly rigid recommendation that there should be a separation of users from the source of the cells. Clearly there will be no sort of pressure on any hospitals or doctor, or indeed any individual, to supply a fetus or cells for the purposes of research. The research, of course, is mostly in virology and in various forms of cancer research. Ethically it seemed to us to be very similar to cadaver transplantation and the ethics to be the same. No more and no less. Our discussion centred upon abortion and we were aware that this was not within our remit. We were all rather unhappy about the present working of the

Abortion Act in this country but this was not part of our remit and nothing that we could do anything about. We did not discuss maternal consent for a number of reasons. Firstly the separation of users of the tissue from the source had been emphasised and it did not seem right to disturb this. Secondly, we learnt that the pregnant women do sign a consent form saying they have no views as to the disposal of the fetus and allow its use for research. The third reason is that the hospital staff at the Midlands Centre of Neurosurgery have a great deal of experience in the problems of donor transplantation. We have a lot of brain deaths and provide organs for transplantation. We felt that the ethical problems of fetal transplantation were very much easier than these. They pose fewer difficulties given the country's present abortion policy.

The resultant publicity rather surprised us in its intensity. Much of the critical comment has been rather muddled suggesting that the fetus would be grown especially for transplantation. This is, of course, not a probability or even a possibility.

Of letters we received on this, only two out of some thousands have not been extremely supportive. We have also been telephoned by a number of pregnant women offering their fetuses.

References

Pappworth, N. (1967). *Human Guinea Pigs*. Routledge & Kegan Paul, London.
Peel, Sir J. (chariman) (1972). *Report of the Committee on the Use of Fetuses and Fetal Material for Research*, HMSO, London.

Fetal brain cell transplants. One gynaecologist's view

[As explained in the Foreword, clarifications of some of the points raised in this chapter are interpolated in the text at the relevant points. *Eds.*]

By way of introduction I would like to say that I am not going to argue the case against transplantation as such. I would also like to say that these thoughts have been prepared at short notice and most of my information has been gleaned from media coverage of this topic. I would like to divide what I say, just discussing basically theoretical objections and then moving on to perhaps the practical ones.

Theoretical objections

Over-riding the whole discussion, of course, is really the question of abortion. It is interesting that, in the light of the current debate around David Alton's Bill, the general public, quite apart from doctors who should know better, are appreciating that the pregnant women is indeed carrying, albeit miniature and albeit dependent on its mother in special way, another human being. We cannot escape that. Whatever we have heard from the philosophers or however we argue it, as we work backwards from the child, to the neonate, through the latter stages of pregnancy, to the middle trimester, early pregnancy, we really cannot pinpoint any specific event. We could consider birth but as we have heard, we might one day have artificial placentas. We could talk about the event of implantation. But these are stages of development and where you actually put your beginning of life (whether it is the entry of the sperm into the egg cell or at the fusion of the pronuclei) I am not going to argue here. I am simply going to state that although abortion is legal that does not make it right and I believe that abortion is wrong.

Now I would like to move on to take up a point raised by Professor Hitchcock's work and by Dr West here. I do not believe that something good can come out of what actually is morally wrong in the first place. I do not believe that the ends justify the means. It is all well and good for Professor Hitchcock to say that he is unhappy with abortion but since these fetal brains and here, let us use them.

I would like to move on to discuss Dr John Dawson's remarks made on television and his distinction between embryos, for instance, that are produced deliberately for research and those that happen to be spare. I think it is a very fuzzy distinction. If you are practically involved in an IVF unit and you are supervising these embryos in a freezer, can you really distinguish between ones that happened to be left over and the ones that may have been created deliberately. What is the difference actually? As Dr West has intimated, there could come a point where this loss of distinction might be extended to fetuses. The thought is abhorrent that women would deliberately become pregnant in order to offer their fetuses. We have just heard that women have been ringing up saying that their fetus could be used in this way. They did not deliberately get pregnant this time to do that but there is a very fine dividing line. We could imagine the niece of a man with Parkinson's disease who, if there was a shortage of fetuses, might feel that it would be a self-sacrificial and a good thing to do to get pregnant to provide a brain to help him.

I would like now to move on to the question of consent because this has been raised and discussed in free communications at this conference (Dalton & Bromham, 1988). Normally, when talking about kidneys, for instance, it is an adult rational person who actually carries a donor card or gives consent prior to death, or it may be sought from the relatives. If we are talking about a kidney or a heart being used from a child then obviously it is the parents who give their consent. I would like to refer to the Peel Report (1972) here which makes distinction between a viable fetus (note, this could include anencephalics because they may be alive at birth) and one which is not. The Peel Report states that if the fetus is not viable then consent is not normally required. I would like to take that point up in a minute when we go on to discuss the more practical aspects

Finally, under the theoretical aspects, I would like to raise a point that I have simply gleaned from the newspapers and it is again a theoretical objection although one that could probably be sorted out. There is obviously some dispute amongst neurosurgeons themselves as to whether this treatment is actually a good treatment. Now obviously medical progress through the decades has been challenged by this kind of objection. When kidney transplants were first done there were objections, similarly with the first heart transplants. There might be objections simply because it is new and people do not know whether its going to work.

Before I leave the theoretical objections and perhaps just recapping on the question of consent. It is interesting that in Sweden where they have apparently hammered out some guidelines, maternal consent (that is the mother of the fetus) is sought and it is laid down that the person donating the fetus and the person receiving the tissue should not be related.

[British Medical Association Guidelines have been published since the conference (*British Medical Journal*, **296**, 1410, 14 May 1988) and on this point recommend that 'There should be no link between the donor and the recipient'. *Eds.*]

Practical objections

Moving on then to the more practical objections. My first, as a gynaecologist, refers to the mode of abortion. Perhaps Dr West can clarify? Are intact whole brains required? How are you going to get those at 8 to 10 weeks? Usually at 8 to 10 weeks you are doing a termination that results in brains coming out all mashed up. So presumably we are talking about hysterotomy specimens?
[WEST (responding from floor): I do not know. My only source is *The Sunday Times* (17 April 1988, *Eds.*) where we are assured that they are not. We have been taking pains to separate ourselves from the source. This is for obvious practical reasons. If I am asked where it is from I can lay my hand on my heart and say, 'I do not know'.]
[Professor Hitchcock has since clarified this matter. He is able to use the products of a standard vacuum aspiration termination. *Author.*]

We all know how fragile an 8-week-old fetus is, and we have all seen the normal methods of termination with fetuses of this age, so I would like to know how on earth they get an intact brain with a normal abortion method at 8 to 10 weeks. I have read that hysterotomies are being done. I cannot see how you can do a hysterotomy, as opposed to a suction termination, without the consent of the woman. Obviously one is exposing the patient to much greater risk with the former operation. I wondered whether some of these were perhaps combined with sterilisation; we should not combine the two procedures given the increased risk of deep vein thrombosis and pulmonary embolus.

Another very practical point is that has been raised is that it isn't just Parkinson's disease that may be treated be fetal brain cell transplants. We are also talking about Alzheimer's disease and post-measles encephalopathies, for instance. Now this is huge number of people in our population. My colleague, Nigel Cameron, informs me that he heard at a recent conference in Finland that it is estimated in Sweden that they are going to need 20 000 fetal brains a year for this kind of work. I just do not know what sort of numbers we are talking about in this country. Can you use one brain for several patients, or indeed *vice versa* do you need several brains or one brain per person? If it is just a matter of transferring cells perhaps one brain may be used for more than one patient.

I assume that you need a very fresh brain. Obviously autolysis and tissue breakdown occurs very quickly after abortion and presumably you cannot use tissue from spontaneous abortion, both because the fetus has been dead for a while and because they are probably damaged in the course of miscarriage.

Presuming that fresh brains are needed, and accepting the report in *The Times* that hysterotomy specimens were used, I would like to draw attention to the Peel Report, paragraphs 41 & 42, which makes a very fine distinction between whether the fetus is alive at birth or whether its not. Paragraph 42 refers to the non-live fetus and says that we do not need consent to use its tissues. I would maintain that, if you are lifting a fetus out of a uterus at 10 weeks, it is actually alive at the time.

The gynaecologists here, and I certainly have, may have operated on the occasional tubal pregnancy which had not yet ruptured resulting in the death of the embryo. I have myself in such an operation actually held a fetus in the palm of my hand at 8 weeks and seen the little heart beating away through the transparent chest wall. I do not know whether any of you have experienced it. You realise that this thing is alive and there is nothing you can do to save it, obviously you had to do the operation to save the woman. In a hysterotomy you are lifting the fetus out of the uterus. It is alive until you clamp the cord and you are not going to do anything to the fetus, to disrupt it physically, because you want an intact brain. You want it extremely fresh and the Peel Report makes the comment that where we are dealing with a live fetus, and this would include anencephalics as well as these early ones, you do actually need maternal consent.

Regarding consent I might just quote from paragraph 42 of the Peel Report: 'there is no statutory requirement to obtain the parents' consent to this research but equally there is no statutory power to ignore the patients' wishes'. So I suppose the kind of consent form referred to has, in a blanket fashion, covered all eventualities.

The Peel Report disapproves of a close liaison between the supplier of fetal tissue and the user. Who actually dissects the brains in these cases and where is that done? Well, the Peel Report says that the dissection of the fetus should not be on the same premises as where the abortion is being performed. I would call it a rather sinister relationship between the neurosurgeon waiting to grab the tissue and the gynaecologist providing it. In other forms of transplantation it is often the same surgeon who goes and gets the heart, heart/lung or even the kidney. They would rather take it out themselves and then put it into the recipient. Obviously this cannot be done in the case of the gynaecologist who really has to be doing the operation. The ordinary transplant surgeon is not responsible for the death of the donor.

Lastly, very briefly, I would just like to express my slight disquiet about commercial interests. I know this does not apply so much in this country but there is transport of fetal material and sale of fetal material on the continent and one worries and wonders about commercial interests even here. Peel himself refers to this and he says here, and this is 1972, that there is public disquiet about the use of fetuses and fetal material and people who have been influenced in part by the suggestion that financial transactions are involved.

In conclusion, then, I would just like to argue the case for a complete moratorium on this kind of work while there is time for adequate public discussion and debate and obviously a consensus will emerge. People like me will remain in the minority, I am sure, but at least we will have a chance to voice our opinion.

References

Dalton, M. & Bromham, D. (eds.) (1988). *First International Conference on Philosophical Ethics in Reproductive Medicine – Abstracts.* University of Leeds, Leeds.
Peel, Sir J. (chairman) (1972). *Report of the Committee on the Use of Fetuses and Fetal Material for Research.* HMSO, London.

Discussion   Chairman: Raanan Gillon

Gillon: There is a useful approach to analysis that depends on looking at principles; respect for autonomy, beneficence and non-maleficence and justice. If one is trying to analyse this particular problem there are three categories of human entities to consider. The first is the potential recipient of the brain transplant, the second is the fetus and the third is the donor or mother of the fetus. I do not think there is much moral problem about the recipient. The person's autonomy is respected, there is a reasonable balance of potential benefit over harm in the proposal and it is just, in the sense that distribution of resources are not unjust in the case and the rights of the person are not over-ridden. As far as the mother of the fetus is concerned – is her autonomy respected in the sense of her consent being obtained, consent being an autonomy-respecting obligation? It seems to me that the answer given by the Ethics Committee Chairman is that it has, in the sense that she has signed a form saying that she has no interest in what happens to the aborted fetus. Whether or not mere signature of a form is sufficient for real respect for autonomy it is a genuine opportunity to say 'YES I do have an interest'.

As far as the woman is concerned, Dr Sims has asked whether a more dangerous form of abortion has been performed which is certainly something to be taken into the moral balance. So far as justice is concerned, if her rights are respected and there are no distributive justice issues no problem arises.

The problems arise on the question of the fetus – what the moral status of the fetus is. On your answers to that question will turn so many of the moral conclusions to be developed. For those who believe that the fetus is one of us, morally speaking, then it is unacceptable to do the abortions in the first place. Whether, having done the abortion, some good can be salvaged or not turns on precisely the question: 'Are you prepared to try to derive good out of bad or is this so wrong that you must not condone it by using the 'material' that derives from it?' If you believe that the fetus is not a person, and it is morally legitimate to do the abortion, not very much remains in the way of a moral problem about using tissues for the benefit of others. If you do not believe that it is legitimate to do the abortion you are going to have to find some very special moral justification to say that it is not justifiable to implant it into others.

Robinson: I am not against termination of pregnancy or research. However, I think it is quite inadequate to have only one lay member on an Ethics Committee. You did not discuss consent. Ethics Committee members have to be able to publicly justify the decisions they take. I would not have been prepared to justify such a decision as yours. Pregnant women had signed a consent form saying that they had no wishes about the disposal of the fetus. That has never been part of the normal abortion consent; in whose interests was that form produced? When a woman is going for a termination it is very difficult for her to say no to anything. Another issue is this tissue tested for the AIDS virus. It is equally wrong to carry out that test on the woman without her knowledge and consent. This fetal brain tissue is going to build into a market of enormous commercial value. Once women realise what the issues are they are going to be very angry indeed that the mother who consents to the abortion has not been given any voice in the use of this tissue.

West: Our Committee is constituted according to the recommendations of the DHSS. I personally would feel better if there were two lay members. However, It is not a popular function. The Committee was properly constituted according to the recommendations of the DHSS. We did not discuss consent at length because, in line with the recommendations of the Peel Committee, the material was obtained from an entirely separate source. There would be no question of any influence of Professor Hitchcocks' needs upon that source. He managed to be completely separate from it. He had not got the exact form of consent but did in fact sign a consent form.

Bromham: Dr Sims believes that it is necessary, for the health of the mother, for her as a gynaecologist to end the life of an ectopic pregnancy. How does she equate this with her respect for life and her denial of the possibility that termination of an intra-uterine pregnancy might also be justified for the benefit of the mother?

Sims: I would perform an abortion to save the mother's life. I look at an operation on an ectopic as a life-saving procedure. If you do nothing you are going to lose both lives.

Serr: The ethical committee may be set up according to the Helsinki guideline with regard to composition but it is a local ethical committee to deal with local problems. However, the issue under discussion is above the ordinary everyday scientific investigation. It should be referred to a national higher committee when the issue concerned is completely revolutionary and requires public discussion. As regards the fetus the old Roman law said that the fetus is a person when the matter under consideration is for its benefit.

H. Murray: I am the only lay-member of the North Manchester District Health Authority and it does not bother me a bit. I am a representative of the Community Health Council and have the benefit of the experience and practical advice of the CHC that I represent. We did have a sightly similar case and I took this back to my committee to discuss the implications. Most important was the consent of the mother for the use of human tissues. In the recommended code of practice in the Peel Report (section 3; subsection ii) it says that: '. . . The use of the whole dead fetus or tissues from dead fetuses for medical research is permissible subject to the following conditions . . . where there is no known objection on the part of the parent who has had an opportunity to declare any wishes about the disposal of the fetus.'

You cannot say that the mother has had an opportunity to do this if you do not explain that medical experimentation is an option. The mother's wishes must be the over-riding consideration, however benevolent the end.

Jackson: Dr Sims on her gloss says 'the end does not justify the means' meaning that out of something wrong good cannot come. If abortion is wrong then it is not made all right if it is done to help people with Parkinson's. But if it is going on independent of you that does mean that you cannot make something good come of that.

Greengross: There should be tightening up of the consent form, and women undergoing abortion should have more opportunity of knowing what is going to happen. As a general practitioner having seen enormous numbers of women about to have an abortion I think their over-riding emotion was one of guilt. Given the opportunity to understand what the implications were, they would be very relieved that some good would come of it. You have got to be careful about the enormous numbers of terminations done in the private sector. The whole question of legislation about the sale of human tissues must be taken on board very seriously. On the question of good coming out of evil, if we extrapolate from what Dr Sims said, then the tissues of people killed in road accidents or as a result of assault could not be used for transplant purposes.

Garnett: There seems to be a considerable element of patronage in the way in which women are looked at in these arguments. In the current situation there is an element saying that if a women is presented with a consent form that sets out the possible actions, and, assuming she is in full possession of her wits, she signs it, that should not be taken very seriously. I find that very difficult to take on board.

Gorovitz: I have heard a lot of arguments in the last little bit that strike me as peculiar. One of them is the notion that the process of using fetal brain tissue therapeutically is troublesome in that it might do so much good for so many people that a shortage could result. That seems to be an odd line of attack. It is true that organ transplantation, particularly kidneys, has that characteristic; there is a shortage of transplantable organs and there has been much discussion about it and what might reasonably be done in order to increase the supply because kidney transplantation helps a lot of people. Many proposals have been examined but rejected on the basis of the exercise of social policy judgement. There is a collective capacity that we have to both acknowledge the reality of the shortage and to set limits to the lengths that will meet the shortage. I find it very peculiar to hear it offered as a criticism of a form of therapy, that it might actually work and work well and do good and make us wish we could do more of it.

Sims: The criticism, because I believe that an unborn human life is a life, is the spectre of the fetuses being created for this.

Gorovitz: I see that as being quite parallel to the spectre of poor people selling one kidney as a means of simultaneously being uplifted out of their poverty and reducing the shortage of kidneys.

Millican: The two main objections seem to hinge on maternal consent and abhorrence for abortion. These rather conflict. Maternal consent is important if you consider the fetus to be an organ of the mother; if you consider the fetus to be an independent life it is not clear why maternal consent should be so important. If a mother's child dies it is reasonable that she should have a say in the disposal of the body but if she actually kills the child it is far less clear that she should have a say. I do not think that you can emphasise both of those objections at the same time.

Sims: She has abrogated her responsibility in that she wants rid of it and once it is removed from here body is it really hers or is it the hospital's? I hear what you say but my overwhelming principle is my complaint against abortion.

Gillon: I think probably that last remark summarises the moral problems.

Part 5

Clinical trials in obstetrics

Pregnant guinea pigs; the consumer perspective

There are problems in consent to research with pregnant women – practical problems which we need to address if we are not to have criticism and researchers in trouble.

For three years I was involved with a patients' association and dealt with about a hundred complaints a week. Virtually the only complaints that I got about receiving treatment which had specifically been refused were in the field of obstetrics. For example, women said they had been given pethidine when they had specifically said they did not want it.

I got the first grant which the Patients' Association ever had from the DHSS on the grounds that the letters I received from women about their experiences of induction of labour were so horrific that ethically I could only use women who had completed their family and therefore I needed to be able to pay them. Doctors only accept anecdotal evidence which they have produced themselves. However extensive and well analysed the evidence, they do not accept it from lay people. So I went to Dr Anne Cartwright, the Director of the Institute of Social Studies in Medical Care, and persuaded her to do a survey on what mothers though of induction.

Anne Cartwright found that only half, 54%, felt that they could have refused induction on labour. While 66% of social class I felt that they could refuse, only 46% of social classes IV and V felt that they could. There was evidence from other sources such as a study by *Parents* magazine. This was a self-selected sample, but the study showed again quite clearly that a number of women were given pain relief and subjected to practical procedures which they had not wanted. Sheila Kitzinger, in her study, 'Some Women's Experience with Epidurals', pointed out that 'Some women were bullied into agreeing to have one'. So there is evidence that women who enter hospital to have their babies had less freedom, and were treated as having fewer rights than other sane adults in this country. One aspect of this was the Medical Defence Union's (MDU) advice to its members that when a woman entered hospital to have a baby she gave implied consent to 'any necessary form of treatment'. At that time induction rates were well up in the 40–70% range which presumably obstetricians regarded as necessary forms of treatment. The MDU was in fact advising doctors that they could act unethically. The MDU booklet was later revised but I and the Association for Improvement in Maternity Services (AIMS) remain unhappy with it. Women feel extraordinarily vulnerable when they are in labour.

From the contents of *The British Journal of Obstetrics and Gynaecology* for the last two years, it is quite clear that women are now asked for consent but they are asked for their consent when in labour. One cannot expect to get valid consent at such a time. One of the functions of the husband during labour seemed to be to act as support against the staff when they tried to inflict on her things she did not want. There are stories concerning women in labour, accompanied by the husband. The senior person comes in and asks the husband to leave. The woman is asked to take part in a piece of research. She is in labour. She gives her consent. The husband is then allowed back. This is unacceptable.

The Central Oxford Districts Ethics Committee was reformed after three years' pressure by the Community Health Council (CHC). We wanted and got the right for the researcher to appeal against a turning down of his or her project. Many are aware that Professor Smithell's proposal for a randomised clinical trial of vitamin supplements for woman at risk of giving birth to a child with neural tube defects want to a number of Ethics Committees. It was turned down. As a result a non-randomised study was done which was not accepted by many people because it was not a 'proper' study. We then had a difficult ethical decision to set up another study. The appeal procedure was used only once during 6 years and the researcher was still turned down, nevertheless it was an important right.

We insisted that immediate consent should not be expected when people were asked to take part in research. Ideally there should be a delay of at least 24 hours, during which they could discuss the project, with written information, with whomsoever they chose. This, was particularly important for pregnant woman. If you are researching during the process of labour, the only ethical time to obtain valid consent is at the antenatal clinic. Women have to have time to discuss it with their partner because it concerns their unborn child. The father should also be involved in the decision. The woman then has time and she can change her mind at a later stage. It is difficult if you are recruiting for a trial of premature labour but it is the only ethical way to do it. Women who are in labour should not be approached by a researcher. It is no longer acceptable and increasingly womens' organisations are recognising that.

CHC nominees on the Ethics Committee were not regarded as delegates and I certainly did not see myself as a delegate of the Council. Initially the District Health Authority had said they wanted three names to choose from. The CHC fought this and they only got one name. At that time we did not have a confidentiality rule. However, a researcher does have that right of confidentiality and projects should not be discussed outside the Committee itself. When considering issues which had considerable public importance I was free to discuss, with the CHC, principles of ethics in general terms.

The sole lay member on an Ethics Committee acquires more medical knowledge but also acquires medical ethos. So on the Ethics Committee I asked myself, 'Could I defend this if it was suddenly blown up on the front page?' That has stood me in very good stead with the blow-up on the study of anaesthesia for babies. Sir Bernard Brain and a number of members of Parliament condemned, as barbaric, the trial into which I would have entered my own child. It concentrates the mind wonderfully finding yourself put in that category. I found myself defending those who carried out the trial to the GMC but I declined to take part in any consideration of this complaint as I sit on the Professional Conduct Committee of the GMC. The children were, with the consent of parents having written information, randomised to have what was then the standard analgesia for that surgery, nitrous oxide, or to have nitrous oxide plus a drug called fentanyl, a narcotic. Sir Bernard was condeming for giving the narcotic to half the patients although the other half had the standard care given to patients all over the country. I think it would have been totally preposterous to give everybody fentanyl without doing a randomised study. Any patient asked to consent to a non-randomised study can only give valid consent if told that 'this trial is so designed that we shall learn less from your contribution than if it were designed with randomised treated and non-treated groups'.

An enormous number of changes in the care of pregnant women and the newborn have been introduced without this kind of research being done. I would mention studies on antenatal ultrasound to which almost every unborn child in this country is now exposed, sometimes for long periods of time for research activities. In 1981 I wrote to Dr Gerard Vaughan, the then Minister of Health, asking for a properly designed randomised clinical study of ultrasound. He said that the Medical Research Council had considered it and since there was no reason to believe that the use of such techniques was likely to lead to any increase in the incidence of gross anomalies in offspring, the trial would have been unlikely to have done more than show whether these techniques were responsible for any subsequent anomalies that might appear. However, such anomalies are extremely difficult to assess and the use of ultrasonic techniques has become so widespread that a controlled trial along the lines originally proposed would no longer be ethically possible. So it seems to be more ethical to expose every unborn child to antenatal ultrasound without any adequate knowledge of its safety at all. The results of the long term follow-up in Denver suggest, but do not prove, the possibility of an increase in dyslexia in children exposed to antenatal ultrasound.

We are not adequately researching many new changes to which unborn children are exposed and although we do not know the long-term consequences to them, we are not doing long-term follow-up. All of us, of course, remember the lessons of stilboestrol which resulted in the development of clear cell carcinoma of the vagina of exposed girls. It was only picked up because a few young women developed what was an unusual cancer. Had they been developing squamous cell cancer of the cervix, nobody would have noticed. Martin Vessey, Professor of Community Medicine in Oxford, examining records that had been kept at the University College Hospital, was able to look at the long-term outcome of the exposed group and controls. He discovered that there was significantly more mental illness in the exposed than the unexposed children. Valerie Beral found that the boys exposed were less likely to marry. These are more subtle effects but they would not have been discovered or sought but for the fact that a few girls had developed an unusual form of cancer. Yet we are introducing many changes in the treatment of pregnant women and children without a properly designed randomised clinical study and without long-erm follow-up, which I regard as absolutely essential. If researchers get 'out of synch' with what the public will understand and accept they get into trouble.

We who represent consumer organisations want to work with researchers, to exchange ideas and help in presenting them to the public. However, there is a *quid pro quo*. I am unhappy about the ethos of much of reproduction research. The subjects interest researchers and, of course, equipment manufacturers and drug companies. They are not priority subjects fo the users – mothers, fathers and children. We want a share of the power and we want a say in how these studies are done. There are also practical problems. I came across a report on early termination with the use of prostaglandin pessaries. We were concerned about the women being able to refuse if asked to take part. One of the researchers, a distinguished man, felt that every women had quite freely given her consent. The research nurse also felt that everybody freely gave consent. Given this information there was nothing further we could do. However, just a few weeks later a local women's group came to me with a tape-recording from four women who had been involved in this particular research. What was quite clear from the tape was that women had not freely given consent, despite the best intentions of the researchers who were ethical people. It is not bad doctors who necessarily get into trouble it is good doctors as well. What had happened was the women had not been referred to the normal gynaecological out-patient clinics but directly to the research unit and were told: 'The pro-staglandin termination system is what we are offering, you don't have to have it if you don't want to'. That involved either consenting, not getting a termination at all or a delay because you had to be referred to someone else. They should have been referred to an ordinary clinic where it was put to them that they could have procedure A or procedure B. Incidentally that was a large non-randomised study funded by the WHO. Although there were some pieces published on it, we did not have any details on the outcome of this physically or emotionally for the mother. The reaction from the women was that great pain was involved. They had been given the prostaglandin pessary and sent home with analgesic tablets. Prostaglandins induce nausea and vomiting and as soon as you took your tablets you vomited and had no pain relief whatsoever. One girl living alone in a multi-occupied house described stuffing a towel in her mouth to prevent herself screaming throughout. There was no research on the emotional effect involved. What the receiver thinks of the particular procedure is often not built into the research protocol. It should be and should be done by an independent team of sociologists or psychologists.

The problems in consenting to treatment in obstetric care indicate that there are particular problems in the consent to research. Some of this involves the attitude researchers and doctors have towards women. We know from some research, for example a comparison of interviews with male and female patients, that whereas they ask the same number of questions, the male patients are given information but women patients are given reassurance and doctors are less inclined to pass information to them. I would like us all to examine those issues and to be particularly aware of them. Encourage the development and knowledge in our consumer organisations in order to encourage them to take part in the choices of research. Encourage a greater willingness to share power and decision-making both in treatment and in research on the part of the medical profession.

Disadvantages of random controlled trials as a clinical research technique in reproductive medicine

Introduction

There is little doubt that the double-blind random controlled clinical trial is a useful technique in clinical research and that it will so remain. On the other hand there has been a regrettable tendency in recent years to suggest that it is the only acceptable approach to clinical research. Worthwhile projects have been rejected by potential sponsors because they did not conform to this pattern – even though to employ it would have been unethical. Sound papers have been rejected when submitted for publication by journals, because of lack of random controls, when the results obtained are valid, correct and important. It is this attitude that needs redress. It is therefore opportune to draw attention to some of the disadvantages of double-blind random controlled trials, whilst accepting that they eliminate one source of bias that may confound the results with other techniques.

The double blind approach

This is often taken to mean that neither the doctor prescribing the treatment nor the patient are aware of which of two treatments, one of which may be a placebo, is being applied. In practice this is seldom possible. If there is any meaningful different between the two treatments, even the taste or texture of pills, this rapidly becomes apparent to both doctor and patient. In many trials the nature of the treatment is immediately revealed to both, for example, in a comparison of vaginal delivery with Caesarean section. It is the *selection* of the treatment which is supposed to be double blind. That is, neither doctor nor patient has any knowledge of which treatment is selected before the decision is made. Such blindness is difficult and expensive to achieve. Simple manoeuvres such as sealed envelopes which can be held up to the light or drawing numbers out of a bag are easily circumvented by non-compliant junior doctors who consider that their own views on patient welfare take priority over a trial.

Double-blindness can be achieved by having a telephone system whereby when a case arises a call to an individual totally unconnected with doctor or patient makes the decision on patient allocation, but this often means providing a 24-hour on-call structure. None of these approaches will cope with the doctor who feels a given treatment might be inappropriate to a certain type of case and forgets to include the patient, or finds an excuse for excluding her from the trial. Nor are they capable of excluding bias created by patients who exclude themselves by refusing to comply when the nature of a treatment is revealed to them. An attempt is currently being made to run a trial, wherein all appropriate patients are asked when they book for antenatal care to participate in a trial concerning mode of delivery if they go into pre-term labour, later in the pregnancy, when they will be allocated at random. This procedure is very likely to be defeated by doctors who decide when the circumstances actually arise that the patient, for one unforeseen reason or another, is unsuitable for the mode of delivery selected. More important will be the patients who change their minds at the last minute and refuse to comply with the protocol. The things that make them withdraw from the trial will be the things that create a bias. In particular, those ill-informed or lacking understanding as to their ethical right to 'opt out' will bias the results.

Random allocation

The word 'random' is a noun, an adjective or an adverb. Its meanings include 'impetuosity, great speed, force or violence; and impetuous rush, a rapid headlong course; at great speed, without consideration, care or control; in a neglected or untended condition; heedlessly, carelessly; having no definite aim or purpose'. In the present context we may take the meanings 'at haphazard; without aim, purpose or fixed principle; not sent or guided in a particular direction; made, done, occurring at haphazard' (Shorter Oxford English Dictionary, 1985).

The words 'randomise' or 'randomised' do not exist in the English language, and for a good reason – they are tautological. They would be derived from a transitive verb, implying taking deliberate action – the antithesis of the random process!

In clinical trials the process of random allocation simply means that the selection of treatments is decided by chance, and is not revealed to doctor or patient until the decision is made. In practice, resort is often made to the Fisher & Yates (1963) tables of random numbers, which were selected by a process sufficiently tortuous as to be acceptable, for all intends and purposes, as random.

The first problem that arises is that of 'runs' (Tables 5.2.1). The two blocks of 20 in the table were selected as random (*sic*!) from Fisher & Yates (1963) and it will be seen that there is a run of eight As in the first block and one of ten Bs

196 Clinical trials in obstetrics

Table 1 *Random numbers* (Fisher & Yates, 1963)

Two blocks of 20, selected at random
(a) BBABBBAAABAAAAAAAABB = 12 × A; 8 × B
(b) AABBBBABAABBBBBBBBBB = 5 × A; 15 × B
Alternate case
    ABABABABABABABABABAB = 10 × A; 10 × B

Table 2 *Betamethasone and respiratory distress syndrome* (Liggins & Howie, 1972)

Babies under 30 weeks			
Betamethasone	No	RDS	Died
Females	7	2	2
Males	5	1	2
Controls	2	1	2
Females	6	4	6
Males			

in the second block. The occurrence of such runs, perhaps coinciding with a spell of adverse climatic conditions or one individual's week on duty in the labour ward, could completely confound the results of a trial. The extensions of this problem can lead to greater complexities of interpretation. In Liggins & Howie's (1972) random trial of antepartum glucocorticoid treatment for the prevention of respiratory distress syndrome in premature babies, in the high risk group less than 30 weeks pregnant six of the eight babies in the control group were boys, who are at greater risk, and they all died. In the high risk group allocated steroids, only five out of 12 were boys and only two of these five died (Table 5.2.2). The positive result in favour of steroids depended on this result, and had to be verified in multivarate analysis trials before it became generally acceptable.

The second problem was also reflected in the Liggins & Howie (1972) trial – it is the inequality of groups when the trial is complete. In the blocks in Table 5.2.1, the two groups of 20 cases led to twelve As in the first and only five As in the second. In a small trial, random allocation can lead to imbalance of data such that the result may become insignificant.

These problems can sometimes be partly solved (D. R. Waud, personal communication, 1988) by instituting a rule that if there is a run of more than three cases in one treatment group, the individual allocating the groups passes on to the next allocation in the other group. This also results in a smaller imbalance in numbers at the end of the trial.

The rule is valid because the doctor is still blind to the allocation of the case when the decision is made. On the other hand, it is not applicable when the treatment selected becomes apparent to the doctor before the case is concluded and documented – and this is the situation in the majority of trials. This is so because if he is given three A allocations he will know in advance that the next will be a B.

Alternate case designs

Chalmers *et al.* (1983) have ably demonstrated the effect of blind random designs with respect to controlled trials of the treatment of acute myocardial infarction. They found that at least one prognostic factor was maldistributed between the test group in 58% of studies where controls were not selected at random, in 27% where they were selected at random but the doctors were aware of the nature of the treatment selected when they decided whether or not to include a patient, and in only 14% of the blind random studies. Whilst this points out a feature of random allocation, properly applied multivariate analysis at the ends of the trials would have isolated maldistributed factors and validated the result. Of course, there are imponderable factors but these can crop up in any sort of clinical trial. The only defence against them is to verify that the findings really make sense and that they agree with findings by other workers using different techniques in different environments.

Alternate case designs may not be rigorous with respect to the liability of the doctor to exert selection bias on inclusion or exclusion of patients according to which treatment is designated, but they do have advantages. They are administratively economical – all one needs is a book in which suitable patients are inserted, and accorded the appropriate treatment, as they present. It is easier to verify compliance of doctors with protocols – deviations may easily be detected if date and time of admission are recorded, whilst the events are fresh in the minds of those concerned. Control of temporal variables – climatic condition, subtle or overt changes in management policies – is better; there is no problem with runs coinciding with changing conditions. Optimal use is made of case material; the trial can be stopped at any point with approximately equal numbers in the groups. There are valid and effective calculations for missing data items.

The alternate case principle is readily extended to more sophisticated and economical designs such as the use of blocks of cases in blocks of four or more, enabling two treatments to be examined at once, such as prophylactic β-sympathomimetics alone, prophylactic antibiotics alone, both or neither, in pre-term rupture of the membranes (Dunlop *et al.*, 1985); examining four different doses of a drug; or obtaining good comparisons of potency of two drugs using two dose levels and deriving therapeutic ratios in various respects. In particular, the use of latin squares is possible with blocks of 9 or 16 patients.

Numbers of cases and multicentre trials

A weakness of all prospective controlled trials where the 'blind' principle is applied is the number of patients required to achieve a result. For ethical reasons, if patients are not to be consulted about which treatment is to be applied, the difference to be detected must be small. Lilford (1987) gives examples of the numbers of pregnancies needed to study the effect of various forms of management on perinatal mortality, for the trial to have a power of 80% in detecting a difference at the $p<0.05$ level. With screening all patients *versus* selected patients for gestational diabetes 92 000 cases would be required; with home versus hospital delivery for low risk women, 704 000; with induction of labour of postmaturity, 394 000; and with Caesarean secftion for very premature babies, 1 100 000. With such studies, the question being asked is malconstructed, and the technique of prospective controlled studies inappropriate. For example, to answer the question: 'In what percentage of apparently normal pregnancies, at term or after, where there is a perinatal loss, is postmaturity a factor, and in what percentage is it the primary factor?' only takes 100 cases and a multivariate analysis to answer. We have already examined the outcome in 200 babies delivered at 23–28 weeks, and determined by stepwise logistic regression analysis that mode of delivery, whether the presentation is cephalic or breech, is an unimportant factor with respect to survival (Bloomfield & Hawkins, unpublished observations, 1988).

The numbers of patients required in large-scale prospective controlled studies involves a multicentre approach with extensive administration and funding. This means blunting the quality of the data, and between-centre inconsistencies, although it may be good news for out of work administrators. The prospective Collaborative Study of more than 50 000 pregnancies from 12 centres in the United States of America over the years 1959–1965 was extremely costly. The data on the relationship of drugs in pregnancy to birth defects finally appeared in a volume over 500 pages in length (Heinonen *et al.*, 1977), without a meaningful new statistically significant result in it. The prospective random trial of cervical circlage – a procedure which tens of thousands of obstetricians have found to be of value in cervical incompetence over the last 25 years – had to be confined to low risk cases in which the obstetrician was uncertain as to whether or not the circlage was indicated, for ethical reasons. The results were quite predictable. After 7 years an interim report involving 200 obstetricians in nine countries, and 905 patients has appeared. There was a small advantage to inserting the suture, of marginal statistical significance (MRC/RCOG Working Party, 1988). No money would have been needed for half-a-dozen small studies of higher risk patients in single centres, and multivariate analysis would have revealed the prognostic factors.

The importance of the study

The need for a double-blind random controlled clinical trial is inversely related to the importance of the point under study. Real advances in obstetrics – the lower segment Caesarean section, the use of antibiotics, ergometrine and control of the third stage of labour, intensive care in major obstetric problems, epidural anaesthesia, laparoscopy for suspected ectopic pregnancy, amniocentesis, ultrasound scanning, prostaglandins, intensive care of premature newborn, fetal monitoring, β-HCG to detect ectopic gestation, the roles of endogenous oxytocin and prostaglandins in normal labour, the use of adequate doses of progesterone and of a specific oxytocin antagonist in premature labour, have not needed controlled trials to establish their effectiveness. Controls merely provide an estimate of 'background noise' in such situations and the useful function of controlled trials is to sort out details of management. Double-blind random controlled studies have their greatest value in determining optimum doses and deciding between variations in technique where the answer is really unknown.

Informed consent

Ethical committees vary in their interpretation of the need to obtain informed consent from patients being incorporated in a controlled trial, depending rather more on the composition of the committee and their opinion of the integrity of the investigator than on the merits of the case. A comparative trial in which the results of one clinician who treats patients one way, vary from those of another who treats patients a different way will usually be taken not to require patient consent. The clinicians are exercising their clinical prerogative, but the results are highly susceptible to a wide range of biases. If a clinician changes his treatment after, say, 6 months with a view to comparison, this again is his clinical prerogative, but there is some susceptibility to bias. If he conducts an alternate case trial, then he may be able to convince an ethical committee that he really does not know which of two treatments is best and that informed consent is not required. The moment the subject of random allocation is introduced, most ethical committees have no hesitation in requiring informed consent.

It would be informative to be a fly on the wall when informed consent is obtained. 'We are making a study which will help women get the best management for themselves and their babies' – but could it help *that* patient? 'I have not encountered any untoward side effects' – from a house surgeon appointed a week before, who is anxious for a good reference! 'There is no way in which you are being used as a guinea-pig' – a lie! 'This is the way we do it at this hospital' – with no mention that the patient can go to another hospital! 'You could not obtain this new treatment elsewhere' – and so on. I suppose I myself have been guilty of most of them over the years. These days I apply the simple criterion, readily forgotten by the great majority of doctors involved in clinical trials: 'Would I be completely happy for *my* wife or daughter to be included?'.

The time at which informed consent is obtained creates problems. If it is obtained well in advance, the patient must be given the opportunity to opt out at a later stage and this will create bias. On the other hand, in a trial involving management of acute situations, consent can rarely be informed, in the proper sense of the word.

Ethical problems

The ethical validity of random allocations is inversely related to the importance of the difference being examined. Such trials are ethically limited to situations where the clinicians concerned really do not know which of two treatments is best, or if a treatment is of any value. In the 1960s, when the Medical Research Council planned a placebo controlled trial of anti-D immunoglobulin prophylaxis of rhesus iso-immunisation, it was left to the late Professor R. J. Kellar to insist the proposal be dropped because it was unethical. The efficacy of the treatment had already been established by a Combined Study (1966) which had started off on an alternate case basis but because of logistic difficulties was completed with comparable controls. The eventual Medical Research Council study was concerned only with optimum dose, which really was not known.

Table 3 Treatment of eclampsia (Menon, 1969)

		Cases	Maternal deaths
1950–51	Rectal bromethol	80	5 (6%)
1951–52	Intravenous thiopentone	75	12(16%)

The difficulty can be particularly acute when concerned with matters of life and death. It should not be forgotten than 12 women out of 75 died to prove that intravenous thiopentone was lethal in the treatment of eclampsia, compared with rectal bromethol (Table 5.2.3).

It is surprising how blind, responsible and well-intentioned doctors can be to ethical principles when involved in the search for knowledge. The Medical Research Council's comparison of chorion villus biopsy at 9–10 weeks of pregnancy with amniocentesis at 16–18 weks in the antenatal detection of fetal abnormalities may be thought to have been ill-conceived from the start. Chorion villus biopsy is primarily concerned only with finding chromosome abnormalities, whilst amniocentesis involves detection of neural tube defects and other anatomical malformations as well. Be that as it may, the original study was planned in four groups, subjects to patient selection: (a) chorion villus biopsy; (b) amniocentesis; (c) random allocation between the two; and (d) no investigation. It having been explained to the patients that if an abnormality was detected, abortion at 11–13 weeks would be possible, whilst with amnio-centesis abortion would have to be at 18–22 weeks, all the patients elected either group (a) or group (d). The trial was then redesigned. In a revised patient information pamphlet, prospective patients were first informed that a 19–20 week legal abortion for an abnormal fetus is 'a bit more difficult' than a similar procedure at 12 weeks – surely a masterpiece of understatement. In addition they were told that, in their area, the only way they could obtain the test for fetal abnormality was to agree to participate in a random trial of chorion villus biopsy versus amniocentesis. As far as my area of London was concerned, this was a lie. The patients were more intelligent and more informed than had been anticipated. They tended to tour London, seeking a hospital where 'they would not be randomised'! It is interesting to note that in the current version the information pamphlet has been amended for participating hospitals to read 'Termination of pregnancy, if necessary – amniocentesis – later and more difficult – CVS test – earlier and easier'; and 'CVS at this centre is only available within the study we have described'. The italics are in the document. Recruit-ment is still slow, presumably being confined to those who do not read the women's magazines. Meanwhile, large scale uncontrolled studies elsewhere have established the safety of chorion villus biopsy (Rhoads et al., 1988).

The demonstration in 1980 and 1981 that reductions in recurrence of neural tube defect in a subsequent pregnancy by preconception administration of folic acid to the prospective mother was probably the greatest single advance in preventive teratology of this century. The result came from controlled trials in two different centres with three different approaches. Smithells et al. (1980) used supplementary vitamins, minerals and folic acid. Laurence et al. (1980) used dietary advice involving increased folic acid intake. Laurence et al. (1981) used just folic acid. The corresponding reductions in recurrence of neural tube defects were from 5.0 to 0.6%, from 18.0% to nil, and from 11.8% to nil, respectively. Coupled with the knowledge that folic acid is intimately involved in early development of organs in the embryo, that deficiency of folic acid will cause fetal abnormalities, and that folic acid antagonists will cause fetal abnormalities, the case was unequivocal. Professor Smithells and his colleagues have since made up the numbers of patients involved in these studies to many hundreds, with similar results. The inclusion of a placebo group, to be given minerals only, in the subsequent Medical Research Council multicentre random controlled trial was considered by many obstetricians to be unethical. There is a word for the publication of the long article denigrating every aspect of Smithells' work, and intended to defend the trial, in a reputable obstetric journal whose editor happened to be an employee of the Medical Research

Council. Recruitment to the trial is sluggish, as most eligible women who have had a baby with a neural tube defect have already had folic acid treatment instituted before they attend a collaborating hospital; and it is estimated that it will take another 5 years to complete the study (Harris, 1988). Even then, the patients will mainly be confined in Great Britain to those who do not understand the news media and whose general practitioners do not read the medical literature; and to women abroad who are less well informed.

I, myself, was approached a few years ago about a comparative trial of analgesic to be employed in the relief of postpartum episiotomy pain. It was proposed that there should be two different doses of each analgesic, which was fine as there was no information as to which was better and what was an appropriate dose. Very considerable research funding was involved. Then came the request for a control group given only placebo for their pain. This was of course unacceptable. The managing director of the drug company concerned came to see me with his minions, and agreed with me that the placebo group was unethical. A few weeks later I had a polite letter saying that the drug company's statisticians had insisted on the inclusion of the placebo group and my collaboration would not be needed, the trial was being done elsewhere!

Another ethical problem that faces doctors involved in random controlled trials in which they are blind to the nature of the treatment they are giving is lack of knowledge of the – often potent – medicines they are giving. This might be described as using a 'secret remedy', of unknown composition. The practical problems that can arise are obvious. If a patient suffered serious side-effects, or lost her baby or even died, how would the courts look upon the doctor who did not even know what drug he was using? Mechanisms are often built into trials to 'break the code' and stop the trial if a serious problem arises. In real life these are just a sop to Cerberus. The logistics are cumbersome and the doctor is under pressure not to wreck the trial.

New approaches

The introduction of new statistical techniques of multivariate analysis into obstetric research offers an alternative approach which will reduce the need for random controlled trials with all their problems. Stepwise logistic regression analysis is a form of multivariate analysis which enables primary aetiological and treatment variables which affect outcome to be isolated from ordinary uncontrolled but well-documented retrospective or prospective clinical studies. The analysis is so good that, used with some thought, it almost belies the old 'garbage in, garbage out' dictum about computer work – it throws the garbage out for you! The approach was used by Nelson & Ellenberg (1986) to isolate the antecedents of cerebral palsy and is being widely applied to obstetric research. The other multivariate statistical method of great interest in its potential for unravelling the complexities of obstetric data is that of path analysis. This was used by Rogers & Chang (1987) to determine factors leading to perinatal asphyxia.

Conclusion

Double-blind random placebo controlled trials are the approach to obstetric research which is most free from bias and are a valuable tool. They have a number of disadvantages and their applicability is limited by clinical and ethical considerations, cost, the large numbers of patients needed and delay in obtaining results which may have little meaning. They cannot replace established methods of clinical research in obstetrics such as smaller well-controlled trials and simple prospective and retrospective clinical studies which do not commit patients to unsuitable management. New methods of multivariate statistical analysis are now available to extract valuable information from the data generated from clinical studies.

References

Chalmers, T. C., Celano, P., Sacks, H. S. & Smith, H. Jr (1983). Bias in treatment assignment in controlled clinical trials. *New England Journal of Medicine*, **390**, 1358–61.
Combined Study from Centres in England and Baltimore (1966). Prevention of Rh-haemolytic disease. Results of the clinical trial. *British Medical Journal*, ii, 907–14.
Dunlop, P. D. M., Crowley, R. A., Lamont, R. F. & Hawkins, D. F. (1985). Pre-term ruptured membranes, no contractions. *Journal of Obstetrics and Gynaecology*, **7**, 92–6.
Fisher, R. A. & Yates, F. (1963). *Statistical Tables for Biological, Agricultural and Medical Research*, 6th edition, Longman, London
Harris, R. (1988). Vitamins and neural tube defects. *British Medical Journal*, **296**, 80–1.
Heinonen, O. P., Slone, D. & Shapiro, S. (1977). *Birth Defects and Drugs in Pregnancy*. Publishing Sciences, Littleton, Mass.
Laurence, K. M., James, N., Miller, M. & Campbell, H. (1980). Decreased risk of recurrence of pregnancies complicated by neural tube defects in mothers receiving poor diets, and possible effect of dietary counselling. *British Medical Journal*, **281**, 1592–4.
Laurence, K. M., James, N., Miller, M. H., Tennant, G. B. & Campbell, H. (1981). Double blind randomised controlled trial of folate treatment before conception to prevent recurrence of neural-tube defects. *British Medical Journal*, **282**, 1509–11.
Liggins, G. C. & Howie, R. N. (1972). A controlled trial of antepartum glucocorticoid treatment for prevention of the respiratory distress syndrome in premature infants. *Pediatrics*, **50**, 515–25.
Lilford, R. J. (1987). Clinical experimentation in obstetrics. *British Medical Journal*, **295**, 1298–300.
Menon, M. K. K. (1969). Pre-eclampsia and eclampsia. In: *Modern Trends in Obstetrics 4*, ed. R. J. Kellar, pp. 307–10. Butterworths, London.
MRC/RCOG Working Party (1988). Interim report of the Medical Research Council/

Royal College of Obstetricians and Gynaecologists' multicentre randomised trial of cervical cerclage. *British Journal of Obstetrics and Gynaecology*, **95**, 437–45.

Nelson, K. B. & Ellenberg, J. H. (1986). Antecedents of cerebral palsy. Multivariate analysis of risk. *New England Journal of Medicine*, **315**, 81–6.

Rhoads, G. G., Simpson, J. L., Elias, S. & Jackson, L. G. (1988). Presentation of NIHCHD chorionic villus sampling collaborative trial. Thirty Sixth Annual Clinical Meeting, American College of Obstetricians and Gynaecologists, Boston.

Rogers, M. S. & Chang, A. M. Z. (1987). Perinatal asphyxia: the use of path analysis in its explanation. *Journal of Obstetrics and Gynaecology*, **8**, 29–35.

Shorter Oxford English Dictionary (1985), 3rd edn., reprinted, Clarendon Press, Oxford.

Smithells, R. W., Sheppard, S., Schorah, C. J., Seller, M. J., Nevin, N. C., Harris, R., Read, A. P. & Fielding, D. W. (1980). Possible prevention of neural-tube defects by periconceptional vitamin supplementation. *Lancet*, **i**, 339–40.

Discussion   Chairman: Professor Richard Smithells

Lilford: Could I briefly explain what is meant by equipoise in a situation in which you are truly unsure as to which treatment is best? One is seldom sure but usually has a hunch. If we follow the 'gold standard' as if treating one's own daughter, then one would end up doing an experiment. Although experimentation would be infinitely better 'you do not have to treat a patient like your own daughter' and you could rather be influenced by the 'general body politic' of medical practice. The term 'collective equipoise' has been advanced, meaning that informed opinion as a whole is equally divided on the issue. This still leaves a problem because seldom will doctors be equally divided on an issue. We have been doing some experimentation about what the public thinks about how much equipoise doctors should have, how many should think the same way before it becomes ethical. It is much less than 95.5, the implication of that being that trials should not run until $p < 0.05$. It should start before that and that will be much closer to people's acceptance of equipoise.

Serr: I speak in my capacity as a member of the European Safety Committee for Ultrasound, which was set up by the European Federation for Ultrasound in Medicine, which is answerable to the WHO. It is not fair to say that ultrasound has not been examined, we have been carrying out trials for over 15 years and the Safety Committee has examined every publication. Most studies are *in vitro* or animal studies. In humans statements have been issued at the European, American, Australian and other Committees for the Safety of Ultrasound and nothing has been found in humans to show any deleterious effects. The only one quoted, from Denver, is an uncontrolled and very unreliable study. We are really following this very carefully. We will not see a repetition of the radiation issue that Madame Curie studied.

Robinson: What alarms me is that obstetricians have unequivocally been saying 'it is so'. We do not have evidence unless we have a large scale randomised study, with long-term follow-up, and we look for more subtle possibilities because the animal studies do suggest it. The intensity of the exposure by machines used routinely in Britain on women varies by 5000 per cent. I find this worrying. As consumer groups we have tried to be responsible. We could have put out, on the basis of that Denver study, alarming information which could have been misunderstood. We have not done that, we have been responsible, but the obstetricians have not.

Gardner: If we go back to that stilboestrol-induced vaginal adenocarcinoma, many of the cases occurred when the girls were past the menarche. So you have got an interval of 15 years or more to look at. Now the benefits of ultrasound in diagnosis are incalculable. Are we to say 'we are not going to do them until everybody is over 15 years' because it may be that time before we know? The safety of ultrasound in obstetrics has been followed to the best of our skills but how can we research a procedure if we do not do it?

Robinson: If the proper studies had been done at the very beginning we would be getting evidence now. The use of stilboestrol declined once a randomised clinical trial showed it did not work. Suppose it had actually been effective in preventing miscarriage. We should still have had those adverse long-term effects on children when they were grown up and came to reproductive age themselves. Unless we actually think of research long-term and we begin and plan for it from the beginning, we are never going to know the answer. I think as women who are becoming pregnant, and bearing and raising children, we are now asking something quite different from obstetricians and are no longer going to accept false reassurance.

Mott: On the importance of written information. I have worked both sides of the Atlantic. In California we had, by law, to subject parents of the children, who had cancer, to 20-page documents about all the very vaguely possible ramifications for their child, aside from whether or not they were cured of cancer. In contrast the informed consent you get from parents here, sitting down and talking to and assessing those individual parents and being able to answer their questions, is infinitely more valid than the 'informed' consent we were getting in California.

Robinson: I agree with you on this. In the USA written consent is regarded as a legal safeguard for the doctor. We are much more able to be concerned with ethical consent than legal consent. Studies of some of the consent forms in the USA showed that you needed a postgraduate degree in order to understand them. People threw up their hands and said' 'I leave it all to you doctor'. The quality of consent was in fact worse. Written information is important if we make sure that information is in a simple form. It was a very good exercise for the researcher to prepare this and it would of course be supplemented by verbal information. There have been remarkably few studies of what happens in practice actually watching what the doctor says and what the patient understands.

Somorjay: Who sets the research agenda? We have heard a great deal aobut research being done at the frontiers of technology. There is an awful lot of research still needed which is much less glamorous. The sorts of concerns I hear about at the NCT are really poles apart from the things that are being discussed here. What is going to be done to address the concerns of the consumers?

Robinson: We have to think about where the research money is coming from. With less and less free research money we are less and less going to meet the needs of the consumer.

Chalmers: People that have the money will wield the power in determining what the research agenda should be. A recent trial compared the use of intravenous streptokinase with placebo in men who had had a myocardial infarction. Because streptokinase is a potentially profit-making drug the trialists were also able to include the use of aspirin compared with placebo in the same trial, but only because of that, there is no commercial interest in aspirin. A similar reduction in the mortality risk was achieved with streptokinase. It is a good example of the way that money actually pays in setting the agenda.

Millican: I understand Professor Hawkins to say the more important the medical advance, the less need of a randomised trial. If we always knew which were the important advances there would be no need for a trial at all. When uncertainty is equal I would say the more important the issue the more need of a trial.

Hawkins: I was talking not about trials *per se* but about random controlled trials. There is a need for a trial in all the circumstances. It is the technique that is in question.

Chesney: I am a midwife. I feel we have portrayed a somewhat jaundiced view of the obstetric services. The majority of the complaints were a decade ago. The service did listen, has changed and is continuing to change to meet the demands of the public. Is it not good that the mothers feel safe enough to criticise? On the whole, Mrs Average is more than pleased to take part in non-invasive research for the help of her follow woman.

Greengross: I still put a lot of these problems down to communication and the way people speak to each other. What we must do is talk more in terms that ordinary people, who have not got particular technical skills, understand. We are all ordinary people in most walks of life with particular expertise in one. Until wearing our consumer hats, we can demand of other people that they talk in terms that we understand the problem will just continue.

Hawkins: People hear not just what you say, they hear either what they particularly want to hear or do not want to hear. You have the example of the consultant throwing the husband out of the room to obtain consent. Mrs Robinson is placing the worst interpretation on this. I have seen it done for a very good reason – to obtain the wife's decision, whichever way she chooses, in the absence of her husband, who is going to dominate her one way or the other.

Part 6

Informed consent

What is informed consent?

Introduction

The concept of informed consent implies not only allowing patients to make choices that concern themselves but providing the information required to do so. The definition may be extended further by requiring that the clinician not only provides them with the information but does so in such a way that it can be understood and, therefore, used for rational decision-making. The clinician's role, in this context, may be seen as that of a teacher; this observation is not new. In this submission, I will consider the inherent limitations that human beings have in coming to rational decisions. Having explored this area, both from the basis of our own research and by review of the published literature, I will ask the question: Where does this take us morally? I will show that human beings have serious limitations in their ability to make rational (internally consistent) decisions, but I shall also argue that this does not take us very far morally. The corollaries of impaired ability to make rational decisions affect procedural ethics (e.g. the best way of providing information to patients) and not the substantive ethics of whether patients should be allowed to make their own decisions. I shall also discuss the relevance of the psychological and philosophical principles to the question of consent for clinical experimentation.

Limitations on human rationality

There is a poster in the waiting area to my consulting rooms which shows a confused wire-haired terrier dressed in cloth-cap and jumper, which bears the caption: 'The more I think, the more confused I get'. The psychology of choice has been analysed by a number of workers, such as Amos Tversky and D. Kahneman (Tversky, 1974; Kahneman & Tversky, 1979; Tversky & Kahneman, 1981). The concern here is that people may make choices in ways that are completely irrational. This might not matter a great deal, indeed I will take this line of argument later on. Here, I am merely concerned whether it is true that people make irrational choices.

People are sometimes accused of making irrational choices when we simply do not agree with them, for example, a person may be accused of having an irrational preference for coal power stations over nuclear generators, even though that person might accept that the nuclear alternative is safer. This point of view is not necessarily irrational since there are other factors, apart from safety, which may influence the preference for one form of power generation over another. Here, we are talking about decisions which are irrational in the sense that they can be shown to conflict with previous choices. These can be described as errors due to failure to process information in a logical fashion. A famous example concerns lung cancer and the choice between two treatments, surgery and radiation therapy. Subjects were told that, of 100 people having surgery, 10 died during the operation, 32 were dead after 1 year and 66 after 5 years. Of 100 people having radiation therapy, none died during treatment, 23 died of cancer within 1 year and 78 after 5 years. Subjects were then asked to choose radiotherapy or surgery. When this question was posed to a group of physicians, framed in terms of mortality rates, 50% of respondnts favoured radiation therapy. But when the same information was presented in terms of survival rates, radiation was preferred by only 16%. Surgery is somewhat risky at the outset but has better odds of long-term survival. This was not the predominant influence on choice, which was influenced instead, to a disproportionate degree, by whether the question was phrased in terms of risk of death or survival. There are a great number of examples of this type of irrationality, all demonstrating the limitations of the human mind in processing information. Of course, it could be argued that the particular problem encountered in the above example is easily remedied, simply by presenting information in both forms. Unfortunately sequence of information provision is also very important. Consider a hypothetical court case in which mitigating and incriminating information is fairly equally balanced. If the incriminating information is given first, then most subjects find in favour of the prosecution, while if the mitigating evidence is given first, then most find in favour of the defence. It is interesting to ask whether more intelligent people are less prone to these 'faulty heuristics'. I have no information on this point. However, there are a number of numerical exercises, also designed to show the limitations of human intuitive reasoning, and it is known that mathematicians make the same intuitive mistakes as other subjects when asked to guess the answer to statistical riddles. I think it has to be admitted that our evolution has not equipped us with the mental capacity to make the kind of choices which our own inventions have thrust upon us. An example based on a research project in my own area of clinical work will explain this further. This work concerns one of the principle choices to which people are now exposed in large numbers. This is the choice to accept or forego prenatal diagnosis for Down's syndrome, and the particular type of diagnostic procedure if one is desired.

Chorion villous biopsy (CVB) (Lilford *et al.*, 1987) or amniocentesis can both be used for the prenatal diagnosis of Down's syndrome. Patients choosing CVB pay for the advantage of earlier diagnosis with a less accurately defined risk of miscarriage – procedure-related abortion (PRA). Rationally, the choice should be made on the basis of objective probabilities of the probable outcomes and subjective assessment of the desirability (relative values) of these outcomes. Considerable data is available concerning the PRA risk and the age-related risk of chromosomal abnormalities, and we are now getting better information on the comparative risks of amniocentesis and CVB. There is, however, no specific information on how patients make value judgements in this area or the extent to which they are able to assimilate the numerical information on which this decision should, rationally, be based. We (Thornton and I) therefore performed a study of decision-making. The aim was to test the internal coherence or consistency of these choices.

Seventy-three women of child-bearing age were interviewed, including: 16 doctors and medical students; 21 nurses, midwives and pupil nurses; 21 women in immediate puerperium (two professional, five skilled, ten semi-skilled and four unskilled from postnatal wards of two Bradford Hospitals); and 15 paramedical workers. British women were interviewed as follows: each was given factual information about the different tests and told the clinical situation we wished her to consider. As a crude test of coherence, she was asked to place in order of dislike the following possible adverse outcomes of pregnancy:

birth of a live Down's baby;
accidental abortion of a normal baby at 18 weeks after amniocentesis;
accidental abortion of a normal baby at 12 weeks after CVS.

She was then given preliminary information and asked to perform lotteries for three hypothetical choices:

(1) Whether to have amniocentesis or no prenatal diagnosis at various risks of Down's syndrome, at a 5 per 1000 (1/2%) miscarriage risk from amniocentesis.

(2) For those women who would accept amniocentesis at a Down's risk of 5 per 1000, whether to have CVB rather than amniocentesis at various relative PRA risks for these two procedures.

(3) If amniocentesis was not available, whether to have CVB or no prenatal diagnosis at various risks of Down's syndrome.

The reason for the last question was to enable us to test coherence. Coherence may be defined as the ability to predict the outcome to a third gamble, from the answer to the first two gambles.

Coherence

If necessary, during the lotteries, the subjects, attention was drawn to the fact that their response was not consistent with their initial ranking of the three adverse outcomes. They were then allowed to change either the levels of indifference or their original ranking of the outcomes. We then made a formal calculation of the internal consistency or coherence (Llewellyn-Thomas *et al.*, 1982) of the three lotteries as follows: we developed an equation whereby we could calculate the choice of a totally coherent subject from her answers to the first two gambles.

Results

The mean duration of interview was 30 min and all subjects appeared to understand the choices.

In lottery 1 the range of indifference was between risks of Down's of 0.05 per 1000 and declining amniocentesis at any risk. The median indifference was at a risk of Down's of 1.3 per 1000, or 1 in 750.

The levels of indifference varied between 5 per 1000 PRA risk in lottery 2 and 100 per 1000. The first choice would imply that the subject would not accept any increased risk in order to get the earlier diagnosis of CVS, whereas the last would imply that the subject would accept a 20 times greater risk of abortion for the perceived advantages of CVS. The median value, however, was 10 per 1000 indicating, *for this genetic risk*, that half the subjects would accept a doubling of PRA risks for the advantages of CVB. Twenty women were excluded from the study because they would not have accepted amniocentesis at a Down's risk of 5 per 1000.

In lottery number 3, women were asked to state the various Down's risk at which they would accept CVB with a 20 per 1000 PRA risk, assuming that amniocentesis was not available. Again the range was wide, but the median risk level of indifference was now 1.8 per 1000.

Coherence was measured in 53 subjects, whose level of indifference for amniocentesis on the first lottery was less than or equal to Down's risk of 5 per 1000 and we were thus able to perform the second lottery at this Down's risk. We had the problem now of deciding how close the answer to the third gamble should be to the expected answer from the first two gambles, in order for the subject to be declared coherent. We decided empirically that if the risk of Down's syndrome on the third gamble was within a halving or doubling of the risk calculated by the equation, then we felt that this subject had understood the choices reasonably well and could be categorised as internally consistent or coherent. A very small number of subjects could not be tested for coherence because they anchored their answers at the extreme of the range. Of the remaining patients, 55% were coherent by our definition and 45% were not. Some of the latter were very incoherent indeed. Some of the incoherence can be attributed to a fault in our coherent measure itself. If subjects do not visualise risk on a linear scale, in other words, if a risk of 1 in 200 is not viewed as twice as bad as a risk of 1 in 400, then subjects will appear incoherent on our measure. Nevertheless, the extent of the incoherence in 45% of subjects is so great that we must attribute this to poor understanding of the numerical choices offered, rather than a fault in our measure itself.

All our subjects paid close attention during the interview and did their best to give answers consistent with their own true values. In the presentation of our risk cards, we were careful to present cards alternatively from the higher and lower end of the range, to minimise 'anchoring' towards the initial end of the scale.

We believe these observations are important, since they underpin genuine difficulties which are inherent in choices which all women may now be offered in pregnancy. The evidence which we have presented from within my own speciality, along with an entensive study of psychological literature, confirms that human choice is very far from rational. What is the importance of this observation? What are the moral consequences?

Moral significance of impaired cognition and decision making

Ethical issues are sometimes subdivided into substantive and procedural ethics. Substantive ethics relates to whether a particular procedure or method can ever be ethical. Procedural ethics discusses the provisions and controls, i.e. safe-guards, which should be imposed if a course of action may be ethical under some circumstances. Of course, these two are not completely separate. If a course of action is substantively ethical, but no adequate procedures can be developed, then it will become substantively unethical by virtue of the fact that no acceptable procedure can be devised. Nevertheless, the broad distinction is a useful one, particularly with reference to the implications of imperfections in human decision-making ability. Our argument is that these observations have little or no substantive ethical importance. There are a number of reasons why the inherent inability of human beings to make fully rational or coherent decisions is not of great substantive ethical importance: all the alternatives are worse. If people are not able to make their own decisions, albeit incoherently or irrationally then somebody else must make the decision for them. Not to offer the choice is no solution to the problem, since this itself is a reflection of a decision taken on behalf of other people. Rational decisions taken by care providers on behalf of individuals might be preferable to an irrational individual choice if there was any one right answer, i.e. if the range of human values was very small. This, however, is not the case. Even among totally coherent subjects in our study, there was an extremely wide range of opinion. Many subjects clearly regarded a Down's baby as an infinitely worse outcome than losing a normal baby from a prenatal diagnostic procedure. Others, by the same token, would not wish to have prenatal diagnosis at a risk of around 1%, even if the chance that the baby had Down's syndrome was 1 in 2. It is, therefore, quite clear that human values vary enormously and cover virtually the full range of theoretically possible opinions. Let us imagine that for each individual there is a true set of values. We would have to assume, therefore, that irrational personal choice, while it may end up wide of the mark and be a poor reflection of these intrinsic 'true' values, is nevertheless more likely to be representative than a value set by someone else. Furthermore, there is no guarantee that if choice is made by a third party, for example, doctor or Health Authority, that this itself will be any more rational. As mentioned before, Kahneman found that statisticians, if asked to guess the answer to numerical problems, are little better than people who had not been mathematically trained. Similarly, although medical workers and doctors were slightly more coherent than other subjects in our study, they nevertheless exhibited a large degree of incoherence. Thus third-party decisions have two clear disadvantages over individual decision-making:

(1) they are also prone to irrationality, (incoherence) and are, therefore, imperfect reflectors of the 'true' values of the third party;

(2) there is a high probability that the values of the third party will be quite different to those of the individual, given the wide variation in human values.

It is worth noting, in addition, that in our study of decision-making and prenatal diagnosis, the same range of values was expressed by medical and non-medical people. (The Mann–Whitney U test revealed no difference between these groups with respect to acceptance level for prenatal diagnostic tests.)

There are, of course, still further arguments against third-party decisions. Denying patients the right to make their own decisions is an affront to their autonomy. However, there may be some situations where these principles are over-ridden by other factors, and where placing the full burden of a decision on patients is undesirable.

Clinical circumstances which affect the burden of decision-making between patients and doctors

Limited resources

I shall deal first with the issue of constraint due to limited resources. Our study of prenatal choice (above) shows that fully half of all patients would like to have prenatal diagnosis by amniocentesis even if the risk of Down's syndrome was as low as 1 in 750 and many people would wish to have prenatal testing at much lower risks than this. However the current practice in all developed countries is to offer amniocentesis down to a risk of 1 in 300. Some textbooks say that this is because the risks of amniocentesis and Down's syndrome roughly equilibriate at this age. This is a completely specious argument, which would only apply if both outcomes were perceived to be equally bad. Since about three-quarters of patients perceive Down's syndrome as a worse outcome than loss of a normal baby, we must answer the question: Why do we not offer amniocentesis to all women? The answer is that we are limited to this cut-off risk by resource constraints. Our laboratories, insurance systems, etc., are only financed to deal with risks down to this level. More by coincidence than design, this risk cut-off, at least when risk is calculated on maternal age alone, is also the point down to which amniocentesis is 'cost effective'. Thus, the issue of distributive justice within fixed resources is the first factor which limits full patient autonomy in the exercise of individual values in decision-making. I would like to move on to further areas where there are limitations on the amount of information provision, not because of restricted resources, but because of other practical and ethical restraints.

Practical limitations to patient autonomy
The most obvious of these practical constraints is lack of time or inability of the patient to make a decision. I always teach the medical students that the amount and detail of information provision, and the importance of patient autonomy in making decisions, varies with the clinical situation. At one end of the spectrum I invite them to consider a pregnant patient, unconscious (say from eclampsia), who has been brought into casualty unaccompanied. Under these circumstances, there is only one person who can make a decision and that is the medical attendant, who must treat the patient according to the golden rule – as they think they themselves would wish to be treated under the same circumstances. Next I ask them to consider patients who are in distress and who need emergency surgery. Such patients are in no position to take in complicated information or to make difficult decisions for themselves and at best surrogate decision-making by a friend or relative might be required. An example in this category would be fetal distress or some other complication during labour, when it is believed that an emergency Caesarian section is the best treatment.

A much greater level of information provision and autonomy for patient decision-making is required when there is somewhat more time and the patient is in little or no distress. Imagine a patient with a breech presentation in the last week of pregnancy, where the decision is between elective Caesarian section and trial of vaginal delivery. The trade-offs involved may be very complex and the time to make a decision limited to about a week. Under these circumstances, I give patients a three-way choice. While providing every opportunity for fully autonomous decision-making, and disclosing all relevant information, I am also happy to make the decision for the patient if this is what she wants. The patient's decision in this case would be to have elective Caesarian section, trial of vaginal delivery, or to pass the decision on to me. At the other end of the spectrum, however, are patients who are required to make a difficult value trade-off and where there is essentially no time constraint. This is the situation in the prenatal diagnosis/genetic counselling clinic. Here a large number of counselling sessions can be devoted to making important decisions, and there is little or no urgency.

Decisions where values are more or less important
A further consideration, which influences medical obligation for detailed disclosure, is the extent to which the diversity of human values is likely to influence a decision. We showed in our example of prenatal diagnosis for Down's syndrome, that human values are extremely diverse. In many other situations, however, complex value play-offs are not required, and essentially all patients would wish to be treated in the same way. Where a life-threatening condition is concerned, it is sometimes reasonable to assume that that a patient's overriding wish is to maximise her chance of survival. Thus agonising over the small print of each rare complication of appendicectomy would not seem to be necessary if this operation is required as a life-saving procedure. We can refer to decisions which are not appreciably influenced by value considerations as situations of probabilistic dominance – the decision is dictated almost solely by the probabilities of outcomes with different methods of treatment. I do not wish, however, to imply that maximising chances of survival is *always* the overriding criterion; values are often important, even in the treatment of life-threatening conditions and the legitimate refusal of Jehovah's witnesses to accept blood transfusion is an example of this.

In the example given above concerning radiotherapy versus surgery for the treatment of lung cancer, patients were asked to compare a lower chance of survival with radiotherapy against a higher chance of immediate death with surgery. It has been shown that people wish to make a trade-off between immediate death and overall chances of survival, and that most people will sacrifice years off the ends of their lives in order to lower immediate risk. Decision theorists refer to this as pure risk aversion, and it is an indication that people value the years immediately ahead above those in the more distant future. Younger women are also prepared to sacrifice their chances of survival on behalf of their unborn children. I shall illustrate this with a story from my own practice.

As 36-year-old woman, in her first pregnancy, was found to have an early (stage 1B) cancer of the neck of the womb. Normally, this is treated by either radiotherapy or radical hysterectomy. At the time lesion was discovered, so was 20 weeks pregnant. It is widely agreed that in very early pregnancy treatment should proceed and that the pregnancy should be sacrificed. It is equally agreed that, if the pregnancy has reached 28 weeks, it is legitimate to wait another 2 or 3 weeks until the baby is sufficiently mature to have an excellent chance (over 95%) of surviving early delivery. Twenty weeks is a grey area for decision-making. When I told this patient and her husband of the diagnosis, they indicated clearly to me that they wished to have a say in the decision, although I indicated that I would be prepared to make the decision for them if they wished to relinquish it to me. I think by this stage of the conversation, they were aware that my choice would have been to get on with the treatment of the cancer and this would have meant loss of the pregnancy. The patient asked me what her chances of survival were if she went ahead with immediate treatment. I told her that there was an 80% chance of complete cure. She asked me how long she would have to wait in order for the baby to have a 95% or more chance of survival, and I told her that another 10 weeks would be required. She then asked me the crucial question; to what extent would she jeopardise her chances of survival if she waited those 10 weeks? I said I did not know, and that the world literature on the subject was quite inadequate to provide accurate probabilistic figures. I said, however, that I would be prepared to make a guess on the basis of my knowledge and the biology of cervical cancer, if she wished me to do so. I told them that I thought they would diminish the chances of survival by between 2 and 20%, and came down on a figure of 10% as my own best subjective probabilistic estimate. She said that, in that case, she would like to keep the pregnancy, and she did. Her husband's reaction was interesting. He said that 10% worsening of the chances of survival was far too high for him, and urged immediate treatment. Of course, we do not know whether he really felt this, or if he felt that he ought to say this; guilt is a very important human motivating factor. When she was at 30 weeks of gestation, we gave the mother some injections which would help the baby's lungs to mature, delivered her daughter by Caesarian section and proceeded immediately to radical hysterectomy. This particular patient comes to see me in Leeds each year, the original treatment having been given in London, and I think that she is cured. However, if the tumour had recurred and she had died, then the decision would still have been right, since decisions are correct or wrong in prospect, not in retrospect. This point cannot be reiterated too often, especially in the presence of our legal colleagues!

We have done some formal work in the area of trade-offs that women are prepared to make with their own chances of survival, in order to preserve their potential for having children. There is a disease called microinvasive cancer of the cervix. This is a cancer of the neck of the womb at a very much earlier stage (indeed earlier than that described above) where the tumour has just started to invade the tissues. If the invasion is to a depth of less than 3 mm, then the chance that the tumour will have spread beyond the mouth of the womb is less than 1%, and everybody agrees that conservative treatment is preferable. If it has spread beyond 5 mm, then the chances that it has spread are well over 5% (probably 10%) and again there is wide agreement that radical treatment should be given by radiotherapy or surgical removal of the womb and the surrounding lymph nodes. Between 3 and 5 mm, the chances of spread, all other things being equal, are between 1 and 5%. Radical treatment is usually carried out and this is certainly correct for people who have completed their families. It could be argued that we should not be influenced, in treatment of a life-threatening condition, by reproductive potential. This is not so. We have taken some measurements of value trade-offs between chances of survival and retention of reproductive potential in women with no children. It is difficult to make accurate trade-offs. Indeed the first part of this chapter showed how difficult it is for people to comprehend these trade-offs, especially where the probabilities of bad outcomes are very low. Nevertheless, one can test for coherence in the process of measuring values, and one can make the measurements in many different ways in order to reinforce the validity of any conclusions.

Our findings show that the median point of indifference (i.e. the risk, up to which, half the people would accept in order to retain their capacity to have children) is 15%. For those of you who are interested in the technology of decision theory, we derived these estimates by certainty equivalence multiple gambles. (Again, for those of you who are interested in this subject, the linear analogue method showed that women are prepared to run even greater risks of death in order to preserve fertility, but this method is notoriously unreliable.) Some people were surprised at the risks women were prepared to run to preserve fertility, and indeed we are not asking you to take these at face value. One thing we can be sure of, however, from our large sample of women of various walks of life, is that people place a very high priority on fertility, and I would have certainly been prepared to run up to a 15% risk with my own life in order to have my children. Of course, these figures change once one has children: now that I have a family, I am far more averse to risk and I have given up private flying for precisely this purpose. This difference in attitude between people who have children and do not have children was brought home to me recently when I admitted under my care a patient with very high blood pressure in pregnancy due to a tumour of the adrenal gland (a phaeochromocytoma). She was the mother of two children, and made it abundantly clear to me that she did not wish to run any risk whatsoever on behalf of her unborn child. As things turned out, Caesarian section was required a week later for fetal indications and we were able to remove the adrenal tumour at the same operation. Again, I am happy to report that mother and baby are doing well, but again this is irrelevant to whether or not the decision was correct prospectively.

A particularly interesting value trade-off concerns the risk of fetal death or brain damage and the indications for Caesarian section. Consider, again, the breech presentation at term in a mother with no apparent adverse factors for vaginal delivery. In a detailed review of the subject, we found that trial of vaginal delivery under these circumstances would be successful in leading to vaginal delivery in 65% of cases, but that intra-partum (in labour) Caesarian section would be required in the remaining 35%. As intra-partum Caesarian section is about three times as dangerous as elective Caesarian section, both in terms of mortality and morbidity (Bingham & Lilford, 1987), there is little or no *physical* advantage to the mother in trial of vaginal delivery. The additional risk of fetal brain damage or death, in such apparently low risk cases, from vaginal delivery is 1 in 100 to 1 in 200. Does this mean than women would choose the pain, inconvenience and other psychological disadvantages of elective Caesarian section in preference to trial of vaginal delivery?

Again, we have carried out a number of detailed value trade-offs in order to shed further light on this issue, and have interviewed 100 women for this purpose. One-third were postnatal women of mixed social class, one-third medical or paramedical workers and a further third were women who had opted for home delivery. The latter were identified through the local branch of the Natural Childbirth Trust. We carried out value trade-offs in which we asked women to imagine themselves in a situation that they were being offered a choice between elective Caesarian section and trial of vaginal delivery (Thornton & Lilford, 1987). We told them that, because of the risk of failure of the trial of vaginal delivery, and the higher mortality of intra-partum compared to elective Caesarian section, morbidity and mortality were the same with both choices. Alternating from high to low risks, we carried out a series of multiple gambles to determine the risk of fetal death which they would be prepared to accept in order to avoid the psychological disadvantages and pain of Caesarian section and also to lower their chance of requiring operative delivery in any subsequent pregnancy. The median point of indifference was 1 in 4000. In other words, even when the risk of fetal death was as low as 1 in 4000, half of our subjects would opt for Caesarian section. Interestingly, the subgroup requiring home delivery had a point of indifference in the range 1 in 100 to 1 in 1000, suggesting that these women have a different system of values in addition to any difference of opinion about the probabilities of adverse outcomes.

This line of argument has a bearing on a woman's request for elective Caesarian section. A baby was born with brain damage following normal delivery in New York (Feldman & Frieman, 1985). There had been no signs whatsoever before the delivery that the baby would be born brain-damaged. However, the baby had lacked oxygen during labour, and this had not been detected because of false negative test results. In Court, the obstetrician was asked whether earlier Caesarian section would have prevented this brain damage. He pointed out that in all probability it would have done, but that there was no indication for Caesarian section and that the corollary of this kind of argument would be Caesarian section for all cases. (As I said before, decisions are right or wrong in prospect not retrospect.) To the amazement of all concerned (at least I hope it was to their amazement) the lawyer wanted to know why, in that case, his client had not been offered a Caesarian section. After all, her value system may have favoured this operation to lower the minute chance of brain damage. This is, of course, *a reductio ad absurdum*. Elective Caesarian section is more dangerous than trial of vaginal delivery for normal women because the risk that an intra-partum Caesarian section will be required is less than 10% (or at least it should be). Secondly, the risk of intra-partum death or brain damage is much lower (1 in 1000 to 1 in 2000) than in the case of breech delivery (1 in 100 to 1 in 200). For these reasons, I think that all women requiring breech delivery should be offered a Caesarian section. I do not, however, think that this should be extended to all women, but what about the woman with no special indication who actually *asks* for elective Caesarian section? This issue has caused much recent debate in *The British Medical Journal*. Even though I have contributed to this debate, I cannot help but reflect that the amount of interest in this topic greatly exceeds its practical importance; in 15 years of professional practice, I have only once been asked to carry out an elective Caesarian section purely on the basis of patient preference.

I personally do not believe that one can legitimately withhold Caesarian section from an intelligent and mentally well-balanced patient who specifically requests the operation. Some may argue that the very act of asking is, of itself, a manifestation of emotional disturbance or low intellect! This does not follow, since it is quite possible to have a particular emotional aversion or phobia to vaginal delivery, while being in other ways psychologically normal. It does not follow from this that I would sanction or aid a patient suicide, or assist her in anything she might want, e.g. termination on the basis of fetal sex only. However, the additional risks to the mother from elective Caesarian section are very small (about 1 in 10 000) and I think a patient should be free to run a risk of this magnitude provided she understands that she is doing so but feels that the emotional benefits of Caesarian section are sufficient to warrant this small risk. Indeed if, like myself, one gives considerable (but not overwhelming) support to the principle of respect for patient autonomy, then one must be prepared to accept many of the consequences of this when the patient's value system is at variance with one's own. All these arguments show that values are of enormous influence in decision-making in my field and demonstrate the importance of information provision so that choice can be influenced by the values of the patients concerned.

The fear of causing excessive anxiety
The last limitation that I would like to mention to the principle of informed consent is one which is very well rehearsed, and which I will not go into in detail here. This concerns the perceived trade-off which undoubtedly sometimes arises between the obligation to beneficiance versus respect for autonomy. It has, probably correctly, been argued that doctors have made too much of the defence against information disclosure on the grounds that this information might upset the patient. It is perhaps sufficient to say that I believe that the obligation of autonomy is very important and that very often the obligation to

do one's best for the patient and not harm him or her actually corresponds very well with one's obligation to respect autonomy. At the same time the simplistic rule that autonomy should always have precedence is not true. Indeed, if this were so, there would be no reason for ethical debate at all, and we could dismiss this volume out of hand.

I would like to share some of my thoughts with you on the possible conflict between beneficiance and autonomy in my own subject of perinatology. Prenatal diagnostic tests frequently reveal minor variations which are of doubtful importance. A good example is the tiny brain cysts called choroid plexus cysts. When these are small and the rest of the scan is normal, the outlook for the fetus is excellent and probably no different to normal. Similarly, amniocentesis or chorion biopsy may show minor variations in chromosomes which are again believed to be of no prognostic importance. One of the most famous of these is a so-called pericentric inversion of chromosome 9. This is a minor variation in the structure of chromosome 9, in which some of the genetic material is upside down. As this is of no functional importance, we do not usually mention it to patients. I believe we are justified because a number of observations have shown that many patients find it very difficult to place this kind of information into perspective, and the thought that something as fundamental as one of the chromosomes is not normal, may grow in parents' minds and cause considerable and prolonged anxiety. My paediatric colleague, Peter Dear, tells of a patient where disclosure that a cyst was present in the brain has caused continuing parental anxiety which his reassurance has not been able to dispel. In this case it was necessary to inform the patient, as follow-up was required, and I mention this case merely to illustrate that severe anxiety may persist and interfere with patient–child relationships despite sensitive and detailed counselling.

You will have gathered, from what I have already said, that I believe that empiric evidence has a bearing on ethical decisions; indeed good ethics starts with good factual information. We have an ongoing project at my hospital of group counselling for parents to help them better understand the full range of prenatal diagnostic tests which modern medicine has made available. The majority of our patients, when asked whether they would like to know of minor anatomical variants which we believe have no prognostic importance, say that they would rather not know and state that this would cause them unnecessary anxiety. My own view is that doctors should have a high degree of conviction that any unusual feature is not associated with a bad outcome, before withholding this information. Any variant, which has been shown to have or which is likely to have an association with an undesirable outcome, should be fully disclosed and discussed with parents who would otherwise have a legitimate complaint that information had been withheld. It is only when we believe the variation from the usual is not associated with any bad outcomes that we are justified in non-disclosure.

Informed consent for clinical experimentation

A full discussion of the ethics of human experimentation would be far beyond the scope of this chapter. Clearly, there is a need for properly designed experiments in clinical medicine and many gross mistakes were perpetuated because of failure to conduct adequate randomised studies following intro- duction of new treatments. Those who do not study history are bound to repeat the mistakes of the past, and we should be constantly mindful, not that thalidomide caused phocomelia and that stilboestrol caused vaginal cancer, but rather that they did so to a far greater extent then necessary because they were not tested by randomised controlled trial at an early stage. The potential harm to patients outside trials, due to side-effects of ineffective treatments, is much greater than the potential harm to control patients within studies. Thus more trials should be carried out. I shall not go here into the substantive ethics of trials. In other words, some trials are inherently unethical because the weight of evidence for or against one of the treatments is already so strong that equipoise (i.e. existing belief) is disturbed to a degree that patients should not be offered entry in the study.

I talk now about the procedural ethic; what safeguards and controls should we employ, once we have decided that a trial is substantively ethical? The procedural ethic of trials revolves largely around this question of informed consent. I have already said quite a lot about this issue and the main topic we need to discuss now is whether a different level of disclosure is required for patients in trials than that which is required in conventional practice. There is an intuitive feeling amongst most people that more information provision *is* required for clinical experimentation then for ordinary practice. However, insistence on a higher level of disclosure for trials has led to accusations of the practice of a double standard: that the uncontrolled experimentation of random variations in practice requires less information provision than that required for proper controlled trials. Areas which can be legitimately addressed by trials, namely those which are substantively ethical, are areas where clinical practice already varies considerably. The treatment is determined largely at random since it reflects the personal preference of the individual doctors or midwives who happen to be looking after the patient. Therefore, a double standard is imposed if we insist on a higher or different level of consent for trial entry in comparison to ordinary practice. The counter argument to this is that patients should give consent for trials, even if this is not required for standard practice. This argument hinges on the assumption that, while patients accept that there is considerable variation and controversy in medical practice, they nevertheless are reassured by the impression that their own doctor or nurse will do what she or he thinks is the best treatment.

I shall illustrate this controversy with an example. In the labour ward at my hospital approximately half of our midwives believe in routine rupture of membranes once labour is established. These midwives tend to be day staff, and the other half of our midwives, mainly night staff, tend to leave the membranes intact until very near the second stage of labour by which time most will have ruptured by themselves anyway. Behind this variation in practice is a legitimate difference of opinion as to which method of treatment is best. We are, therefore, planning a randomised trial in which patients will be entered at random (providing they fulfil certain entry criteria) to have membranes ruptured at ±5 cm of cervical dilatation, or much later in labour. This trial is substantively ethical, but what about the question of consent? On discussing this in our labour ward committee, it was suggested that consent should be obtained from all mothers for the trial. I asked if consent was obtained at present and was told that it was not. On further discussion, we decided that this issue should be disucssed with all mothers, and consent should be obtained either way, whether or not the patient was in a trial. This left us, however, with a further problem. I have already said above that patients in labour are frequently not in an adequate state of mind to discuss an issue, absorb relevant information, and make an informed judgement. The only way to resolve this issue of giving all patients necessary information and choice, including the choice not to choose, and not do this under the stress of labour, is to discuss this with all patients before labour. This question has since been taken to the Ethical Committee, and they have decided that all patients who might be eligible for the trial, which includes almost all antenatal patients, should be informed about the trial antenatally and before labour. Patients will then have the choice to opt for ruptured membranes, membranes to be left intact, or for the randomised trial.

This scenario shows that where it is decided that enhanced information provision is required for trial purposes, then one will often find that inadequate information was previously provided as part of routine clinical practice. Nevertheless, I think patients should be asked to give consent to enter most trials, even if such consent is *not* obtained in practice. This is necessary, even if it leads to accusations of the practice of a double standard, because patients assume that their doctor or midwife has chosen the treatment which he or she marginally prefers and they could legitimately complain that a deception was practised if consent was not obtained. There are also powerful symbolic or even political reasons for requesting a higher standard of consent for trials. These relate to the public perception of the duty of doctors to their patients and the intuitive fear of human experimentation, especially covert experimentation.

The situation is a little more difficult when third-party consent is required, especially if adequate time for discussion is not available. I have in mind here trials in neonatology where treatment must be initiated urgently. Under these circumstances, it is impossible to get surrogate consent from parents, and yet these trials are vitally necessary.

A suggested solution to this problem is to ask all mothers if their babies may be entered in the relevant trial antenatally. I am convinced of few things but I am strongly of the opinion that this idea is wrong. Firstly, these treatments are required for very premature babies and would, therefore, apply to less than 1% of the pregnant population. Since the trial is likely to involve a complex medical issue, it is simply not practical to discuss the issue with the whole pregnant population in sufficient depth for any consent to be meaningful. Furthermore, given that the probability of requiring this form of treatment is so small, it is very doubtful if consent given hypothetically about an event which is most unlikely to concern individual parents has any validity in the acute situation. The important thing here is that the trial should be substantively ethical. This should, of course, be confirmed by an Ethical Committee and under these circumstances, but no others, I would think it legitimate for the Ethical Committee to act as an independent giver of consent. It would be interesting to study any opinions of prospective patients on this point of view, although I am fairly certain that the majority of people would agree that the above course of action is appropriate.

Conclusion

The research of many others concerning human choice in general, and my own work on choice within the speciality of obstetrics and gynaecology, indicates that the majority of people are not able to make highly rational decisions, and that this may manifest itself as incoherence. However, these frequently irrational individual decisions are much better than the often equally irrational decisions which may be made on behalf of individuals. I think the value and importance of individual autonomy is the single most important ethical principle when choices have to be made. However, there are situations where, because of resource constraints, practical factors, or because values are not really involved, where detailed information provision and the requirement that the decision be taken by the patient herself, is not required. I believe that ethical debates on this issue are strengthened by first-hand experience of medical practice, and a measurement of public attitudes. I have referred to the measurement of public opinion by means of attitude surveys as 'ethicometrics' and, although I do not believe that ethics is determined entirely by the consensus opinion of citizens, nevertheless, I do not think that public opinion can be ignored.

Lastly, this chapter bears the title 'Informed consent' and I hope that this is the last time this term is ever used. I do not believe it is possible to give consent if you have not been informed and, therefore, 'consent' should be enough. However, I do not even like the word 'consent', since this implies that the patient is doing something to doctor wants. If there is a possibility of withholding consent then this immediately implies that there are at least two possible courses of action. If there is more than one course of action then there is a choice. It is as legitimate to ask patients for their consent not to operate or not to do a forceps delivery, as to ask their consent to carry out these procedures. Indeed, doctors are more often sued for failure to do procedures than for carrying them out when they were not indicated. Thus the debate, and indeed this chapter, is not really concerned with consent at all; what we are concerned with is choice. If there is a choice then a decision must be made. The whole question of so-called informed consent should be seen as a component of the growing science of decision theory. From now on we should discuss not how much informed consent is required, but how much information should be provided.

References

Bingham, P. & Lilford, R. S. (1987). Management of the selected term breech presentation: assessment of the risk of selected vaginal delivery versus Caesarian section for all cases. *Obstetrics and Gynecology*, **69**, 965–78.

Feldman, G. B. & Frieman, J. A. (1985). Prophylactic Caesarian section at term? *New England Journal of Medicine*, **294**, 703.

Kahneman, D. & Tversky, A. (1979). Prospect theory. An analysis of decision under risk. *Econometrica*, **47**, 263–91.

Lilford, R. J., Irving, H., Linton, G. & Mason, M. K. (1987). Transabdominal chorion villus biopsy: 100 consecutive cases. *Lancet*, **i**, 1415–17.

Llewellyn-Thomas, H., Sutherland, H., Tibshirani, R., Ciampi. A., Till, J. & Boyd, N. (1982). The measurement of patients' values in medicine. *Medical Decision Making*, **2**, 159–62.

Thornton, J. & Lilford, R. J. (1987). When a woman asks for Caesarian section. *British Medical Journal*, **294**, 703.

Tversky, A. (1974). Assessing uncertainty. *Journal of the Royal Statistical Society, Series B*, **36**, 148–59.

Tversky, A. & Kahneman, D. (1981). The framing of decisions and the psychology of choice. *Science*, **211**, 453–8.

Informed consent

Introduction

My charge was to speak about informed consent. There is not much that is new to say. There is an immense literature and many of you are familiar with much of it. I hope it will be useful to consider some of the general issues having to do with informed consent and then ask whether there are any special features in the context of human reproduction that make informed consent in any way a different issue in that context. I will make a limited number of points and hope to have time for some discussion because proceedings are most effective when there is a considerable opportunity for interaction.

General issues

I will begin by referring back to the 'Baby Doe Hotline' that I believe Professor Campbell mentioned (Chapter 3.1) when he described the case of an infant whose parents declined consent for corrective surgery that would sustain the life of their Down's Syndrome child born with douodenal atresia. The Federal Government was quite rightly concerned about this kind of episode but in a severe over-reaction sought to address the problem by the intrusive mechanism of requiring that every hospital, recipient of Federal funding, post a notice indicating that, under the laws covering rehabilitation and handicap, all infants must be treated vigorously. Anyone who suspected any infant was not being properly treated could anonymously call a toll-free number or hotline to the Federal desk that was monitoring this issue in the interests of protecting the infants who otherwise would be left unprotected against the capricious whim of self-serving parents and physicians. Thus, as a matter of governmental policy, parental consent was not judged to be definitive in the treatment of infants.

Four or five years ago, just before speaking to another audience, I became curious about that hotline, which had been in effect for several weeks. (Later a Court finding dismissed the plan and its operations as arbitrary and capricious, enjoining the Government to cease and desist.) I called that hotline and I said that I was interested in finding out how business had been. They said: 'You may only call this line to report a suspected wrong-doing in the delivery room or nursery. But if you call a different number, or write to us, we would be glad to give you the information.' I said: 'I'm on in 20 minutes and that won't be of much help.' To my astonishment, an officer of the Department of Health and Human Services did return my call in ten minutes. She said that they had received at that point approximately 500 calls on the emergency hotline. About half of them had been questions about social security, a lot had to do with the veterans administration, and most of the rest were about the national parks. It turned out that a free line to the Feds was a very popular innovation. From the point of view of the populace, the government is the government.

Twelve callers claimed that an infant was being improperly treated. In eight of those instances, investigation failed to reveal the existence of any actual infant as described. There were four cases of infants existing as described. There was some basis for enquiry in at least one of the other four cases. In Baltimore, Federal Marshals and police, to their own discomfort, entered the nursery, had no idea what to do once they arrived, were viewed and viewed themselves as being intrusive and withdrew unable to confirm that anything amiss was occurring. I mention that story just to provide some continuity with the references to it that Professor Campbell made, and also to emphasise how much more there is to the unfolding of events than just the question of mutual agreement amongst physicians and family.

I want to insert at this point a brief editorial on the methodology of philosophy and bioethics. In the early days of modern philosophical medical ethics, about 15 years ago, some philosophers engaged in self-indulgent and utterly unhelpful philosophical work focused on medicine, and some of it had the character of developing sustained arguments about what physicians ought to do. The case was advanced on grounds of autonomy that the physician should treat the patient as an independent rational agent worthy of respect and entitled to make his or her own independent decisions about health care. The physician, therefore, was a provider first of information and second, and subsequently, at the direction of the patient, a provider of services as ordered.

Now that struck physicians as simply loony, because physicians had some sense of what patients are like in all their diversity, in their capacities to handle both information and the responsibility of making decisions. So physicians responded to those philosophical admonitions by quite rightly thinking that however well-crafted that argumentation is from abstract points of view, it has nothing to do with physicians or the world in which they struggle and strive. Bioethics, unlike pure philosophy, must be formed by awareness of clinical realities. Not only is that good for making contributions to medical ethics, it is very healthy for philosophers.

Having made that remark, I want to agree that the case for making informed consent is, as Dr Gillon mentioned (in the Discussion on fetal brain transplants following Chapters 4.3 and 4.4), an autonomy-respecting case, but it is more than that. It is also doctor-protecting, and much of the motivation for adhering to meticulous standards of informed consent is as a protection against future liability that is independent of respect for the patients' autonomy. A third factor is that there is some case for informed consent on the grounds of therapeutic utility. There is, at least in a wide range of contexts, reason to believe that patients who understand what is happening and who endorse it do clinically better as patients; that is a dimension of informed consent that should not be overlooked.

The complexity of informed consent hangs on the fact that it can go wrong either in the informing or in the consenting. Those are quite distinct functions. The requirements of the standards of informed consent change with time, and they vary substantially with place and with culture. In the United States we have seen them evolve away from a standard determined primarily by prevailing practices within the profession – at least within the relevant specialty, to a standard of information provided at a level and in a manner in that a reasonable person would want and expect. That is not the same standard, because in some instances a reasonable person might want more information than the conventions of practice were providing. In the Canterbury case, the standard was ratcheted up just a little bit further to the question of whether the information was provided to the extent to which and in the manner to which this *particular* patient wanted it to be.

That is just a glimpse of the way in which standards evolve in one place. Standards also vary very much from culture to culture and, as Professor Lilford (Chapter 6.1) indicated, some patients are happy to elect the 'you decide doctor' option. The likelihood of that choice being elected or even insisted upon varies substantially in the United States from one ethnic group to another. Anglo-saxons are more insistent on being involved in medical decision-making than Italians or Hispanics, for example. That is just a descriptive fact about different attitudes toward medical decision-making.

I said that things can go wrong in a variety of ways; I am going to cite a couple of those ways because when one is interested in getting something right it is often useful to turn one's attention to examples of how it goes wrong. With apologies to any of you who have already read this, I am going use some text in the interest of efficiency (Gorovitz, 1985).

> An unmarried and uneducated woman gave birth to an acutely ill baby. Its survival was in doubt from the outset. On the third day after delivery the physician came in to see the mother. 'I am terribly sorry,' he said, 'your baby didn't make it. We did everything we could, but it just wasn't enough. I would like to do an autopsy, and I'll need your permission for that.' The mother granted permission, later confirmed by her signing an appropriate form. The next morning the physician stopped in to see how she was doing and to discuss her release from the hospital. 'Oh, doctor, I am so glad to see you,' she said. 'I've been so upset and worried. They gave me pills, but I couldn't sleep much anyway. Tell me please, how is my baby? Did the autopsy help?'

The stunned physician realised at once how completely he had failed. He had then to explain to the women that her baby was dead and to inform her that an autopsy is a post-mortem examination often conducted to confirm the cause of a death. Troubled by the episode he related it to his resident, from whom I later heard the tale.

The mother's failure to understand the physician's message was due in part to the fact that she did not know what an autopsy is – but only in part; it is also due in part to the physician's euphemistic language. She thought that the message was: all the standard interventions that we are at liberty to use without special permission are insufficient so we want to do something non-standard for which permission is required. Now that's one illustration of how naive the philosophical admonition is to treat every patient as a thoroughly well-informed and rational decision-maker. It is also a cautionary tale to physicians about assuming too much by way of background understanding.

Let me give you one other illustration. An attending surgeon sought permission to repair the heart of a newborn baby. In explaining to the mother that there was a leakage from one side of the heart to the other he drew a rectangular diagram to illustrate the chambers. 'The heart,' he said, 'has two chambers, the left and the right, and in your baby's case, the two sides are connected by a little hole that lets blood get through from one side to the other. That's no good, and if we don't fix it, your baby won't do well at all and may not live. But that's the kind of problem we can fix. We just go in and sew up that little hole so that the blood stays on the side it should be on. Then your baby will probably have a completely normal life.'

Later the surgical resident went to see the mother to confirm her understanding of what was being done and why. He asked her if she understood; she said she did. 'I want to make sure,' he said, 'so I'd like you to tell me in your own words what the problem is.' 'The problem' she replied, 'is that my baby's got a square heart.'

It is quite a challenge to achieve the desired ideal level of understanding given the range of diversity in patients' background knowledge. The physician who wished to adhere to a high standard is engaged in a very complex enquiry. We had some indications from Professor Lilford of some of the judgements that have to be made in the process of striving to achieve informed consent. It might be useful just to review a list of some of the questions a physician must ask in this process. How much understanding can this patient achieve? What is the patient's background information on which to build that understanding? What will it cost in time and effort to achieve that understanding? What are the psychological barriers to understanding? Does the patient want the information? What is the likelihood that the information will harm the patient if provided for him, either directly or by impeding the process of recovery? How much of what the patient could be made to understand is necessary for reasonable and appropriate levels of informing in the actual circumstances?

What portion of the information, if any, must he be made to understand independently of the patient's interest in or desire for information? How much of the physician's uncertainty about the relevant information should be revealed to the patient?

We heard some information yesterday about the fallibility of research reports based on insufficiently large samples, which should ensure the physician has substantial scepticism about what appears in the medical literature. How much of that scepticism should be revealed to the patient by way of providing full information? And finally, when all that is sorted out, when and how should the information be provided? So it is a very complex undertaking.

Human reproduction

What about the context of human reproduction? Are there any special features of that context which make the situation even worse? There is surely a more complex array of legitimately interested persons than is often the case in other areas of medical practice. There is a gradation from the simplest case of one individual, adult, competent, independently-functioning patient from whom the physician seeks consent after providing appropriate information and achieving the appropriate level of understanding. Quite commonly, the individual patient is not functioning entirely independently. Maybe there is a spouse who is very much involved, concerned and interacting. The situation is rather more complicated when the patient is a minor and consent is sought from parents. (In the United States, for research protocols, the child is viewed as an independent decision-maker from the age of seven and must agree as well to the protocol. That is not the case for clinical intervention; for minors, parents consent.) But parents do not always agree, and some of the most difficult cases are those involving difficult treatment decisions that must be made on behalf of a minor whose parents disagree about what ought to be done. The complexity is in part rooted in the fact that there is not just a single undivided locus of decision and of provision or withholding of consent. In the context of human reproduction there are inevitably multiple legitimate interests and variables. Somewhere in the story there is at least a male, a female and, depending on how one counts, the diffuse notion of the interests of the child who may come to be.

Let me give you some specific examples in which the provision of treatment has been complicated by the complexities around consent. Here is a real case. A woman sought an abortion in the USA this year under conditions in which she was clearly entitled to it. The father, if you like that term in this context, or the male responsible for the pregnancy, if you prefer that it be put that way, did not approve. He sought and obtained a court injunction barring the abortion on the grounds that he as an ancestor had legitimate rights in respect to the potential child. There is not, traditionally, symmetry between male and female interests in such matters. That case landed in the courts.

In assisted human reproduction, where we can have a sperm donor, *in vitro* fertilisation, an egg donor, a surrogate mother, and a commissioning couple, there are many primary players apart from the various doctors and lawyers who participate. We have no clear idea of what the notion of informed consent means in the context of that kind of complexity. With respect to issues in human reproduction, do we also need, in order to proceed, the consent of those who are not principals, not directly involved, but whom we might view as the sensitively interested or the offended? Some would argue that agreement among all the would-be participants in some of these arrangements is insufficient, no matter what the level of information and nature of this consent, because some of these procedures threaten to change the fabric of social relationships and therefore require some sort of societal consent as well. For that reason, consent in the context of human reproduction is doubly complex. It retains all the levels and layers of complexity that I referred to in the general case, but has this additional overlay.

There is one other aspect in which consent in the context of human reproduction may be more of a challenge. It can be argued that it requires, because of its subject matter, a higher degree of self-knowledge that most other contexts. Some would argue that consent with respect to innovative methods of human reproduction requires a higher level of self-knowledge than can be achieved. Let me cite two illustrations. One is the infamous case of Baby M (see Chapter 2.1). Mary Beth Whitehead agreed to participate in an arrangement on behalf of the commissioning couple for a fee. She believed that she would be affected in certain ways, would have certain reactions, but, by her account subsequent to the delivery of the child, she simply was wrong about how she would react to the experiences that followed from her decision. She did not know herself well enough.

Another example concerns one of the more vigorous participants in the sperm bank programme where he was a medical student. He went to Medical School in a community that was limited in size and he was suddenly beset, some years later, by the perception that the young couples that he saw in the park, engaged, one Spring, in the sort behaviour that young couples engage in in parks in the Spring, for all he knew, might well be both of them half his. By his retrospective calculations, there were many adolescents around who were products of his entrepreneurial approach to financing his medical education. He was very upset by the thought that half-siblings, who did not know they were half-siblings, were making sport, unaware of their genetic inheritance. Here is an instance in which someone wanted these people to be informed of their biological heritage to protect them against what he saw as a highly undersirable risk.

I was much impressed by Professor Lilford's accounts (Chapter 6.1) of how, in the specific context of his clinical and research practice, judgements, that the cognitive psychologists have demonstrated so effectively, play out and are illustrated. I want to emphasise – and I know that Professor Lilford agrees with this, although he did not make this point explicitly – that the judgemental biases, the reliance on judgemental heuristics, the various weaknesses of intellect demonstrated by that kind of research are not characteristic specifically of pregnant women, but of human minds. In particular, they are as easily demonstrable when the tested population are physicians as with any other sector, and that is one of the reasons why respecting the patient's right to play a primary role in decision-making is a preferable alterntive to having the physician make the judgement. There is not much reason to believe that the physician making the judgements, in a wide range of areas, would be making them in a better way. I readily grant that within certain areas, where the question is essentially medical, that is not the case.

I will cite a little bit of research I did myself as an amateur, *ad hoc* social scientist. I asked a group of about 40 health care providers, physicians and nurses primarily, to imagine that they had been screened for a disease. I described both the incidence of the disease in the population and the screening test. The screening test was one with high selectivity and sensitivity, numerically over 95%. I asked them – and gave them an hour to turn in their answers – what the probability is that they have the disease, given that they have a positive test result. Only two physicians got it right; nearly all said that the probability was over 85% when the actual probability was 4.6%; which is demonstrable in minutes once one goes through the calculations.

That is just another example of the striking ineptitude with which we all handle statistical and risk-related information if we are not being meticulous. The nurses, incidentally, were meticulous. They did considerably better than the physicians on this examination.

One of the lessons that one learns is the importance of paying attention to the current working of cognitive psychology. It is not just about college sophomores and other typical experimental populations, it is about us all. When I teach in related areas, I always re-do some of the experiments in class to emphasise that it is about *them*, about the students' own minds. But they do not believe that until they participate in the experiments. That is another kind of bias that we have, that statistical information is always about others, not about ourselves. As Professor Lilford indicates, taken properly into account, such information powerfully influences what the approach to informed consent ought to be. It changes the way information is packaged and provided, and it changes the way its transmission is tested, to a way that requires an interactive process.

Informed consent is valuable morally and therapeutically, is legally necessary, is challenging and difficult to achieve, and it can never, in any situation of any complexity, be satisfactorily achieved in a perfunctory or bureaucratic fashion. Unfortunately, in the USA, it is not a 'billiable service' so it tends often to be approached in a minimalistic way, much to the detriment of both physicians and patients alike.

Reference

Gorovitz, S. (1985). *Doctors' Dilemmas: Moral Conflict and Medical Care*, pp. 19–39. Oxford University Press, New York.

Whose consent?

Introduction. Evolving medical law & ethics

I first addressed doctors on the law and ethics of reproductive medicine in the early dark days of 1985. They felt under seige in the wake of the Court of Appeal's ruling in December 1984 in favour of Mrs Victoria Gillick's campaign to prohibit the contraceptive treatment of under-sixteen-year-olds, even in exceptional cases, without parental consent. I said that the decision would be reversed by the Law Lords. They did not believe me. They shared this scepticism with many unlikely bedfellows, principally monks, who must be the unlikeliest of bedfellows. I had at the same time written an article in the Catholic press, criticising the Court of Appeal and Mrs Gillick's campaign. One or two monks wrote to me and the press, accusing me of incompetence, malevolence and (from an enclosed monastery) of living in an ivory tower.

The doctors who invited me quite frequently to discuss the Gillick case as it progressed through the courts only explicitly consented to my analysis of that particular issue. I disregarded their wishes and also insisted on mentioning three other topics which some doctors were perhaps less keen to hear. First, I said that while some Catholics like myself might disagree with Mrs Gillick on the legal position with regard to teenage contraception, this should not be taken as siding with doctors who imagined that they would win the arguments on the then recent Warnock majority with respect to embryo experimentation. Second, nor should it be taken as siding with those doctors who supported the present Abortion Act. Third, I warned that the litigation which they should really worry about was not Gillick but Sidaway, a case which seemed at first sight to have nothing to do with reproductive medicine but which in fact I claimed had everything to do with developing a doctrine of informed consent throughout the practice of medicine and beyond.

Prophecy is a hazardous business but one's apparent success rate is enhanced by selective memory. Thus, my recollection might have been hazier in other circumstances – if, for instance, just one Law Lord had changed his mind and

Mrs Gillick had won. She lost by the narrowest of margins, 3–2 in the House of Lords, having in fact gained a 5–4 majority of all the judges who heard the case. You can fool some of the judges all of the time ...

But the point I wish to stress by way of introduction is that all the four issues which I then raised still have much to do with my topic today: 'Whose consent?'. Indeed, this title was chosen in the light of those issues, well before the 1987 decision of the Law Lords to authorise sterilisation of a mentally handicapped teenager which now gives the subject even greater poignancy. It is salutary to remember that this conference was planned two years ago and that the title 'Whose consent?' was in fact selected, initially without my consent (although once doctors have decided what we should consent to, the rest seems inevitable), in 1986 in the post-Gillickian euphoria of the medical profession. It is salutary because it shows both the permanency and the flux of medical law and ethics. We have heard little about Gillick this week whereas only recently that case was the preoccupation of such conferences. On the other hand, the issue of 'Whose consent?' will not date. New contexts will come and go but the problem will remain.

The context of the sterilisation case to which I have referred, Re B, is also central to my theme. It was also predictable as one sketched out an emerging doctrine of consent in medical law and ethics back in 1985. Even this week's issue of fetal tissue for brain transplants has long been anticipated by philosophers and others (see, for example, Jonathan Glover in *The New York Review of Books* in 1985). And as the Warnock saga threatens at long last to reach the statute book, there are many more issues as to 'Whose consent?' which deserve our renewed attention. The public debate on Warnock has not yet reached some of the issues of consent latent within that Report. In contrast, the public has moved onto the question of consent in relation to another topic, AIDS.

I will first try to put all these different phenomena into some kind of structure so that we can see how the parts connect to make up the whole doctrine of consent. Then I will focus on the questions of who should consent when the person most directly affected is incompetent and on what principles should such consent be given or withheld. Finally, I will suggest that this provides a good test of what we think about the ethics of many procedures in reproductive medicine, whether or not consent by proxy is involved, and I will point out that since we all have to take decisions for others, there is a duty to educate ourselves and our students towards assuming that onerous responsibility.

By way of of an example to keep at the back of our minds throughout all this, we might take a non-medical problem. It is a dilemma for anyone who fits the category which I dubbed, in my book on *Law and Morals* (1986), the trendy, liberal, Guardian-reading, Hampstead-living person. One such reviewer, Rabbi Julia Neuberger, who lives in Clapham, suggested that I myself had much in sympathy with such a caricature. Would that I could afford to live in Hampstead. I can only just about afford to buy the *Guardian*. Anyway, the problem concerns such people's children's education. Suppose only two schools are in consideration. An unimpressive state school and a spectacular fee-paying school to which the parents can afford to send the children. I do *not* in any way suggest that this is the normal relative status of state and fee-paying schools. If the parents decide their children's schooling in what they think is in the best interests of the parents themselves, they might send the children to state schools so as to preserve their liberal credentials. If they were deciding in the interests of the community as a whole, they might reach the conclusion because they would bring middle-class parental pressure to bear on improving the school and because their brilliant children would radiate Hampstead values which would benefit children from sub-Hampstead suburbs (I should explain that anywhere north of the River Thames is now Hampstead in estate agent-ese but there is Hampstead and then there is Hampstead). But they could still believe that if they really ought to decide in the interests of their children, the best result could be to send them to an independent school which could cater for the special talents their children possess. Whose consent is it? For whom? By whom? Even the decision to let the children decide is a decision itself which many parents will see in this context as a heaven-sent opportunity to deny responsibility. In this and in many other daily dilemmas, we have constantly to address the question of whose consent is it anyway?

Still working towards a jurisprudence of consent

Immediately after the House of Lords ruling in the Gillick case in 1985, I wrote my contribution to the third series of *Oxford Essays in Jurisprudence* which finally saw the light of publication in 1987. My paper was entitled 'Towards A Jurisprudence of Consent'. I tried to piece together the various strands of different common law decisions and suggested that six questions needed to be answered to provide a full, coherent doctrine of consent:

(1) Does the person concerned have the capacity to consent?

(2) If not, who is in the best position to act as proxy and on what criteria should the proxy decide?

(3) Is the 'consent' voluntary?

(4) Is the 'consent' based on information as to the risks of the course of conduct?

(5) Is the 'consent' based on information as to the alternative courses of action?

(6) Even if the above conditions are satisfied, is there any over-riding reason to invalidate the consent?

I see no reason radically to revise the questions. But what about the answers?

I was at pains in that essay to stress that, for lawyers, the concept of consent is a tool which they can use in various ways. We manipulate the doctrine of consent to reflect our values and our interpretation of the facts. The search is not for the right meaning of a word. The search is a more fundamental one, a quest for the holy grail of the perfect, or least imperfect, patient–doctor relationship. So consent is in most cases a technique for safeguarding patients' autonomy or a doctrine which acts as a corrective to the doctor's power and professional paternalism. In cases where the absence, or limited nature, of autonomy, precludes any autonomy-based explanation for a requirement of 'consent', proxy consent is at least a reminder that the decision-maker should have at the forefront the interests of the patients and should bear in mind the different grounds on which decisions could be taken, as in the fee-paying school example.

I must also stress that the *legal* doctrine of consent is a means to two distinct ends. Litigation begun after some medical event and based on the absence of consent can be undertaken either to gain monetary compensation and/or to set standards for future medical care. These functions are distinguishable. A system of no-fault compensation would be a more than adequate surrogate for the former role, and effective, fair disciplinary procedures could perform the latter role. Unless and until the medical profession (a) lobbies for no-fault compensation and (b) sets its own internal disciplinary house in order in the wake of the outrageous show trial of Wendy Savage, then the legal doctrine of consent will be manipulated to serve divergent ends. The court will in many cases be swayed by factors which ought to be irrelevant.

There is another proviso before we address the main questions. The choice in Gillick was not between autonomy and paternalism. It was a choice between medical paternalism, parental paternalism and legal paternalism. I should add that, with a nod in Mrs Gillick's direction, I would be happy to use the term 'maternalism' if that is preferred. By the time we reach the sterilisation case, Re B, the choice is between medical, parental, legal or state paternalism, once the local authority steps into the debate.

There are thus different dimensions to the question: whose consent? We must ask: consent by whom and for whom and on what principles? In terms of my earlier structure, we are principally concerned with the first two questions of a doctrine of consent; whether the patient has the competence to decide and, if not, who should act as proxy and on what criteria? But the other questions are also relevant. For example, the more we require patients to understand about the risks and alternatives, then the higher the hurdle for the capacity to consent.

Finally, in this second section of preamble as to developing a doctrine of consent, with particular reference to 'Whose consent?', I must stress that for the most part we are dealing with a common law area in which the judges gradually fill in pieces of the jigsaw as litigation provides analogues to my six questions. There are occasional statutory interventions, as in the Data Protection Act, but by and large this area of the law is judge-made.

Now, it has emerged in this conference (if not from time immemorial) that lawyers sometimes speak a different language from medics and philosophers. To take one example, I find philosophical papers on surrogacy difficult to follow when they talk about 'contracts'. They often argue as if those who wish to renege on some contractual commitment are always forced to follow it through. A moment's thought will show that this not so. To use an example from the Small World of international conferences, if you buy a ticket from Timbuctoo to Leeds and then at the last moment decide that you do not want to go to Leeds, no court will force you onto the plane. They might make financial adjustments as between you and the airline. But then we begin to talk about the airline's duty to mitigate the loss by getting another passenger. The analogy with surrogacy then becomes different from the impression conjured up by misusing the pseudo-legal concept of a 'contract'.

But I must warn you that not only do medics and philosophers have difficulty in understanding lawyers, so do lawyers themselves. There is as yet no satisfactory theory of how judges decide hard cases. All that may change on 23 October 1988 with the publication of a book entitled *Judging Judges* (Faber & Faber). For the moment, we are beset by what one might call common law myths. Lawyers explain judicial decisions according to the fairy tale, the noble dream or the nightmare.

The judging of judges is a curious business. The fairy tale, put about by many judges, is that there is an Aladdin's cave in which the answers to the common law can be found on saying the magic password, not 'Open Sesame' but 'precedent' or 'statutory interpretation'. The noble dream is Professor Dworkin's elaborate and sophisticated development of that idea. He claims that there are principles or rights inherent in the law which will guide judges to the one right answer in what seems to be a hard case. Judges are, for him, chain novelists trying to develop a story while keeping faith with the plot as laid down by earlier writers. The nightmare, suffered by Professor Griffith, is that, on the contrary, judges have freedom which they exercise to decide in the interests of their class. Judges are old, white, male, rich, upper-middle-class, public-school and Oxbridge. They think in the same conservative and Conservative way.

Incidentally, our earlier discussions on surrogacy might be short-circuited on this account. Instead of worrying about the gestatory or genetic links, the nightmare thesis would say that what really happens when a court has to choose between mothers is that the court decides in favour of the richer, more middle-class litigant, as in the first instance decision in New Jersey's Baby M case. In a parallel case here, however, a court last year gave the child to the impecunious, single-parent mother living on supplementary benefit and denied access to the middle-class, professional couple who had asked her to act as their surrogate.

The fairy tale, the noble dream and the nightmare distort reality. This does not mean that they are without interest. To use a pretentious phrase much-loved in jurisprudential circles in the USA and which alludes to Monet's studies of the cathedral at Rouen, each theorist is presenting one view of the cathedral of law. Those looking from the right or the left cannot see the whole picture. But in painting what they see, they give us insights, not only to the cathedral but also to their own vantage point. The process of a conference such as this, or the dialogue between theorists of judicial behaviour, involves wandering around the cathedral, seeking to understand the perspective from which people paint as much as the picture which they produce.

The reality is that judges are influenced by three factors. First, their view of the past law (precedents, statutes and principles). Second, their evaluation of the future consequences of alternative decisions. Third, their view of their own constitutional role. Should they be activist judges trumping the first factor with the second? Or should they defer to the legislature and wait for Parliament to trump the first with its more representative view of the second factor? This is not the place to develop a theory of adjudication but it is important to stress the controversy which surrounds the judicial role in hard cases and to highlight the variety of factors which can influence the development of doctrines such as consent.

Contexts for 'Whose Consent?'

I can think of at least ten issues where those concerned with reproductive medicine have to ask: 'Whose consent?'

   teenage contraception
   abortion
   sterilisation of the mentally handicapped
   withholding neo-natal care
   testing for HIV
   experimenting on human embryos
   AID and surrogacy
   eligibility for IVF
   transplanting fetal tissue
   using anencephalic babies as organ donor banks.

Let me add that, while the list is obvious, we could ask various different questions about any one of these illustrations. We could ask who is the proxy under British law and on what criteria should the proxy decide. Or we could ask what *should* the law say about this problem. Or we could ask what would be the morally right solution. For example, under the heading of abortion, one might ask whose consent is needed under the present British law. The answer would be: the mother's, two doctors', Parliament's and occasionally the judges' consent. This came out in the Oxford student abortion case, C *v*. S, in the early months of 1987. But one of the issues in that case which the courts did not get around to discussing was whether we should add another consent to that list, namely the father's. 'No' would have been the answer at the level of what the law is but there might be at least some disagreement at the level of what would be morally preferable or even legally preferable. And in case you think that you have the answer to that one for all time, bear in mind the possibility that in the future there might well be babies who have been brought to term without ever being in a human womb. I imagine a laboratory with a bank of microwave wombs. The embryo is popped in, the timer is set for nine months, the parents can watch the embryo grow through the door and when the bell tolls, it tolls for thee. Suppose in that context, the fetus is handicapped or the parents are splitting up or the parents become psychiatrically ill, whose 'consent' ought to be required for an abortion which would involve pulling the plug out of the electricity socket?

Returning to the present law on abortion, it is far from clear that the different consents are to be given or withheld on the same grounds. The mother might well think of the issue as her giving consent to something happening to her. Society, through parliament has placed the requirement of the consent of two doctors for a complex amalgam of reasons, some to do with the mother's best interests, others to do with the fetus's, others perhaps to do with society's. Who is acting for themselves and who is a proxy for someone else, and on what criteria?

Or to demonstrate another dimension to the problem, the eighth example which I gave, eligibility for IVF, reminds us that consent is a necessary but not a sufficient condition in many contexts. The case last year of a woman refused a place on an IVF programme shows that while she may consent to IVF, in a world of limited, society-funded resources, society may not consent to her as a suitable candidate for the treatment. That is one reason why my original structure insists on a last question as to whether there is any over-riding interest in society which trumps the consent.

So whose consent is good enough? This is the case which I refer to as decommissioning the commissioning couple. I suppose that more accurately, it should be regarded as the case of refusing to commission the would-be commissioning couple. Towards the end of last year a judge decided a case (R *v*. St. Mary's Hospital, ex p Harriott) in which a woman who wished to have a child but who was infertile applied to be considered for *in vitro* fertilisation under the National Health Service. She was refused treatment and she challenged her rejection in court. Mr Justice Schiemann decided against her but his judgement opens up several questions of interest to medical law and ethics. As the judge said, 'This I believe is the first ocasion when a decision to refuse treatment for an illness, and for the present purposes infertility may be regarded as an illness, has been the subject of an application for judicial review.' He declined to decide the questions of principle as to whether an ethics committee or a consultant could be subject to judicial review. In the case before him, the judge was convinced that even if review was available in principle, it should not be exercised in practice because the committee and the doctor had not erred in law.

But ethics committee which came to absurd decisions might well find the courts intervening: 'If the committee had advised, for instance, that the IVF unit should in principle refuse all such treatment to anyone who was a Jew or coloured then I think the courts might well grant a declaration that such a policy was illegal.'

Similarly, the judge was prepared for the purpose of the argument to assume that the doctor/patient relationship was within his purview. He also could 'see arguable grounds for criticism of [the consultant's] decision in December 1984 not to treat the applicant (because the patient had not been given a chance to argue that her case was exceptional, and because she was misled as to the true reasons for refusal) but the patient had had a later opportunity to argue her case and now knew the real reasons'.

Those were, incidentally, that the patient's applications to foster or adopt children had been turned down by the social services department, that she had criminal convictions for running a brothel and soliciting for prostitution, and that her husband's children by a former liaison were in care.

One might well ask whether the reasons to refuse treatment in this case were appropriate. Of course, society's interests are mostly to do with the allocation of scarce resources. But still, did these reasons reflect the human rights law which lurks in the background? What about Article 12 of the European Convention, for example, which guarantees that 'Everyone has the right to marry and to found a family subject to the national laws governing the exercise of this right'? Does this Article mean that everyone has the right to found a family except those who are infertile and who used to run brothels? When Parliament comes to legislate on the Warnock proposals, it ought to face the question of eligibility for treatment which Warnock raises. One factor to bear in mind is that sooner or later someone who is refused treatment will be 'taking their case to Europe'. Not that many people seem to know where in Europe such cases are taken since the European Court of Human Rights in Strasburg is frequently confused by the media with the European Court of Justice at Luxembourg. It is the former which is preoccupied with human rights issues and the latter which is the judicial arm of the EEC and thus preoccupied, for the most part, with trading issues.

What I propose to do is simply take two of these many contexts as examples of judicial resolution of the question 'Whose consent?' and then switch to the legislature for some final thoughts about the ways forward in a further context.

I shall choose the two House of Lords' decisions of recent vintage on the law and ethics of reproductive medicine, Gillick and Re B. Then I shall use the Warnock legislation as a very brief spur to our final discussion of the conference.

Gillick

It is possible that at some point I shall tire of this example. Indeed, I am becoming so weary of it that I will pare my discussion down to a few paragraphs and refer you elsewhere for more detailed discussion.

Victoria Gillick sought a declaration that a DHSS circular was unlawful in that it permitted doctors, in exceptional circumstances, to give contraceptive advice and treatment to under-sixteen-year-olds without parental consent. She lost in the High Court, won a unanimous decision in the Court of Appeal and lost 3–2 in the House of Lords.

I have analysed Lord Scarman's judgement in some depth, showing how his one great principle which he claimed to have found within the law was actually rendered in six different formulations by the judge, with different rationales. Even within one of Lord Scarman's formulations there is plenty of room for judicial manouevre. We could, for example, lay down a strong or a weak test of what is meant by capacity to understand what is involved, pitching the requirement of understanding at different levels. Lord Scarman seemed to place a very high premium on understanding, setting a standard which perhaps very few adults could meet:

> When applying these conclusions to contraceptive advice and treatment it has to be borne in mind that there is much that has to be understood by a girl under the age of 16 if she is to have the legal capacity to consent to such treatment. It is not enough that she should have understood the nature of the advice which is being given: she must also have a sufficient maturity to understand what is involved. There are moral and family questions, especially her relationship with her parents; long-term problems associated with the emotional impact of pregnancy and its termination; and there are the risks to health of sexual intercourse at her age, risks which contraception may diminish but cannot eliminate. It follows that a doctor will have to satisfy himself that she is able to appraise these factors before he can safely proceed on the basis that she has at law capacity to consent to contraceptive treatment. And it further follows that ordinarily the proper course will be for him, as the guidance lays down, first to seek to persuade the girl to bring her parents into consultation, and, if she refuses, not to prescribe contraceptive treatment unless he is satisfied that her circumstances are such that he ought to proceed without parental knowledge and consent.

Moreover, there is still room for discretion here in the meaning we attach to the verb 'to understand' throughout that passage.

And again, the width of the exceptions to the need for such capacity and consent (e.g. where there is parental abuse of the child, Lord Scarman thought that a doctor could exceptionally act without the parental consent even if the patient did not have sufficient capacity to understand) contribute to the overall picture of the significance of consent. A judge can concoct a mixture of tests and exceptions to suit his vision of how the law should be tackling the problem of teenage contraception. What is important for our present concern is that the previous legal material is not the sole determinant of the strength of the mixture which any particular judge adopts. Although Lord Scarman spoke as if he was searching for something which was latent in the case-law, Lord Templeman, dissenting, ignored case-law. Their disagreement is at least as much a disagreement as to the future consequences of their decisions as a disagreement on precedent.

The charade of the case was that counsel and judges argued as if the social consequences and moral judgements were irrelevant and that the past law was decisive. In fact, however, it was the unarticulated assumption about consequences and values which determined the judicial disagreements. The judgements are the justification for the decision, not at accurate account of the thought process which led to the conclusion.

The outcome of the case in practice may be that girls do not really match up to Lord Scarman's criteria but doctors may say that they do. I do not know. But I suspect that the tussle between legal, medical and parental paternalism goes on, and that the real decisions are taken behind closed surgery doors. Now I approve of the majority decision. But I would just comment that it was the public suspicion of what was going on behind the closed doors which generated some support for Mrs Gillick. I imagine that her supporters were sceptical of how doctors acted as proxies, as to whether they were really thinking about the best interests of the particular girl or whether they were thinking about society's interests or the interests of the medical profession. In many ways that was a lesson worth learning. People care about the question 'Whose consent?'

Sterilising the mentally handicapped

But once the lessons of Gillick have been absorbed then the central case for 'Whose consent?' is Re B, the sterilisation of the mentally handicapped teenager. In Re B the Law Lords gave leave for the Official Solicitor to appeal against a decision of the Court of Appeal to authorise the sterilisation of a mentally handicapped 17-year-old girl. The girl had a mental age of 5, so the experts said. When she had been of the physical age of 4 years she had been described as a 'wild animal' by social workers. Her behaviour had improved but she would never be capable of consenting to marriage. She could not understand the link between pregnancy and childbrith. She could not care for a child, but she was becoming sexually aware. Those who looked after her, a local authority and her mother, decided to ask for permission to sterilise her. In wardship proceedings, the judge at first instance, the Court of Appeal and the

House of Lords all consented to the sterilisation of the girl without her consent. They acted as proxies. They argued that the only criteria needed for that decision is the family lawyers' phrase: is it in the best interests of the child?

The case sped through the courts at an unprecedented rate because there were only weeks to go before her 18th birthday at which point even the judges might have become unable to act as a proxy. On some views there would then be a power vacuum: nobody might be able to consent. Why? The courts' powers here depend on a statute which enables them to make children wards of court but the wardship jurisdiction is extinguished at the age of 18. Some of us would claim that the wardship procedure is only a statutory manifestation of an inherent, prerogative right in society to look after those who cannot look after themselves, known in the legal trade as the *parens patriae* jurisdiction. The judges did not want to risk finding out that we were wrong. Nor did they want to risk establishing a contraceptive regime which required daily administration (or 3 monthly injections or whatever) after the 18th birthday in case that too would be unlawful. The medical evidence was that there was a 40% chance of a contraceptive pill regime being successfully established. But that would have run into these uncertainties as to life after 18.

I should confess a tangential involvement in this case in so far as Professor Ian Kennedy and myself wrote an article in *The Times* on the day before the case was argued in the House of Lords and that article was much discussed by their Lordships. Times have indeed changed since I was a student a decade ago. In those days, some lawyers still claimed that only the textbooks of now deceased academics could be cited in court. The only good legal academic was a dead legal academic, a feeling with which you might have some sympathy. But reports of our deaths are much exaggerated. Unfortunately, the Law Lords rejected our arguments. Indeed, they were quite indignant at our article and particularly its heading – 'This rush to judgement'. I would still maintain, however, that the Law Lords did rush to judgement, that they would have been better advised to pay more attention to the Canadian precedents as we urged and that they were only storing up trouble by avoiding the question of the *parens patriae* jurisdiction, as I shall explain shortly. Sure enough, the *parens patriae* point has now arisen in a recent case, T *v.* T, and we will inevitably be the poorer for the failure of the Law Lords to anticipate that. Extraordinarily, the Canadian case was not even discussed before the first instance court or the Court of Appeal. It was only after the publicity which the Court of Appeal's decision attracted, that the barristers concerned were told by academics about the existence of this case. I was present at the oral argument in the House of Lords. It took one day. The only case discussed was Re Eve, the Canadian decision. The only other material, other than the decisions of the courts below and the argument of counsel, before the Law Lords was the newspaper article. Instead of thumbing through dusty tomes, each Law Lord was rustling through yesterday's newspaper and saying things like. 'Look at the paragraph to the right of the picture'.

I am not here concerned with the result of Re B or T *v.* T, I am concerned rather with the decision-making process, the question of whose consent is in issue and how it should be exercised on behalf of an incompetent person by their 'proxy'. I think the Canadian Supreme Court's approach in Re Eve was preferable to the Law Lords' efforts and that the Canadian provincial court's approach was better still.

In retrospect, it might seem surprising that the Law Lords even bothered to hear an appeal in Re B. Their judgements seem to suggest that the result was obvious. But the case came hard on the heels of another *cause celebre*, the Oxford student abortion case, C *v.* S, which had also aroused much public disquiet. The Law Lords had declined to hear that appeal but now they were faced with academics and journalists calling the Court of Appeal's determination in Re B all sorts of names. A professor from another London college went on the radio to denounce it as a 'Nazi decision'. Germaine Greer seemed to be denouncing it everywhere.

So should a court authorise the sterilisation of a mentally handicapped young woman? The answers are responses to the second issue within my framework – who is in the best position to act as proxy and on what criteria should the proxy decide?

Some parents, doctors and social workers might believe that they themselves should be able to decide whether or not to sterilise a mentally handicapped teenager who is under their care. But the Court of Appeal and the House of Lords rightly rejected that view. To that extent, their judgements are to be welcomed as a tightening of the law and practice. Yet all the judges who heard this case at all levels were prepared to authorise the sterilisation of this particular 17-year-old. They said that they were acting in 'the best interests of the girl' as a matter of last resort.

At this point, several objections could be made. First, some critics believe that the compulsory sterilisation of those unable to give or refuse consent, is always unacceptable. Second, some believe that sterilisation should only have been contemplated for therapeutic or medical reasons, and not merely as a form of contraception. Third, some would accept other forms of contraception but believe that the irreversible nature of sterilisation makes it the wrong choice. Fourth, some accept the need for sterilisation in some such cases but fear a drift down the path towards eugenics (a link which the judges strenuously denied) and bemoan the insensitive, demeaning discussion which lumps people together under labels such as 'the mentally handicapped'. Fifth, some critics regret the Law Lords' failure to specify the criteria implicit in their vague 'best interests' test and wish that their Lordships had examined the human rights at stake in greater detail. Sixth, some critics feel that the judges missed an opportunity to clarify the law's responsibilities towards the mentally handicapped in adult life, since the ruling was based on a statutory jurisdiction which ends at the age of 18. Seventh, some critics think that the real blame lies at Parliament's doors where legislators consistently duck sensitive moral dilemmas and leave the judges to resolve the ensuing mess. Finally, some people are disturbed by the facts of the particular case and in particular by the fact that the girl in question was sterilised only days before her 18th birthday, at which point the authority of this judgement would expire.

In contrast to the wide range of public concern, the Law Lords themselves had no doubts at all about their decision to authorise the sterilisation. Lord Bridge, for example, claimed: 'It is clear beyond argument that for her pregnancy would be an unmitigated disaster. The only question is how she may best be protected against it. The evidence proves overwhelmingly that the right answer is by a simple operation for occlusion of the fallopian tubes . . . I find it difficult to understand how anybody examining the facts humanely, compassionately and objectively could reach any other conclusion'.

But one might perhaps reach other conclusions for a variety of humane, compassionate and objective reasons. First, would pregnancy really be such a disaster? Second, if it would be disastrous, should she not be protected against sexual exploitation so that the question of pregnancy would never arise? Third, even if one was prepared to tolerate a contraceptive solution to her problems, is irreversible sterilisation the right option? Above all, how on earth does sterilisation help if the real danger is the one of sexual exploitation?

On the first claim that pregnancy would be a disaster, Lord Oliver, for instance, says: 'Should she become pregnant, it would be desirable that the pregnancy should be terminated'. But why? The baby would not be at risk. The mother, according to the specialist evidence, 'would tolerate the condition of pregnancy without undue distress'. Admittedly she would have to be delivered by Caesarean section since she would panic unduly during normal childbirth. The Law Lords were worried that she would pick at the post-operative scar but that hardly seems a ground for an abortion, even within the present legislation.

On the second question of sexual experience, none of their Lordships takes the point that she ought to be protected against sexual exploitation whether or not she could become pregnant. They seem to be contrasting the fear of an unsterilised girl becoming pregnant causing her to lead a restricted life with the greater freedom they would allow her once sterilised. Are these really the alternatives?

On the third point of choosing between various contraceptive measures, there is an argument that the irreversibility of sterilisation makes it even less desirable and even more symbolically degrading. On the other hand, the Law Lords thought that, say, the contraceptive pill would involve a daily violation of the girl's privacy and would be far more risky as a contraceptive and would perhaps have harmful side-effects for a girl with her particular physical problems (such as epilepsy and obesity). That takes us back to the point that everybody in the case seems to have assumed that some form of contraception was inevitable and desirable.

What is particularly intriguing for students of medical law and judicial reasoning, however, is that another final court of appeal, the Canadian Supreme Court, had just examined the same question. In the case of Re Eve, it answered the same question, with the opposite conclusion.

The Canadian Court had three advantages over the Law Lords. First, it had time. It took 5 years for Eve's case to move from the provincial court to the Supreme Court. It took 16 months after the hearing for the Supreme Court to produce its judgement. Here the Court of Appeal reached its decision on 23 March. The Law Lords decided after only one day's argument on 2 April and gave their judgements 3 weeks later. The rush was because everyone in the British case assumed, perhaps wrongly, that if the girl were not sterilised before her 18th birthday on 20 May, nobody, not even the Court, would thereafter have been able to authorise treatment for her since statute decrees that she would then cease to be a ward of court.

The second advantage was that there were several *amici curiae*, presenting the views of interested third parties to the Canadian court so that it could benefit from the widest range of arguments.

The third helpful factor was that the Supreme Court was able to rely on the research of the Canadian Law Commission. The Law Commissions here, however, have consistently failed to address questions of medical law and ethics. Parliament fails to reform the law to keep pace with medical developments and the challenges they pose. The courts meanwhile are left to solve issues of the greatest moral import, often in a rush and without the benefit of considered reflection of public policy. This has happened with teenage contraception and with abortion, it is happening with surrogacy and it may well happen with AIDS. The time for a better method is overdue. The long-term solution must be to follow the French and many others by creating a Commission on Medical Law and Ethics, a Super-Warnock.

La Forest J., giving judgement for all nine members of the Supreme Court in Re Eve, concluded that: 'The grave intrusion on a person's rights and the certain physical damage that ensues from non-therapeutic sterilisation without consent, when compared to the highly questionable advantage that can result from it, have persuaded me that it can never safely be determined that such a procedure is for the benefit of that person. Accordingly the procedure should never be authorised for non-therapeutic purposes under the *parens patriae* jurisdiction.'

The Court agreed that sterilisation may, on occasion, be necessary and lawful as 'treatment of a serious malady'. The crucial distinction is between sterilisation for medical reasons (therapeutic sterilisation) which may be permissible, and sterilisation for non-medical reasons such as for contraception, which was absolutely unacceptable to the Supreme Court.

If the Law Lords were moved to disagree with the Supreme Court's careful, well-researched and long-planned judgement, there should perhaps have been time for more than one day's pause and reflection.

The Canadian Supreme Court said that wardship is but a statutory example of a general common-law principle that the state will take care of those who cannot take care of themselves, known as the *parens patriae* jurisdiction. Lord Eldon's emphatic assertion in an 1827 decision should have been followed by the Law Lords: 'it belongs to the King as *parens patriae*, having the care of those who are not able to take care of themselves, and is founded on the obvious necessity that the law should place somewhere the care of individuals who cannot take care of themselves, particularly in cases where it is clear that some care should be thrown round them.' Clearly, to Lord Eldon this jurisdiction is not limited to the care of children under 18. If the House of Lords had followed Lord Eldon and the Canadian Supreme Court, the urgency would have disappeared. The case could then have been adjourned for more measured examination of the question of sterilisation.

T. was 19 with severe mental handicap. She was found to be 11 weeks pregnant. Mre Justice Wood declared that it would not be unlawful to terminate the pregnancy and sterilise T.

T's powers of verbal communication are extremely limited. She is doubly incontinent. She is epileptic and is on a heavy prescription of drugs. She has no understanding of menstruation. She has become unco-operative and destructive since the death of a grandmother who had helped her mother (the parents are divorced) care for her. Her mental age, we are told, was assessed at 2.9 years when she was physically 13. Her IQ was assessed at less than 30. She is totally dependent on others.

The judge pleaded for the gap in the law exposed by Re B to be addressed. He concluded that nobody could act as a proxy when a mentally handicapped person was over the age of 18. He decided to exercise an unusual power in the extraordinary circumstances of the case and to grant a declaration as to the legal consequences of future actions.

He said that the court (which is, of course, acting as proxy) should ask: 'What does medical practice demand?' He added: 'I use the word 'demand' because I envisage a situation where, based on good medical practice, there are really no two views of what course is for the best.'

The judge ended his judgement with a plea which the Law Lords in Re B should have expected: 'it is abundantly clear that the most suitable jurisdiction is ... the prerogative powers invested in the Crown as *parens patriae* ... I would respectfully urge the Crown ... to give urgent consideration to a speedy restitution of this prerogative jurisdiction.'

Four plausible approaches could have been adopted in Re B.

The first would have been to defer to the girl's mother, guardians and doctors. Some claim that this has been the practice in this country. But Heilbron J. rightly rejected that argument in a case decided 10 years ago. The question is not one of solely clinical judgement since it involves issues of human rights which transcend the competence of doctors.

The second approach was better, and the one which in effect the Law Lords adopted, but it was still unsatisfactory. This is the 'last resort' test adopted by the Court of Appeal. This has the advantages of removing the decision to a disinterested authority, the court, and of emphasising that sterilisation is only to be considered in extremis. But 'last resort' needs defining, otherwise it could slip back into the first approach of what doctors deem to be the last resort.

The third method would have been that of the Canadian provincial court in Eve. The 'best interests' and 'last resort' tests are spelt out in detail. Sterilisation would only be available if a series of 14 difficult steps are taken. The onus is very firmly on those who are arguing for sterilisation to show that it is the only solution to a real problem. They must show, for instance, that the real object of the operation is to protect the girl, not her parents or other carers; that other forms of contraception would be unworkable; that there is a real danger, rather than a mere chance, of pregnancy; and that there is more compelling evidence than the mere existance of a handicap that pregnancy would have a damaging effect. At first glance, this is the most attractive path to take as a compromise solution.

The fourth approach would have been that of the Supreme Court. Even if all the provincial court's 14 hurdles could be surmounted, the Canadian Supreme Court would still not permit sterilisation because as Lord Eldon said: under the *parens patriae* jurisdiction., 'it has always been the principle of this Court, not to risk damage to children which it cannot repair'. The irreversible nature of sterilisation means that although the 14 steps might lead a court towards, say, long-term contraceptive injections for a mentally handicapped girl, they would never justify the final step of sterilisation, a step which could never be retraced.

My own preference would have been for the third, provincial court approach. Why did the Law Lords opt for the second option? They were unimpressed by the argument that there is a fundamental right to procreate which no law can interfere with except where medically necessary for the sake of the girl's present health. This argument does not assert that each woman has a right to bear children. That would fly in the face of reality. It asserts only that the state through the law may not deprive a woman of the opportunity of procreating. As the Canadian Law Commission observed, 'sterilised mentally retarded persons tend to perceive sterilisation as a symbol of reduced or degraded status. Their attempts to pass for normal were hindered by negative self perceptions and resulted in withdrawal and isolation'.

To some this is an absolute right. To others it could be over-ridden if the state could show good reasons. But what reasons could be good enough? Similarly if we focus on another basic human right, the right to bodily integrity and freedom from interference, some would speak in absolutes while others would argue for exceptions. But again, what could count as a good reason for an exception?

Those who find the therapeutic/non-therapeutic distinction helpful might say that the only good reason for an exception to either right is if the operation is needed for the health of the girl. For this to be valid, it must be limited to existing conditions of ill-health requiring treatment. Admittedly, some prophy-lactic measures may be justified, for instance vaccination against a future threat. But apart from such a limited case, irreversible surgery performed for prophy-lactic purposes which are hypothetical and could perhaps be avoided by other means cannot qualify under the heading of therapeutic sterilisation. Yet the Law Lords rejected this approach, finding the distinction between therapeutic and non-therapeutic elusive or unhelpful.

Sterilisation does not of course absolve those with responsibility for the girl from using their best endeavours to protect her from sexual exploitation. And we can still argue for the general principle against sterilisation. The Supreme Court would reject exceptions beyond the therapeutic proviso by saying no, find another way, do not use irreversible surgery to solve social problems, the danger to human rights is too great.

There is a broader danger for human rights if parliament continues to abdicate its responsibilities. As the Supreme Court itself acknowledged in Eve's case: 'Judges are generally ill-informed about many of the factors relevant to a wise decision in this area. They generally know little of mental illness, of techniques of contraception or their efficacy. And, however well presented a case may be, it can only partially inform. If sterilisation of the mentally incompetent is to be adopted as desirable for general purposes, the legislature is the appropriate body to do so. It is in a position to inform itself and it is attuned to the feelings of the public in making policy in this sensitive area.' This is a statement of brutal honesty which deserves our attention when we consider the role of judges as law-makers and as proxies. There are limits to their com-petence and legitimacy.

Hence the wider significance of the Re B argument was that public attention was drawn to yet another problem of medical law and ethics where parliament has failed to guide the judges. In future parliament should take on these dilemmas of modern medicine. And as a first step, it should set up an appropriate body to review the problems and put the arguments before the nation. Although our judges deploy their considerable concern and ability when confronted by these questions under adverse conditions, the present British piecemeal approach to such fundamental problems is inadequate. Issues of human rights deserve more than their day in court.

For an example of the poor argument in court I would cite the unsatisfactory treatment accorded to the European Convention on Human Rights in the course of oral argument. The Law Lords seemed happy enough to be referred to the Convention. But they were not referred to the relevant Articles and the interpretation of the Article which was cited left something to be desired. Counsel for the Official Solicitor, representing the child's interests did not refer to the Convention, nor did counsel for the mother. But counsel for the local authority mentioned Article 12 in order to rebut the argument that the girl in question had a right to procreate. Article 12 is not the most conspicuous success story within the Convention. It runs as follows: 'Men and women of marriageable age have the right to marry and to found a family, subject to the national laws governing the exercise of this right.'

That may not say much but it perhaps says more than counsel supposed. She argued that since the girl in this case did not have the capacity to consent to marriage she did not come within the terms of the Article and thus did not qualify for the right to found a family. Others might suppose that the European Convention would not be interpreted by its own institutions so as to allow the right to procreate only to married couples. And they would suspect that there must be more relevant Articles elsewhere in the Convention. They would be right, Article 8 on the right to respect for one's private and family life, Article 3 prohibiting inhuman or degrading treatment, and even Article 2's right to life, ought to have been considered. Even if the right rights had been pinpointed, some idea of the jurisprudence and interpretive approach of the European Court of Human Rights should surely have been forthcoming. Of course, counsel and the court were arguing at short notice but if the Law Lords really are determining questions of law of general public importance, the principles of human rights law deserve more careful attention.

In practice, as I have suggested, what the Law Lords were really doing was seeking to allay public anxiety over the Court of Appeal's decision. They only partially succeeded. It is central to this chapter that I claim the reason why they were only partially successful has much in common with the reason why Mrs Gillick was partly successful in building a public campaign and that reason is of crucial importance to the future of proxy consents. The common theme is that the public (the patients, teenagers, the mentally handicapped, their relatives, friends and carers) is suspicious when it sees professionals, be they doctors or judges purporting to exercise consent for someone who is deemed to be incapable of consenting for themselves. In Re B there was a worry for many people that sterilisation would be in the best interests of those who have to worry about the care of Jeanette and that they could not necessarily disentangle that from her best interests. Now perhaps they could or perhaps there is no need to do so. My point is simply that the critical public saw no indication that the proxies were being challenged with sufficient rigour and vigour. The law's normal adversarial approach did not seem to work. Nobody in court really pressed the arguments against sterilisation. In that context, many people who criticise the judges are really just trying to remind the professionals of an important question: whose consent is it anyway?

Warnock

'Whose consent is it anyway?' is a question which I predict will recur in the forthcoming debates on Warnock when the government's legislation passes through Parliament. In conferences on medical law and ethics, speakers often talk as if the Warnock Committee was unanimous. It was split three ways on the question of embryo experiments. Fourteen days was the majority position of nine members but two groups dissented, one minority wanted to restrict this to 'spare' embryos, one wanted no non-therapeutic experiments at all. So there was, in some senses, a 9–7verdict. Even where there was a bigger majority, on surrogacy, where two members dissented in the hope of leaving the door open for non-commercial surrogacy, the dissenters have been successful and the government has preferred their caution. So I think that the issues are wide open.

In particular, I think minds will be focussed on such questions as who, if anyone, can consent to embryo experiments. And this leads us on to the point I promised about the wider significance of proxy decisions. Sometimes, the search for a proxy or the criteria for a proxy are so difficult that we reassess whether we want to allow the procedure at all.

To digress to a different, but topical example, it is not inconsistent for some Catholics to say that fetal tissue could be used for brain transplants provided that there is no question of coercing the mother into the abortion and provided that there is no harvesting (by which I mean getting pregnant deliberately to abort). Although the abortion could be seen as a tragedy and morally wrong, good may nevertheless ensue, as when somebody murders a teenager. This is no reason to stop the teenager's organs being used for donation provided that the next of kin consent. The difficulty is that the question here becomes, what if the mother of the teenager had shot her? Should she be the one then to offer consent? Or, returning to the abortion issue, should the mother who has in some sense rejected the fetus' moral worth, then be able to take decisions as to the use of the tissue? Well, yes, and I would predict that the Catholic press in its leaders might well say so. (Rush off to your local church and buy *The Tablet* or *The Catholic Herald*, the two Catholic papers for the Guardian-reading classes, to see if this prediction comes true – the papers come out every Friday.) Indeed, it is in presenting those who have opted for abortion with the knowledge that their fetus has this 'potential for other people's life' that the public might later accept the significance of the phrase that the fetus is 'a human being with potential'. By focussing on the issue of proxy consent, we can be led to re-examine our attitudes to those in issue, be they fetuses or the mentally handicapped teenagers.

Meanwhile, back at the Warnock Report, the very first criticism I made of the Report, in the week it was published back in the summer of 1984, was its incoherence on 'property rights'. Do you remember this passage from the Report para 10.11?

> The concept of ownership of human embryos seems to us to be undesirable. We recommend that legislation be enacted to ensure there is no right of ownership in a human embryo. Nevertheless, the couple who have stored an embryo for their use should be recognised as having rights to the use and disposal of the embryo, although

these rights ought to be subject to limitation. The precise nature of that limitation will obviously require careful consideration.

But surely ownership is nothing more than a bundle of rights, of which the most important are the rights to use and to dispose. The Report denies the concept of ownership but in the very next sentence it bestows ownership on the couple. Now the careful consideration does not seem to have happened. The White Paper says (para 58):

> As far as embryos are concerned, these may not be implanted into another woman, [nor used for research], nor destroyed (prior to the expiry of the storage time limit), in the absence of the consent of both donors. If there is disagreement between the donors the licence-holder will need to keep the embryo in storage until the end of the storage period, after which time, if there is still no agreement, the embryo should be left to perish.

This seems to give a veto right to one side if there is a disagreement. The White Paper might as well have said, in the event of disagreement, toss a coin. That would have given a fifty–fifty chance, instead of a 100–0. But it would have suggested that we had run out of moral argument and concern. But so, on many views, has the White Paper's solution.

My point here is simply that we have to ask ourselves on what criteria should the couple consent or withhold their consent. They are not really acting as proxies for the embryo. It cannot be in the best interests of the embryo that we find our criteria for experimenting or not experimenting. They are really acting on their own behalf, concerned with their own feelings. (I note, in passing, that some would see significance in the existence of such feelings.) Other would argue that the real issue is whether society can benefit from research and the decision to consent or not should be in society's interests. 'Whose consent?' could therefore be argued as the embryo's, the couple's or society's. In arguing for one answer or another, we refine our views on the desirability of any non-therapeutic experimentation on human embryos at all.

Conclusion

I have three concluding observations. First comes the question of the right structure for determining whether a proxy should give consent. The question who is the proxy and the question on what criteria should the proxy decide, are obviously inter-related. Pick your criteria and then choose as your proxy the person best able to apply those criteria. But whosoever the proxy is, and on whatsoever criteria the proxy is meant to decide, one lesson from our arguments during this conference must surely be to bear in mind the lack of consensus, the danger of conflicting your interests in the kind of school your children attend with their interests and, more optimistically, the possibility of argument changing one's initial assumptions. All these point to the need for some element of adversarial debate between the proxy and someone arguing against the proxy's interim decision. This is hardly an innovation, it is nothing more than the plea for a second, critical, opinion. But the second opinion of doctors is not perhaps so adversarial as it might be for this purpose. I am rather suggesting that the medics (if they are to be proxies) steal the vestments of the priests and the lawyers, two groups who traditionally annoy medics on these inter-disciplinary occasions. I would recommend the use, in other words, of the Devil's Advocate. First, becaue I think that if you set someone the task of knocking down your argument, you might prevent some mistakes. Second, because you will, through that process, command more public support for proxy decision. Of course, there are cost implications. Of course, it takes time. Of course, some will claim it is unnecessary. But to the extent that it is modelled on the legal process, let me remind you that the real worry for many in Re B was the rare failure of the legal system to provide any such counter-argument. Many of us who were in court felt very strongly that no-one was really putting the countervailing arguments with sufficient vigour, not because we necessarily believed they should have triumphed but because we know the risks of proxies convincing themselves that they have exhausted all the angles when a Devil's Advocate would ask for more proof. It was this failure which led to so much criticism of the courts and suspicion of the decision. It is the same worry which Mrs Gillick felt about what was going on in the doctor's surgery. In her case, of course, it was the fierce adversarial argument in the courts which convinced many doctors that the issues of proxy consent were being taken seriously. My first conclusion then is that those who act as proxies would be well advised to begin by creating Devil's Advocates to act as their proxy consciences.

What is a Devil's Advocate? Let me quote from Morris West's book *The Devil's Advocate* (Fontana).

A Cardinal is asked by a local Bishop to begin investigating the claim of some that there was a saint in the neighbourhood. There was much at stake. Error would be unthinkable. Morris West says the Cardinal:

> could afford less than others the luxury of error ... He would find the men (for the preliminary investigations) – a Postulator to build the case and present it, a Devil's Advocate to destroy it if he could. Of the two, the Devil's Advocate was the more important. The official title described him accurately: Promoter of the Faith. The man who kept the Faith pure at any cost of broken lives and broken hearts. He must be learned, meticulous, passionless. He must be old in judgment, ruthless in condemnation. He might lack charity or piety, but he could not lack precision. (p. 24)

This should be compared with another passage (pp. 238–9): 'I shall try ... to prove by every possible means that this is not' ('a miracle' or for our purposes, an appropriate proxy consent in the best interests of the patient).

My second observation is that if we reflect on the ten contexts I outlined above and ask on what criteria could a proxy consent to such procedures, this may be a good test of our worries about the procedures even when no proxy is needed. If we ask how should a mother decide whether or not her 'spare' embryos should be used for experimentation and we flounder, that may be because the embryos should not be so used at all.

My third observation is that it is part of the human condition, especially that part of it known as parenthood, to take awesome decisions on behalf of others. It is not an easy duty to discharge. It is one which doctors and judges and ethics committees and legislators have to shoulder to a greater degree than the rest of us. But it is by no means clear that there is anything in their training (if legislators have training) which necessarily prepares them for that task. We have seen the complexities it involves. And there is even less indication that the rest of us have any appropriate education, other than through experience, in discharging the burden when it falls on us to send our children to school or our mentally handicapped children into the community or into the operating theatre for sterilisation.

If I may conclude this conference in a spirit of optimism, however, I would say that this international, multidisciplinary meeting of minds is an invaluable part of that education. We have exchanged ideas. We have met people whom we had previously known through the pictures of medical ethics which they have painted. Now we perhaps understand a little better the perspective from which they see the world.

Discussion   Chairman: Peter Millican

Jackson: Doctors need to be even more alert and aware of the difficulties about giving information when they are addressing middle-class educated patients than when they are addressing others? They are quite likely to be both flattered by having an explanation and inhibited from admitting that they do not understand. It is easy to be misled about what people know about medical jargon. I was recently surprised to find second-year philosophy students coming to ask me what the word hysterectomy meant.

Jarvis: How do you approach a problem where the giving of a piece of information, may prejudice the outcome of the procedure? Operations carry risks. We can understand bleeding and infections. Certain procedures carry complications which may also have a psychogenic origin. For the young man having his colon removed for ulcerative colitis there is a risk of impotence. Should that complication be communicated because a reasonable person would expect to know it in making his decision, or should the information be withheld?

Gorovitz: The awareness of impotence as a known side-effect might well be sufficient to induce impotence. Nothing cools the ardour like terror. Given the reasons for the surgery, the reasonable person would not be deterred. If surgery is done for very powerful reasons which are not likely to be over-riden by that side-effect, a fairly strong case can be made for not providing that information. I would want to know the varieties of impotence and their amenability to treatment. If it is a significant probability and not subsequently treatable then I think the case becomes more powerful for providing the information with a maximum of reassurance that is consistent with some regard for truth.

Bromham: We are very bad at getting points across in language that our patients understand. One thing that worries me a little bit is the use of 'counsellors', who perhaps are interpreters of jargon into lay language. I would prefer to become better as a doctor, in counselling my own patients, rather than delegate one of the prime experiences and skills of a physician, counselling and explanation.

Kluge: I like Mr Lee's rather positive presentation of the case of Re Eve, as to how it was perceived through the courts. One shadowy player whose consent is necessary was ignored. That was the State. Would you not also agree that another shadowy player with respect to informed consent who should be involved is, philosophical difficulties aside, the as yet unborn child?

Lee: With respect of Re Eve I did say that the judges have some kind of state role in consent. In my initial structure of six questions for consent the last is: 'Is there any over-riding reason for society to reject the consent?'. I include the idea that the state has an interest.

Kluge: Over-riding interest tends to be in terms of social policy. How about the parameter of the child-to-be, or the future generations which do not come up under the rubric of social policy *per se*. The ethical perspective as to the use of children for the realisation of potential was focussed on by the judges when they said: 'You may not deprive Eve of that'. That was a unanimous decision that may very well reflect social policy but certainly from an ethical perspective seems to be somewhat questionable.

Lee: The judge in that case was relying on the Canadian Law Commission Report which said that it is an important part of a woman's dignity to realise that she may have some kind of capacity for procreation.

Botros: The more sophisticated the information that a doctor is required to give, the higher capacity to understand must be. Informed consent theorists, though they accept that, insist that patients' consent or refusal of consent, should be honoured.

Lee: It is a very important point. In Gillick, the things that the girl had to understand, according to the judgements, was so extraordinarily high, that she probably would not be able to match that in reality. So some significance is attached to the fact that she cannot do so. So, the higher up you push the necessity for knowledge of risks and alternatives, the more people you take out of the net who can decide and therefore the more proxys have to decide, who are the very people telling you the information and alternatives.

Jackson: When you referred to the woman who was refused infertility treatment, you referred to the alleged right to have a spouse, and children. What kind of right? Many of us are familiar with the distinction between liberty rights and claimed rights. I have a liberty right to sit in this seat when I came into this session, but if someone else had been sitting here I could not push them out. Mr Millican (chairman) had a claimed right to his seat as he is chairing this session. If he had found someone else sitting there, he could say: 'This is my chair. Get out!' Even though he has a claimed right that does not mean that he has a claim to our assistance. Do we have some obligation to pull that man out of his seat? We have faint right to assistance to get a spouse and found a family. In the particular type of case that we are discussing, where resources are scarce, surely the doctor is still entitled to say: 'I cannot give this treatment to everyone wanting it. I therefore I am entitled to use selection criteria.'

Lilford: This is obviously very applicable to *in vitro* fertilisation. Another example is renal transplant. The dichotomy comes up as to when the decision should be made. The majority view is that a doctor and his patient must somehow make it in the consultation, and the other view is that the criteria for the decision should be laid down before the consultations take place. I support the second view as I do not like the idea that the doctor–patient relationship should incorporate a bargaining component.

Lee: I was talking about the legal question. Sooner or later a doctor will be taken to the European Court on Human Rights in Strasbourg. Article 12 of the Convention on Human Rights says: 'Men and women of marriageable age have the right to marry and to found a family according to the national laws governing the exercise of such a right'. Article 14 says: 'No-one in the exercise of these rights should be discriminated against on grounds such as race, sex . . .', and so on. It depends how the court interprets that right. There are clearly some grounds on which the doctor must discriminate when he has got limited resources. Some would be regarded as irrelevant.

Lilford: A woman who had been sterilised came to me asking to be unsterilised. The general practitioner mentioned that her previous children were in care. Medically it was quite possible to attempt reversal. So I asked her permission to contact the paediatrician and social worker involved. The circumstances were that the social services would probably have taken any future child into care. I declined to do it because of resource problems; I did have those resources. A second opinion was the same. I really did not want to reverse her sterilisation but I would never sterilise a person for those same reasons. Is there a difference between refusing to sterilise someone and refusing to unsterilise? At about the same time we were discussing surrogacy and decided that one of the procedural ethics for surrogacy should be that the family would be a loving and giving family to that child. Others agreed that same test can be used in the 'unsterilise' question. Another example would be if I had a son who was a very irresponsible driver, I would have no right to stop him buying a fast car. However, if he came with a standard issue car and asked me to upgrade it, I would have a right to refuse, given his driving record.

Gorovitz: The question of the right to reproduce is basically a right not to be interfered with with respect to reproductive autonomy. The most plausible interpretation is of a liberty. This is why the distinction between involuntary sterilisation and access to assistance is such an important and sharp distinction. The person who is denied access to assistance is not being interfered with, though it may make the difference between ability to reproduce or not. The person who is sterilised involuntarily is being interfered with, and that requires particularly strong justification because it is over-riding a *prima facie* right to reproduce. I think it would be ludicrous to interpret the right to marry and have a family as a claimed right lest one next be in the position of applying to the government for a wife, or a husband, and being provided with one.

Robinson: Professor Lilford was talking about risks of 1 in 200 and information given to patients, 'whether or not they are capable of making rational decisions'. We all have the right to be irrational, particularly as we all are irrational. I am concerned that numerical information is almost always dishonest. The information is almost always of published figures, done at the best centres by people who are confident enought to publish their information. The risks at that centre or in the hands of that individual, is quite another thing. It has been said that 'informed consent should include the question of how many times you personally have done the procedure, doctor'.

Lilford: That is not necessarily correct. A doctor may portray information that he knows is extrapolated from a non-representative series from the literature. I showed those figures as the best assessment of the probabilities, derived in whatever method the doctor thinks. There are two kinds of probabilities in decision theory. Objective ones come from published work. Subjective ones come from what you intuitively feel to be the correct answer. The right way to practise medicine is to give the figures as you really believe they are. The purpose of science is to influence a belief. If your belief is only partially influenced, you must give your best assessment of the overall risk using the paper and your subjective judgement. I often quote two risks: the best guess from the literature and my own figures.

Gorovitz: There is a residual point as to whether patients should be provided specific information on the health care facility and its record. Sometimes people want to know and that information is not made available. The argument for withholding that information is that the information is misleading because there is a learning curve. The hospitals that are in on some procedure early have worse records but are doing the job better. Some hospitals also systematically filter out high risk cases. We are dealing here with a very difficult level and complexity in the nature of information. If we simply say the success rate is *x*, we may, by providing that *true* information, thoroughly mislead.

Greengross: It may be that it is too expensive to spend the time or that the consultants' particular skills may not be best suited to that. The Warnock committee did recommend that there should be independent counselling for all undergoing fertility procedures. The role of the counsellor is in helping people reach situations where they are able to make informed consent.

Gorovitz: In the USA the primary players, numerically, are nurses and physicians. Down the list come patient advocates or social workers. They play a role in education and the process of consent but it is not as highly valued and supported an activity as you might have wished.

Robson: None of us actually come to clear decisions where we are not affected by other psychological factors in our social reality. Missing from this debate is the experimental and psychological input as to how a lot of these processes actually happen and the education that can be put in so that people involved can present the information in more effective ways.

Lindsay: The dilemma is that the doctors are faced with choosing between intervening and non-intervening. If there are too many barriers put in their way the fear may result that whether they intervene or not they are at risk of litigation.

Gorovtiz: That is really ending this conference by invoking the need for another. It is an immense subject. Much of the difficulty is the linkage between an unfortunate or disappointing outcome of a medical situation and the notion of entitlement to compensation. There is a kind of linkage between disappointment, culpability and compensation. It is ill-conceived and ill-advised. I do believe that malpractice is something that is very serious and should be taken seriously. That needs to be utterly separated from the notion of compensation for injury.